THE PRACTICE OF RESEARCH

How Social Scientists Answer Their Questions

Shamus Khan
Columbia University

Dana R. Fisher
University of Maryland–College Park

New York   Oxford
OXFORD UNIVERSITY PRESS

Oxford University Press is a department of the University of Oxford.
It furthers the University's objective of excellence in research,
scholarship, and education by publishing worldwide.

Oxford   New York
Auckland   Cape Town   Dar es Salaam   Hong Kong   Karachi
Kuala Lumpur   Madrid   Melbourne   Mexico City   Nairobi
New Delhi   Shanghai   Taipei   Toronto

With offices in
Argentina   Austria   Brazil   Chile   Czech Republic   France   Greece
Guatemala   Hungary   Italy   Japan   Poland   Portugal   Singapore
South Korea   Switzerland   Thailand   Turkey   Ukraine   Vietnam

Published by Oxford University Press
198 Madison Avenue, New York, NY 10016
www.oup.com

ISBN: 978-0-19-982741-1

Contents

List of contributors   vii

Introduction: The Practice of Research   1

1 **Experimentation   24**
Constraints into Preferences: Gender, Status, and Emerging
Career Aspirations   27
Reflection by Shelley Correll   41

2 **Survey Research   50**
Digital Na(t)ives? Variation in Internet Skills and Uses
among Members of the "Net Generation"   53
Reflection by Eszter Hargittai   62

3 **Survey Research, Analyzing Social Networks   71**
Partisans, Nonpartisans, and the Antiwar Movement in the
United States   74
Reflection by Michael T. Heaney   82

4 **Field Observation/Ethnography   90**
How Elite Students Think about "The Staff"   93
Reflection by Shamus Khan   102

5 **Field Interviewing   109**
Running an Outsourced Canvass   112
Reflection by Dana R. Fisher   120

6 **Research Using Available Data   127**
Racial Self-Categorization in Adolescence: Multiracial
Development and Social Pathways   130
Reflection by Steven Hitlin, Scott Brown, and
Glen H. Elder Jr.   142

7 Research Using Available Data/Historical Analysis   147

Islamic Mobilization: Social Movement Theory and the Egyptian Muslim Brotherhood   150

Reflection by Ziad Munson   160

8 Research Using Available Data/Content Analysis   168

"Close Your Eyes and Think of England": Pronatalism in the British Print Media   171

Reflection by Jessica Brown   182

9 Multiple Methods/Mixed Methods   188

Why Organizational Ties Matter for Neighborhood Effects: A Study of Resource Access through Childcare Centers   191

Reflection by Mario Luis Small   204

Glossary of Terms   213

Acknowledgments

The Practice of Research is a joint project of Shamus Khan and Dana Fisher, but many people along the way made it possible. First and foremost, we would like to thank the Department of Sociology at the University of Wisconsin–Madison—where we met—for helping make us into sociologists. The department provided us with a stellar training and exposed us to great teachers and mentors who taught us methods. In particular, we would like to thank Pamela Oliver and Jane Piliavin for inspiration. We also want to thank M. Patricia Golden for providing a great model in her book, *The Research Experience*, now out of print.

The contributors to this volume were a pleasure to work with. We thank them for buying into our idea and for doing such a wonderful job with their reflection pieces. We would also like to thank Zach Richer for his hard work and research assistance, especially when navigating the world of permissions; Sherith Pankratz at Oxford University Press for her support; and the following reviewers for their insights, in addition to two anonymous reviewers:

Elif Andac, University of Kansas
Xiaojin Chen, Tulane University
Elisabeth S. Clemens, University of Chicago
Anne Figert, Loyola University–Chicago
Kimberly Goyette, Temple University
Melinda Messineo, Ball State University
Wendy Regoeczi, Cleveland State University
Linda Renzulli, University of Georgia
Erin Ruel, Georgia State University
John H. Schweitzer, Michigan State University
Junmin Wang, University of Memphis

List of Contributors

Jessica Brown is assistant professor of sociology at the University of Houston.

J. Scott Brown is associate professor of gerontology at Miami University.

Shelley Correll is professor of sociology and Barbara D. Finberg Director of the Michelle R. Clayman Institute for Research on Gender at Stanford University.

Glen H. Elder Jr. is research professor of sociology and psychology at the University of North Carolina at Chapel Hill.

Dana R. Fisher is associate professor of sociology and director of the Program for Society and the Environment at the University of Maryland.

Shamus Khan is associate professor of sociology at Columbia University.

Eszter Hargittai is associate professor of communication studies at Northwestern University.

Michael T. Heaney is assistant professor of organizational studies and political science at the University of Michigan.

Steven Hitlin is associate professor of sociology at the University of Iowa.

Ziad Munson is associate professor of sociology at Lehigh University.

Mario Luis Small is professor and dean of the social sciences at University of Chicago.

Introduction: The Practice of Research

> We have a habit in writing articles published in scientific journals to make the work as finished as possible, to cover all the tracks, to not worry about the blind alleys or to describe how you had the wrong idea first, and so on. So there isn't any place to publish, in a dignified manner, what you actually did in order to get to do the work. . . .
>
> *Richard Feynman, Nobel Laureate, Physics*

The purpose of this book is to expose students to studies in the social sciences that use a range of methods and to provide accounts of how those studies were done. Such accounts—though not exactly confessional—should help students recognize that research is messy. The structure of research write-ups often suggests that researchers knew exactly what their questions were and what the corresponding relevant literature was before beginning their work. Yet the research process is often far more iterative, where the exact questions of projects and what is important about those questions is finalized once the research is complete and scholars are analyzing and writing up their data.

This fact does not mean, however, that research is haphazard. As the contents of this book will illustrate, there is a method to social science inquiry—one that ensures that the findings reported might reasonably serve as the basis for knowing something about our social world. And at the core of that method is a particular research attitude: skepticism. While much is often made of the differences between **qualitative** and **quantitative** work, in this volume we argue that all studies of the social world that we might consider "scientific" share a key feature: they proceed by adhering to the logic of science, which is not to prove an idea correct. Instead, the logic of inquiry is negation.

For a scholar to feel like she has established a claim as "correct," what she must do is work hard to find evidence that she is wrong. Although this process might seem counterintuitive, it is the basic way in which knowledge advances: we are never certain, but the more times we try to show that we are wrong and cannot, the more comfortable we can feel that our idea has some basis in fact. Whether one is testing subjects in a lab or wandering the hallways of a school observing its inner workings, the basic approach is the same. One seeks to eliminate alternate potential explanations for the observed phenomenon so that the best explanation is the only one that fits.

In this book, you will read the work by researchers who use a variety of methods. Even so, across all the methods used, the research is driven by a common theme: the only way to prove a point is to disprove all other possible explanations. The one supreme lesson we hope you come away with after reading this book is be skeptical. Research is not about affirming your beliefs; it is about being unable to prove them wrong.

THE LOGIC OF THIS BOOK

This book is not a traditional methods textbook. The chapters are not set up to teach about each method by writing about them. Rather than talk about research methods, our emphasis is on illustrating research methods through actual research projects. You will read the results of these projects in the form of excerpts of published research papers and books, but you will also read the authors' personal reflections about how they did the research that yielded the publications. Chapters in this book center around nine different social science research methods, and each chapter has three parts. First, we provide a very brief introduction to the method in question. Second, we illustrate this method with an excerpt of a scholarly paper that uses the method. These papers are written by leading scholars in the field and were chosen because they contain creative ideas, have interesting findings, deploy research methods in thought-provoking ways, and raise critical questions about how to do social research. Following each paper is a personal reflection, written by the author or authors of the paper and specially prepared for this volume; the reflections explore how the research project presented in the paper was actually done, some of the challenges faced, and how they were overcome. These reflections will give a sense of what the authors actually did in their research, why they chose the particular methodology, how they think about that method, and how they overcame obstacles that came up throughout the research process (obstacles *always* emerge).

Our aim is to show students how research works by providing examples of research but also by "pulling back the curtain" on the research process and having authors reveal what is often hidden when we publish papers: our missteps, challenges, and at times failures, as well as the practical solutions that were employed to complete the research project and publish its findings. We hope that this book provides students with a better understanding of research methodology and will help them realize that the challenges they face are not unique. Through seeing how leaders of the field have dealt with many of the same issues that plague all social research, we hope that this volume provides students with a set of practical skills to help them work through common challenges and make their research more methodologically sound.

In this book, we do not advocate any particular methodological approach. Instead, in our introductions we point to how each method works and how specific methods are best suited to answer certain types of questions. For example, if you want to establish a causal claim, you are better served by an experiment than by content analysis; if you want to understand how people interact with one another, you'll likely be better off observing them than surveying them. Each method is good at answering particular kinds of questions, but no method is perfect. Recognizing the strengths of different methods will help students more effectively design research projects and evaluate the projects of others.

For the remainder of this introduction, we outline a variety of considerations when designing a research project. This chapter provides a general but hardly exhaustive introduction to social science research. Yet it will provide students with some basic insights that can guide their readings of the papers in this volume, as well as the design of their own research projects.

ISSUES TO CONSIDER WHEN DOING SOCIAL RESEARCH

Perhaps the most daunting task in doing research is deciding what you will actually study. There are two rules of thumb to follow here. First, what are you passionate about? Research projects require long periods of time: months, often years, and sometimes lifetimes! Though scientific research is frequently presented as the product of a disinterested observer, you must be able to sustain interest in the project through setbacks and timelines that can feel endless. A commitment to your research project is what helps you get over the hurdles of such challenges.

Second, you should pick a project you can actually complete. If you want to study the Yoruba, for example, you will probably need to move to West Africa for a period of time; it would also help to speak Yoruba. If you have commitments in your life that require you to be home at night, you can still do social research, but it makes no sense to develop a project that studies the inner-workings of nightclubs. If you are not interested in mathematical modeling, you are probably not well suited for sophisticated quantitative data analysis. These everyday constraints are important to recognize and keep in mind as you develop your project. Having constraints does not make you a less dedicated scientist; it makes you a human being.

From Topic to Question

Once you have a research topic that you know your interest can sustain for a long period of time and you have confirmed that conducting the research is doable (it fits your life and the research skills you have developed), you are ready to turn that topic into a **research question**. The most important point to keep in mind is that your research question must really be a question. For example, "I want to show that people from different cultures have different ideas of 'the family'" is not a question. First, you might ask, "Who would disagree with me?" It is hard to imagine that "the family" is universal across cultures. Your task is to think about how you could be wrong. Is it possible that different cultures don't have different ideas of the family? If your answer is no, then you've set up a research project based not upon a question, but upon an answer you already have in your mind. This example points to an even greater difficulty: if you say, "I want to show . . . ," you are starting off with the wrong attitude. Remember that the logic of science proceeds by negation. So your aim ought not to be having a point you want to show. Instead, it should be to have a question you want to answer. Staying with our example, you might instead start with, "How do different cultures conceptualize 'the family'?" Now that's a researchable question.

With this kind of question, we could draw on lots of different research methodologies. As we will discuss in this book, some methods are more appropriate choices for answering certain types of questions and dealing with particular populations. Yet for the most part, research questions are "methods-neutral." In other words, many different social research methods could be used to answer the question posed above. We could interview people from different cultures to see how they think about the notion of the family. Or we could conduct an ethnography of family life in a number of cultures. Or we might be able to find survey data that explores attitudes about family life. We could also do a content analysis of journalistic stories about "the family" and see how the stories differ in various countries and media outlets. If you don't know what it means to use these different methods yet, don't worry. By the time you are done with this book, you will.

Units of Analysis and Observation

Once you have a question, you have to decide what you actually want to observe. In other words, you must decide on your **unit of analysis**. Sometimes we are interested in individual people. But not always. We can ask questions about groups of people or about even larger units—organizations, companies, or nations. For example, we might ask how people's incomes are influenced by their education (our unit of analysis for this first question is the individual); or, we might ask how family structure has changed as more women have entered the workforce (our unit of analysis for this second question is a social group: the family); or, we might ask how capitalist nations are able to extract resources from their citizenry compared to monarchies (our unit of analysis here is the nation). You should not think of certain units of analysis as better than others; they simply determine what types of data you must collect and which research methods are more or less appropriate to answering your questions.

Quantitative versus Qualitative Research?

In the process of specifying your unit of analysis, you will also decide *how* you will collect your data: Will you do a survey or a field experiment? Will you conduct participant observation or semistructured interviews? Will you find a dataset that has already been collected and analyze those data? In the process of making this decision, you will also need to decide what types of data you want to collect and/or analyze. The distinction between quantitative and qualitative research really just concerns the difference between types of data you will collect—do the data reflect numbers and quantities or thematic qualities? The research instrument itself does not actually dictate whether the data will be numbers or not. Some surveys include open-ended questions that collect data that are then qualitatively coded, and some ethnographers count things when they do their research.

In general, quantitative data and analyses are better suited for explaining the *what* of a research question. For example, what explains the differential unemployment rates of people from different backgrounds? Qualitative analyses, in contrast, tend to be used to answer the *how*. For example, how do policymakers decide on unemployment benefits? As we will discuss in more detail in the following sections, certain types of quantitative data allow for the broadest array of statistical analyses, whereas you can only do very limited types of quantitative analyses on qualitative data.

Units of Observation: Variables

Deciding on a unit of analysis does not mean you observe only that unit; in fact, your **unit of observation** can still be at the individual level even if you are interested in groups (and vice versa). For example, if you are interested in the second question posed above—how family structure has changed as more women have entered the workforce—you are likely to gather observations at the individual level, such as interview data with women who have recently entered the workforce. If you ask the question about capitalist nations, you are likely to gather information about individual-level tax rates.

Your unit of observation is more commonly called a **variable**. It is the dimension or aspect of your unit of analysis that has various values, which can be either quantities or qualities. These values can be just two (if you're looking at differences between men and women), or they can be almost infinite (if you're looking at people's wealth in dollars, which can go from negative values for someone in debt to figures in the billions). Essential to all variables is that the specified values for each must be *exhaustive* and *mutually exclusive*. In other words, if you are gathering information on a variable, every observation of interest must be possible as a category or value of your variable, and every observation must fit into only one category. For example, let's say you created a value for "level of education" and our categories were these:

- some high school
- high school graduate only
- four-year college graduate only
- professional, master's, or PhD degree

In this instance, there would be concern that the variable is not exhaustive. Why? Well, what do you do with people who have some college education or who have gone to technical school or a community college? These people completed more than high school but did not earn a four-year college degree. In short, not every category is represented in the values of the variables. Before collecting data, you must make sure to design the research in such a way as to avoid this problem. This issue is not as important when the question is open ended. In other words, if respondents just fill in their own answers and do not make a choice on a survey or if respondents are answering interview questions orally, then this issue will be resolved during data analysis.

Once you have ensured that every observation can fit within your variable, you must also ensure that no observation can fit within more than one value. So let's say we're doing a survey and asking people their income levels. We give research subjects the following to choose from:

- $10,000–25,000
- $25,000–50,000
- $50,000–75,000
- >$75,000

There are two problems with our design. First, our variable is not exhaustive. What if you make less than $10,000? You have nothing to select! Also, the categories of our variable aren't mutually exclusive. What if you make $25,000 or $50,000 or $75,000? You have two categories to choose between, both of which "match" your income. Again, we must redesign our instrument to make sure that every answer can go into one, and only one, value for our variable. As a researcher, it is your job to define your variables and make sure the values you collect information about are exhaustive and mutually exclusive.

Although the two previous examples illustrate challenges to survey research with closed-ended questions, similar challenges come up in interview and ethnographic research. Qualitative researchers must define how to characterize their observations and make sure that such observations are complete. For example, if you want to conduct participant observation to understand the economic behavior of gangs in a neighborhood but you did your research only in the morning, you would miss all kinds of activity because you did not make observations across every condition of the variable (during the afternoon, at night, etc.). Your research would not be exhaustive, and your observations would be subject to bias. Further, if a gang operated a "legitimate" business—say, an auto repair shop—you would have to be careful in coding that activity. If the work at the auto repair shop counts as both categories of your variable (gang economic activity and legitimate economic activity), your observations will be too vague and require reconstruction or considerable explanation.

Types of Variables

There are many different kinds of variables, and they allow for different kinds of analysis. This point is particularly important if you want to do statistical analysis on your data. The rules for what types of variables are appropriate for what types of analyses will not be covered thoroughly in this book, but students who are likely to do statistical analyses should consult textbooks or papers that deal with how different types of variables are analyzed. For now, we will cover just four common types of variables and give you some insights into what they mean for doing analysis. The four types are nominal, ordinal, interval, and ratio.

Nominal data are often called **categorical data**, because they are data that deal with categories of things that do not have a meaningful numerical value. Nominal data are classified by category. Eye color would be an example (brown, blue, gray, etc.) or gender (male, female, or other) or college major (sociology, physics, etc.). Again, when gathering nominal data, it is important that the categories are exhaustive and mutually exclusive.

Ordinal data are like nominal data, but some kind of meaningful distance is placed between the values of categories. This value happens through a scale. The scale shows the order of variables but not the distance between one value and another. An example of an ordinal scale might be the final position of swimmers in a race. It would show who came first, second, third, and so on but reveal nothing about the swimmers' times. Did the winner win handily, or was it a photo finish? Who knows? The ranking of items can be important, but not knowing the distance between values limits the kinds of statistical analyses one can do.

Interval data are like ordinal data in that we know the values of categories and they are placed on a scale, but with these data we also know the size of the intervals between the categories. A good example here is a temperature scale. For example, in Celsius 0° indicates the freezing point of water, and 100° is its boiling point. Moreover, the distance between 23° and 24° Celsius is the same as the distance between 15° and 16°. However, such scales do not have a true or meaningful zero. While the freezing point of water may be interesting to know, setting this temperature as 0° is arbitrary. On the Fahrenheit scale, in contrast, the zero temperature value is well below the point at which water freezes. On the Celsius scale, we could as easily set 0° at the boiling point of water or the average temperature in Oklahoma City during the summer months. It is completely arbitrary. To do particular types of statistical analyses, there must be a meaningful zero point.

Ratio data are like interval data in that we have an ordered scale with fixed intervals between values, but something is added: a meaningful, or true, zero point. Examples of ratio data might be your income in dollars, the number of people enrolled in a class, or your height in inches or centimeters. Although there is a big difference between being 187 centimeters tall and 187 inches tall, in both metrics the zero point is the same.

If all of these details make it seem as if social scientists just create categories of data for the fun of it, let us assure you that these differences matter! They particularly matter for the kinds of analyses you can do with data. With nominal and ordinal data, you have limited options, but you can look at aspects of the distribution across your sample. For example, you can look at the frequency of different items (how often you observed different social phenomena), percentages, and modes (the mode is the most common value). These kinds of analyses can be conducted on just about all types of data if they are collected correctly. For example, an ethnographer can count how often a student asks a teacher for help or her interview data can be coded to see how often activists talk about the outcome of a political campaign.

With interval and ratio data you can look at the mean, calculate standard deviations, correlations, and other statistics. So as you seek to gather data on variables, ask yourself what kinds of analyses you want to do on those variables. If you are analyzing data you did not collect yourself—what is called **secondary data**—you must be sensitive to what kind of data you are working with, as this information will determine some of the analytic techniques you can deploy. Again, we will not systematically cover these techniques in this book. For more information about them, consult a statistical textbook or a textbook on quantitative or qualitative analyses.

Making Sure Variables Vary

In order for social scientists to observe relationships, no matter what kinds of variables we are working with, we must observe **covariation**. So let's say we posit a relationship between two units of analysis: building upon our example above, perhaps the relationship is that your education influences your income. In this instance, your education would be an **independent variable**; that is, it is related to the variable you are trying to explain. The other variable—income in this case—is your **dependent variable**; that is, its value or categorization is dependent on the independent variable. To put it more simply, it is the effect you are looking to observe.

When we say that we must observe covariation to observe a relationship, we mean that observations of both the independent variable and the dependent variable must have more than one value. Let's say we observed only people with a high school diploma (nothing less, nothing more). Looking at these people's incomes, we would see lots of variation—that is, many different values of income. A few of our subjects would make a lot of money, most would make some money, and a few would be unemployed. But given that we have only one category of the independent variable—high school education—we could not say anything about the relationship between that variable and our dependent variable, because our independent variable does not vary! However, if we gathered information on people with varying amounts of education, we would be able to say something meaningful about the relationship between our variables.

So when selecting independent variables and dependent variables, we must make sure we have more than one value for each. It is possible that when we look for a relationship, we do not observe any covariation. In this case, it is simply that we do not find a relationship between variables. To take a silly example, we might ask if the length of your thumb was predictive of your income. We could then observe the thumb length of many people (we have variation) and see how this characteristic is related to their income (again we have variation). In this case, it is unlikely that we have any meaningful covariation, so our two variables are not related to one another. Lots of things in the world are unrelated to one another, and sometimes finding out that social phenomena are *not* related can be as important as finding out that they are.

Causal Direction and Spuriousness

Let's say we *do* find covariation. What can we say once we find a relationship between two variables? Do we know that our independent variable has caused our dependent variable? In all likelihood, we do not. Some of you may have heard the expression "**correlation** does not mean causation." There are two potential reasons that this statement is so often repeated. First, just because we have observed covariation does not mean that we have identified the correct direction of the relationship: x does not necessarily cause y; y could be causing x. For example, let's look at two variables: (1) the health of children and (2) the amount of time their fathers spend with them. Doing a study, we find that there is a positive correlation, or **association**, between fathers spending more time with children and children being in good health. The researcher might be tempted to argue that children are more healthy *because* their fathers spend time with them. Intuitively, this explanation makes sense. However, we could have the causal direction completely wrong. In other words, it could be that fathers are more likely to spend time with healthy children than unhealthy children. To establish a **causal relationship** requires considerably more work than establishing an association. One of the ways we can show causality is through research design—for example, through using experiments. (You will learn more about this research method in the first chapter of the book.) Another reason to interpret a causal relationship is if one variable precedes the other (it happens first). For example, to test the problem above (with children's health and fathers' time), we might look for cases where children get sick and see what happens. Do fathers then decrease their parenting time, or vice versa? If fathers begin to spend less time with their children, what happens to the children's health?

Finally, even if we solve the problem of causal direction, the **nonspuriousness** of the observed relationship still needs to be ensured. A **spurious relationship** is one where it looks as if there is a connection between two variables because of observed covariation but in reality there is some other variable that has a causal impact on both our independent and dependent variables. This situation is easiest to understand with an example.

Let's return to the case of the impact of education on income. In this instance, we observe a strong relationship between the two. People with more education make more money. Given that education *precedes* income, we can be fairly certain of the causal direction: education causes higher earnings. So we have a situation that looks something like this figure:

Higher Education   ⟶   Higher Earnings

However, we still have to worry about spuriousness. That is, what if some other variable has an impact on both level of education and earnings? Our worry can be presented in the following diagram:

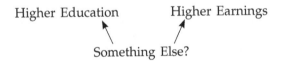

In other words, the association we find between higher education and higher earnings exists, but it is not because education has an effect on earnings. It is because some other variable has a positive effect on both education and earnings. If this explanation is correct, it is possible that we have assumed a relationship where one does not exist. One potential spurious variable might be parents' earnings. In other words, we might find that children of wealthier parents are more likely to have more schooling and are also more likely to make more money themselves. In this case, then, parental earnings might explain both education and earnings. Thus the association between the two variables exists, but education does not explain earnings; instead, parents' earnings explain both level of education and earnings. Social science researchers looking at this particular question have found that if we look at education alone we overestimate the effect of education on earnings, because both education *and* parents' earnings help explain earnings but parents' earnings also have a positive effect on education.

Such spuriousness is a challenge for most social science methods—except experiments. Experiments isolate the effects of a single variable, and so there are few worries of spurious results (they have other worries!). For all other methods, however, an unobserved spurious variable is always a concern. Survey instruments can deal with spuriousness of observed variables by using statistical controls (more about them in later chapters). Qualitative methods often describe social processes (how things happen) more than causal pathways (what variables explain what outcomes); this difference allows researchers to avoid some of the challenges of spuriousness. However, for most research, it is important to keep two points in mind when conducting research: (1) some unobserved variable (the "something else" in the image above) might explain the results, and therefore (2) it is important to gather information on the most likely spurious variables so that you can rule them out as competing explanations.

From Research Question to Hypothesis

Now that we have a sense of some of the basic building blocks of research, we are ready to make our question a little more specific. We are ready to turn our research question into a hypothesis. An hypothesis is simply a statement about how variables relate to one another. Let's stay with the topic above—that of the relationship between education and earnings. In this section we will talk about three kinds of hypotheses: (1) the general form of a hypothesis, which is converted into (2) an abstract form based upon your question of interest, and then into (3) your operational form, which is what you actually study.

The general form of a hypothesis is the form that almost all hypotheses take. And it looks something like this:

For Population (P) in Condition (C), Independent Variable (X) is related to Dependent Variable (Y)

This phrase might seem overly complicated and abstract, but bear with us; it will become clearer! The basic insight here is that for an hypothesis, you need to define the **population** you're interested in studying, under conditions that are of interest relative to variables you think are important. Are you interested in people from the United States or just people from Texas? If it's Texans, there is no point in gathering information about people from California. We rarely want to know about the entire world. In fact, we usually just want to know about a very small part of it. So first, we must define whom it is we want to know about: our population.

We also want to know about what counts as a condition of interest for that population. So again, let's say we're interested in the relationship between education and wealth in the United States. Do we want to gather information from everyone in the United States? Probably not. We probably want to limit our information gathering to people who are of working age; there is no point in gathering information about people who have yet to work a job or whose education is incomplete. So we are unlikely to decide to gather information about people under the age of 18. But we also might not want to gather information from people above the age of 65, since many of these people are retired and not earning money in the labor market anymore. We may also want to exclude people who are presently in college or unable to work because of a disability or because they are incarcerated. These are important research decisions that relate to how we gather information and who is of research interest. How we deal with these questions has implications for the population we can draw generalizations about. We will talk more about these issues when we get to our sampling section, next. But for now, it is important to note that we must specify the conditions of interest for our population.

Next, we need to construct variables that we think might explain a relationship. These are our independent and dependent variables discussed above. In our case, the independent variable is education. Our dependent variable is income. Once we have all of these elements, we are ready to move on to our **abstract hypothesis**.

For Americans (P) who are of working age (C), their education (X) explains how much income they make (Y)

Now we have an abstract hypothesis that tells us whom we are interested in and what a possible relationship might be between the variables of interest. But at this point, we are still not ready to gather any data. We have yet to figure out how we will measure each of our variables. We must, therefore, make some **measurement assumptions**. Such measurement assumptions are how we move from an abstract idea—say, "education"—to something more concrete about which we can gather data.

The most obvious way to measure education is to look at years of schooling. But such a measurement makes all kinds of assumptions about education: that it only happens in schools, that a year at one school is equivalent to a year in another school, that "on the job training" does not count as education, and so on. We can think of many instances where people learn outside school: where people "educates themselves" (say, by learning how to do computer programming or to cut hair), where a very wealthy school might be able to do more by way of educating than one that is a very poor school, or where someone learns a considerable amount through working. By gathering information about years in school, you make certain assumptions about what counts as "education" and what does not. We could have a similar discussion of "income." Again, while it seems clear that we measure income in terms of salary (so we ask about your salary on a survey), this measurement misses important sources of money. What if your parents continue to support you? Does that count as income? What if you receive government support? What if you have investments that give you income but aren't part of your salary? Again, we miss all these factors by assuming that we can measure money as "salary."

Such assumptions about how you will measure your variables are referred to as the variable's **operationalization**. In other words, how do you convert your abstract idea into something concrete that is measurable so you can gather data? Such operationalizations can be better or worse, but it is unlikely that they will be "right" or "wrong." Take another variable that is often of interest to social scientists: social class. There are many ways to operationalize class. We could look at a more quantitative variable and collect data about how much money you have. Or we could use a more qualitative measure and collect data about whether you are in charge of determining how you do your job or if someone else tells you what to do. We could also look at the kinds of items you like to buy: a Ferrari and an antique chair can cost the same amount of money, but if you choose to buy one rather than the other, it might say something about you and your social class! All of these operationalizations of "class" make sense, but they are very different. Making a choice to operationalize class in one way rather than another will influence your research project.

Measurement assumptions (how you operationalize your abstract hypothesis) are not something you can escape. They apply to *all* research projects. But given that they are important for your findings, it is imperative that you are clear about what they are, how you arrived at the operationalizations you selected, and what the implications are for generalizing your findings back to your abstract hypothesis.

After we have made our measurement assumptions, we are finally ready to articulate our **operational hypothesis**, which is even more specific.

Among people who live in the United States, are of working age, and fill out a survey where they report their schooling and salary, those who report having spent more years in school will report having a higher salary than those who report less schooling.

This hypothesis seems considerably more limited than where we started. Although social research aims to answer big questions about social phenomena, the design of research projects is typically narrow. As we move from a general interest to a specific question, we must narrow it to a question we can actually answer. We have made some assumptions along the way—unavoidable ones but ones we must be clear about articulating. We have moved from an interest in education and income to years of schooling and salary. We could have made other measurement assumptions and moved in a different direction, but the practice of research requires that we make such specific choices to get from abstract concepts to particular operationalizations. And this move means making assumptions and narrowing the scope of our work. But being more narrow or specific has its benefits: we are asking a question we can actually answer. And that means that through our answer we will know more about the world than when we started.

This variable-based articulation of an hypothesis may seem closer to what quantitative scholars do than what qualitative researchers do. To a degree, that is true. As you will see over the course of these chapters, the hypotheses that researchers end up with are not always the ones they started with! Sometimes such articulations are created after data are collected and the researcher asks, "What do I have here?" Regardless, the questions we have identified are of equal importance to the qualitative researcher, even if his or her hypotheses are less focused on causality and more on relationships among qualities. In other words, before beginning any research project, you must be able to answer the following questions: What are the relationships that I am interested in studying? How do I decide who counts as part of my population of interest? What are the concepts that I want to study? And what counts as an observation of these concepts? Whether you do an ethnography or an experiment, these are important questions you must be able to answer in order to do your research.

Selecting a Population of Interest

Once a research question has been pared down to an operational hypothesis, it is time to figure out whom exactly you will observe to test this hypothesis. **Sampling** is the way in which social scientists select a representation of their population of interest. It is very rare that we can study everyone we are interested in—or what we call a **population**. Instead, we often have to study a smaller group of people whom we claim are representative of that population. Such sampling happens in quantitative and qualitative work. In qualitative work we might, for example, be interested in the conditions of homelessness. We cannot study all homeless people in the country. Instead, we might do an ethnography of a neighborhood where homeless people live. In this instance, we are not studying all homeless people. We are studying a sample of homeless people (a neighborhood), with the hope that what we learn from our sample can be **generalized** to our population of interest.

In quantitative work, it is most often the case that samples are drawn to be as representative as possible, so that we can generalize to as large a population of interest as is manageable. There are generally four steps to this process: (1) deciding upon a population of interest, (2) creating a study population, (3) deciding on a sample frame, and (4) constructing a sample. We will deal with each of these points in turn.

Your first question when creating a sample is "Whom do I want to study?" This is your population of interest. It could be everyone in the United States or everyone enrolled at your college. The population of interest is the population about which you hope to generalize your research findings.

It is very rare that you can actually study everyone in your population of interest. Instead, you will have to take a sample. In other words, you will have to come up with a plan for how to select some of them in a way that is representative in meaningful ways to the larger population you want to understand. One of the main questions you should ask yourself when you start to develop your sampling is how you actually gain access to the people you want to study? If you cannot access them, then you cannot study them! The group that you can access through your sampling techniques is called your **study population**. If you are interested in the entire population of the United States, chances are you will not be able to access everyone due to time and resource constraints, as well as to the fact that some members of your population may be inaccessible because they will not respond to you or they are unavailable. For example, if your population of interest is the entire United States, it is unlikely that you will be able to access prisoners; so your study population will miss these two million Americans. It is also unlikely that you can access the very, very rich or the very, very poor. People who are living here illegally are similarly likely to avoid being accessed by researchers. As a result of these issues, your population of interest and your study population are rarely the same.

Once you have decided upon your study population, you have to figure out how you will actually access that population. This step involves creating a **sampling frame**. The sampling frame is how you determine who will be contacted to be part of your sample. Let's say you want to study the entire US population's attitudes toward civic engagement. First, you identify your study population; that is, those people you potentially could access. Second, you construct a sampling frame, which is *how* you actually access them. Examples of a sampling frame might be randomly selecting from a telephone book, a voter list, or a mailing list or using random-digit dialing (randomly dialing phone numbers).

Each of these sampling frames comes with challenges. For example, if you decide to use the telephone book, you will not be able to access people who do not list their phone numbers, people who do not have phones, and people who have only cellular phones. If you use voter lists you will access only people who are registered to vote. If you use home addresses, you will miss people who move frequently or who have moved since your list of addresses was constructed. You will also miss those who are in institutions (dorms, nursing homes, prisons), as well as those who do not have homes. Selecting a sampling frame means balancing issues such as cost (some procedures are more costly than others), as well as considering what it is you want to know and from whom. If you would like to know what young people think about an issue, for example, using a telephone directory as your sampling frame may not be wise, as many young people have only cellular phones and are unlikely to be listed in phone directories.

Your sampling frame defines the population about whom you can actually make generalizations. This point is very important. When you draw conclusions from your work, strictly speaking, you cannot draw conclusions about your populations of interest, or even your study population. Instead, you can draw them only about the group of people represented by your sampling frame. So returning to the example above, if we are interested in the attitude of Americans to civic engagement and we decide to use a sampling frame of the telephone directory, then we can make claims only of the sort that say, "Of people listed in the telephone book, their attitudes about civic engagement are . . . [whatever you find]." In actuality, papers are rarely this specific about the constraints of their sampling frame. However, as a reader it is important to pay attention to the limits of findings based upon the sampling frame.

Once we have defined a sampling frame, we must draw a sample. This process can be done either randomly or nonrandomly. If we draw a nonrandom sample, then we are even more restricted in the claims we can make about our sample. For nonrandom samples, if we are being strict and accurate, we can truly make claims only about the actual people we studied and no one else. That is, we have no generalizability beyond our sample. However, a lot of social science work draws upon nonrandom samples and still makes claims beyond the particular people studied. In these cases, scholars argue that even though their sample is nonrandom, it can still be seen as representative of general trends. These types of samples are common in qualitative work like interviews and ethnographies. But they also appear in experiments and surveys. As you read through the papers in this volume, you should pay attention to whether or not the samples drawn are random or nonrandom. If they are nonrandom, you should also pay attention to how scholars argue that even though they cannot make claims beyond their sample, they feel confident in making more generalizable claims. We will not cover all the various types of random samples in this introduction. Interested students should consult textbooks on sampling for detailed information on many different ways to construct both a random and nonrandom sample.

Many scholars, however, in particular researchers involved with many large-scale survey instruments, like the census, use **random samples**, which are often called **probability samples**. All random samples have two elements in common. For a sample to be random, each element of the population must be (1) *known* and (2) have a *nonzero* probability of selection. In other words, if some elements of the population cannot be selected (they have a zero probability of selection), then the sample is not random. An example would be if the sample excluded people who were in the sampling frame (say, a telephone book) because they lived too far away and were, therefore, too hard to reach or too costly to access. Second, to be a random sample, the researcher must know the probability of selection for each unit. If you do a *simple random sample*, this method means that every unit selected has an equal probability of selection.

However, there are other kinds of samples—say, **stratified random samples**—where some units have a greater chance of selection than others.

Scholars do these kinds of samples when they know that there is an element of the population that is comparatively small but that they definitely want to have within the sample. Let's say in your research project you want to make sure that there are Native Americans within your sample (their data are important for your project for some reason). There are not many Native Americans in the United States. So if you do a simple random sample—where everyone has the same chance of being selected—you are unlikely to have many Native Americans in your sample. Therefore, you may choose to oversample on Native Americans to make sure you have enough of them in your sample. In this case, your sample is still a probability (or random) sample as long as you *know* the probability of selection for Native Americans (and all others).

Once you have decided on your sampling technique, you draw your actual sample. At this point, your main concern is what scholars call **nonresponse bias**. If people choose not to respond to your attempts to include them in your research, you have to figure out if there is a systematic reason why the people who are not participating are not participating. In other words, are particular types of people participating at lower rates, and if so, why? If people systematically do not respond for a reason, you run the risk of drawing incorrect conclusions based on a sample that is biased in some way.

For example, let's say you are asking people about their attitudes on sexual behavior. You do a national probability sample—in short, you do a good job constructing a sample that is representative of the American population. What you find when you look at who participated in your study is that people have very permissive attitudes about sexual activity among teenagers. However, you also see that a lot of people have chosen not to respond to your survey. One of the big concerns, then, is that the people who are likely to have permissive attitudes toward sexual activity are also more likely to answer your questions. People with conservative attitudes, by contrast, decline to answer your questions. Even with a well-constructed sample, because of nonresponse bias (where the likelihood of response is systematically correlated with a trait of interest), you cannot be confident in claiming that your finding is valid.

We have covered sampling very briefly in this introduction, but we hope to have given you an idea of what to think about when designing your own sample or when evaluating the sampling techniques of others. The importance of a sample is twofold: (1) you cannot study everyone, so you have to choose; and (2) your choice of how you sample influences the population about whom you can make generalizations.

We end with a final word on sampling, particularly in relationship to qualitative work. As we noted earlier, qualitative work rarely draws representative samples. So what can we learn from this work if, in the strictest sense, we can draw conclusions only from the people sampled by a nonrandom sample? We should remember that different methods have different aims. As we discussed earlier in this chapter, quantitative methods seek to establish associations between variables. So they answer the question "What is the association between these variables?"—say, education and wealth. Qualitative methods also look at associations, but they often address *how* and *why* questions. That is, once we know there is a relationship between education and wealth, we might wonder why that relationship exists. What is going on inside schools or with students that their education helps them earn more? Or we might explore how it is that people use their educational skills to earn more money. To show these processes at work often requires digging—down to more specifics that can be better gained through ethnographic observation or open-ended semistructured interviews. Because of the ways these methods are conducted, representativeness is much harder to achieve, and sometimes it is impossible.

Qualitative methodologists are sensitive to biases that might make their data unique, and researchers often confront these issues directly. But the potential weaknesses in terms of representativeness are often balanced by the benefits of the method: they can also provide a sense of the rich texture of how social processes work that large-scale representative studies cannot. Research does not happen in isolation. Instead, it happens in dialogue with other research. So as researchers develop ideas about how the world works, these ideas can be tested and evaluated in other settings by other researchers. Qualitative research, therefore, may be limited in its generalizability, but it can provide ideas that are critically evaluated by quantitative work that might have validity beyond the few subjects explored. Conversely, quantitative work may limit us by being able only to speak about the association of simple variables in isolation from the context of people's lives, which is the strength of qualitative work. In other words, both types of methods have strengths and weaknesses, but they can work well as complements for one another.

Validity and Reliability

Once you have completed your research project and found an association between two variables, there are two questions you should ask yourself. Both of these questions have to do with the **validity** of the findings. First, is this association really an association, and second, does this finding apply beyond the context of my actual research project? These are two of the driving questions of all research findings. And in this introduction you have seen us ask them again and again.

The first question addresses the **internal validity** of your findings. That is, can you trust that your finding is really a finding, not an artifact of something else? You might recall our discussion of spuriousness: how do we know that the association we have found isn't because some other variable has an impact on both our independent and dependent variables? We call this "something else" an **extraneous variable**. In other words, are we sure we are measuring what we think we are measuring? Almost all research has to deal with the issue of the role that may be played by extraneous variables. The only method that can fully eliminate them is the experimental method—if properly done! For most other methods, however, we are constantly worried about these variables. How do with deal with them? There are many ways, from statistical controls to asking subjects about alternate explanations. Common to all of these approaches is the advice we gave at the beginning of this chapter: be skeptical. Your aim is not to prove you are right, but to try to prove yourself wrong. And being unable to do so, you can feel somewhat confident in trusting your finding. Therefore, our skepticism means hunting for extraneous variables or for alternate explanations for why we found what we have found.

While experiments are good at eliminating extraneous variables, they have one major challenge. How do we know that what we found during our experiment applies to contexts outside our experiment? This issue is the basic question of the **external validity** of our findings. Scholars often call external validity **generalizability**. The basic question of external validity is whether or not the findings in a study can be extended beyond the study itself.

In the discussion above on sampling, we focused a lot of our attention on the generalizability of findings depending upon how subjects were selected to be part of the study. These discussions asked the basic question "How generalizable is the population under study?" or, in other words, are the group of people you are studying a good representation of a larger group? Whom you study influences your generalizability, no matter the actual research method.

But how you conduct the study also influences its generalizability. That is, we might ask how representative the research situation is of an actual situation within which people are engaging in the social world. This issue is certainly of concern for lab experiments, where we cannot always assume that how people act in a lab setting is how they will act in the world outside it. But it is also true for survey instruments, where the attitudes that people express when taking a survey might not be that strongly related to their actual behaviors in the real world. And so while qualitative data are frequently not representative in terms of the people that are sampled, they are often much more representative in terms of the situations that are studied.

Questions of internal validity are ever present for most researchers. And the practice of research means being ever vigilant in eliminating alternative explanations, looking for sources of bias, making sure the operationalization of your concept of interest is justifiable, and dealing with extraneous variables. Questions of external validity are similarly universal. And the balance of having a representative population versus having a representative situation speaks to the advantages of quantitative research in some contexts and qualitative research in others.

In addition to asking how valid our research is, we must ask about the **reliability** of our observations themselves. Reliability is the consistency of the measurements taken. For example, if multiple researchers are interviewing research subjects about their participation on a sports team and what such participation means to them, can we be sure that each of those researchers asks questions in the same way? If researchers ask "Why is participation important to you?" but one researcher uses a tone that suggests that participating is a waste of time while another uses a tone to suggest that it is the best thing you could possibly do, then subjects are not really answering the same question, even though the words are the same. In the former instance subjects may feel the need to justify themselves, whereas in the latter subjects may want to confirm just how great sports are. The result is low reliability, meaning that our measurement of the answer to the question "Why is participation important to you" will not be consistent. A further question to reliability is if all researchers are taking notes, are they doing so in an agreed-upon fashion, so that subject responses are consistently coded the same way? If they are not, then again, our reliability is low, because the same exact answer from research subjects could be interpreted differently by the researchers themselves.

Challenges to reliability are not just for research teams. If we stay with our example but assume that only one researcher is interviewing subjects about sports participation, there can still be problems with reliability. For example, if the interviewer talks to some subjects on the sports field after practice, others in the classroom after school, and others at their job, the responses may be different because the research subject is in a different situation when asked questions. After practice, the salience of the sports team might be more present for a research subject, and therefore their answers might be more biased in suggesting that sports are very important in their life.

Challenges to reliability can also come from problems with the instrument used to collect the data, such as when a survey includes questions that are too vague and open to interpretation. For example, if we surveyed a group of students and asked them, "Is class important to your life?" some subjects may answer about their social class (economic background), whereas others might reply about their experiences in the classroom. When designing research projects, researchers must take pains to ensure that they are asking questions to their subjects in consistent ways, that they are interpreting common responses consistently, and that subjects themselves are interpreting the research object dependably.

Ethics

The first and last consideration of any research project should be the ethics of the research. Research ethics are important for all research, but they are particularly acute when dealing with human subjects.

During the Second World War, German researchers (mostly physicians) conducted violent and often deadly research on concentration camp prisoners. These researchers were held to account for their actions in 1946 at the Nuremberg trials. The courts also established the Nuremberg Code, which outlined 10 basic points for research on human subjects. The first and perhaps most important was that "The voluntary consent of the human subject is absolutely necessary." The code also established that

- Research should yield fruitful results for the good of society;
- Research should avoid all unnecessary physical and mental suffering and injury;
- The degree of risk to be taken should never exceed that determined by the humanitarian importance of the problem to be solved;
- Research should be conducted only by scientifically qualified persons;
- Human subjects should be at liberty to bring their participation in the research project to an end at any time; and
- The scientists should be prepared to terminate their work at any stage if they have reason to believe that there are serious risks to the human subjects.

However, researchers have often ignored the guidelines. And ethical violations have hardly been limited to Nazi scientists. From 1932 to 1972, the Tuskegee syphilis experiment was conducted in the United States. This research sought to study the progression of untreated syphilis in a poor black population in rural Alabama. The study began in 1932 with 600 subjects, 399 of whom had syphilis and 201 of whom did not. For the next 40 years, researchers from the US Public Health Service observed these men. They never informed the subjects that they had syphilis; they simply told them they had "bad blood." Most concerning of all, after 1947 there was a clear treatment for syphilis: penicillin. Even after the establishment of the Nuremberg Code and its acceptance by US researchers, the researchers did not make the subjects aware of this treatment and simply let the subjects' syphilis progress. As a result, many in the group unnecessarily died, gave the disease to their wives, and transferred congenital syphilis to their children. The research was ended only in 1972, when a whistle-blower revealed that ethical guidelines were clearly being violated within a research project that had unnecessarily resulted in human suffering and death for many years.

As a result of these and other ethical failures, today there are guidelines in place to protect the interests of research subjects and the validity and reputation of scientific research. Though most of these guidelines were established primarily in relation to medical research, social scientists have established guidelines of their own that they use to guide their research practice.

Social researchers embrace the basic principles outlined above—particularly the idea of **informed consent**. This principle means that all human subjects must be informed about the research project before they agree to participate. As part of this process, subjects must be made aware of any risks to their person and rewards to general knowledge. A participant's consent to being a research subject is conditional upon that full awareness.

Finally, social scientists do not rely upon researchers alone to safeguard the interests of human subjects and the ethics of research. Today, an **institutional review board (IRB)** exists at every research institution to regulate the research conducted on human subjects. These boards are made up of members of the faculty and administration, and their responsibility is to evaluate impartially the ethical implications of every research project involving human subjects. Before we ever conduct social research, we must submit our research protocols to the IRB at our institutions for their approval. The IRB review is an important step in ensuring that we conduct our research upon human subjects with ethical responsibility.

WHAT TO THINK ABOUT AS YOU READ THE REST OF THE BOOK

We close with considerations that will help guide you as you read through this book and other social research. This list is hardly exhaustive. But it will get you started as you begin to think about how the designs of social research influence the reliability of the claims being made and their overall validity.

For each of these articles, we would encourage you to ask yourself these questions:

- What is the unit of analysis? And what are the units of observation?
- What are the important variables?
- How are those variables being operationalized?
- What is the proposition about the relationship between those variables? What is the abstract hypothesis? What is the operational hypothesis? What are the measurement assumptions to this work?
- What was the population of interest for the paper, and how does it relate to the population actually studied? What implications does the sampling have for the overall external validity of the study?
- What is the relationship between the research situation and the situation within which people live their day-to-day lives? What are the implications of this component of the research for the external validity of the study?
- Are there other issues that make you wonder about the external validity (how the study can be generalized to other situations or people not studied)?

- Are there any concerns about the internal validity of the study? Are there aspects of the research design that make you question the quality of the findings? Does the research deal with spuriousness (or extraneous variables)?

- How reliable are the observations? Are the variables of interest consistently measured?

- Are there ethical concerns to the project? If so, how does the author deal with these concerns?

- How did the author eliminate alternative explanations of the observed phenomena?

In the remainder of the text, each chapter begins with a brief introduction of the method in question, relates it to the topic of the excerpted paper, and ends with questions to consider. Following each introduction is an excerpt of a scholarly article or chapter. Finally, the author or authors of each excerpt have written a personal reflection about the method they employed, how it helped them answer their questions of interest, and how they overcame some of the challenges they faced.

As you move through these papers and discussions, we hope they will help you develop a better understanding of the practice of research.

CHAPTER 1

Experimentation

Experiments in the social sciences seem far removed from experiments you are probably most familiar with: those in natural science laboratories. Social scientists deal with human beings, not test tubes, and there are moral and ethical concerns when researching human subjects (though it is important to note that these concerns apply to all methods). Yet for all the differences between experiments in the natural and social sciences, there is one commonality: the logic behind this methodological technique. Experimental work seeks to isolate particular variables of interest and test their effects. If we want to see causality at work, the experiment is our best methodological tool.

ABOUT EXPERIMENTS

The great advantage of experimental work is its capacity to establish causality. The great challenge of this work is its **external validity**—the capacity for experimental findings to apply to "real world" situations. At their most basic level, experiments work in three steps. First, the researcher identifies an **independent variable**[1] of interest and manipulates it. This process involves creating two groups—a "treatment" group and a "control" group[2]—and assigning each group to one category of the independent variable. Second, the researcher randomly assigns research subjects to one group or the other. Third, the researcher keeps every aspect of the research situation the same, except for the "treatment" and "control." The basic insight behind experiments is as follows:

(1) If subjects are randomly assigned to a treatment or control group, and

(2) every other aspect of the subjects experience is the same, and

(3) the treatment produces different results than the control,
   then

(4) the only possible explanation for the different results is the manipulated independent variable.

The issue of **internal validity** is primarily concerned with questions of design. In order for experiments to work, researchers must be confident in their random assignment. If there is a reason why some subjects enter into the treatment or control group other than random assignment, then that reason, not the independent variable, could explain the outcome. In this instance, the internal validity of the experiment is compromised, and the researcher's capacity to generate a causal explanation is highly questionable. Similarly, if any part of the situation of the experiment differs for the treatment and control group other than the manipulated independent variable, then the experiment is not internally valid. For these reasons, experimentalists spend a lot of time in the planning stages of their work ensuring that they have designed a research project where only the independent variable can explain the outcome.

Questions of **external validity** are even more of a challenge. These questions are about how generalizable the findings of experiments are. Just because we found something in an experimental setting, does it mean that we can be confident we would find it *outside* the lab, in people's day-to-day lives? Experiments create "pure" situations, where one variable (and only one variable) can explain an outcome. Yet we humans live in messy and complicated situations where, more often than not, many forces are always in play. For researchers who do experimental work, a persistent question is how dependent their results are upon the laboratory situation. Researchers often deal with this concern by pointing to similar results, produced outside the lab, using nonexperimental methods. These results can help to establish that the research findings from an experiment are generalizable to the broader social world. This step is particularly important with experimental research where the subjects under study are college students who are being paid for their participation (college students are not particularly representative of the national population).

THE BIG QUESTION OF "CONSTRAINTS INTO PREFERENCES"

We can see all of these elements at play in the paper by Shelley Correll. First, we will warn you: this is a challenging paper. But it is also a wonderful example of the experimental method—one that takes on many of the issues we have discussed above. If you are finding the paper a challenge, you might start with the reflection, read the paper, and then return to the reflection at the end.

Correll begins by noting that men and women often seem to be in different careers. In particular, men are more likely to hold jobs that draw upon skills in science, technology, engineering, and mathematics. Why is this? In the messy world of our day-to-day lives, the answer is "lots of reasons." But Correll sought to take advantage of the "pure" world of experimental research to test directly the causal impact of gender stereotypes upon career choice. She asks, is it the case that men and women might have similar skill levels but that because of stereotypes, they assess themselves differently? For example, if we taught both a man and a woman to knit, and the man and the woman were equally good knitters after a few weeks, the man may assess himself to be "less good" than the woman because knitting is viewed as a stereotyped skill (something that women do and not men). And so the woman might continue knitting, and the man might quit, even if they have the same basic skills.

This example is somewhat far-fetched and silly, but it represents the kinds of insights that Correll seeks to develop—much more elegantly than we have!—to look at math/science skills. What if men and women are equally good at math or science but, because of socialization, men are stereotyped to think they're better? Perhaps even when men and women have the same skills, men are more likely to continue along a math/science trajectory because they evaluate their own skills better than women do. This is the "big question" of Correll's paper, and she comes up with many interesting answers through her experimental work.

ISSUES TO CONSIDER

If we return to the three steps of an experiment, we ask you to think about how Correll achieved each one. You should consider the **internal validity** of the experiment. How confident can we be in Correll's design? What is the **independent variable** of interest, how is it operationalized, and how was it manipulated? How were subjects assigned to "treatment" or "control" groups? Was the assignment random? Was every aspect of the experiment kept the same, except for the manipulated independent variable? Answers to these questions allow us to ask if the only thing that can explain the result is the independent variable. If the answer to that question is yes, then we can be fairly sure that Correll has demonstrated the causal impact of her independent variable.

Even if we are satisfied with the internal validity of Correll's experimental design, what is the **external validity** of this study? How confident are you that the results can be applied beyond the laboratory setting? Correll directly answers this question in her work, and it is important to note how she does so. What are some other ways Correll might have established the external validity of her experimental finding?

Finally, what are the ethical concerns of the study? In the introduction, we argued that when dealing with human subjects, we have special moral and ethical considerations when designing our work. Correll uses deception in her experiments: telling her research subjects things that aren't true. Under what conditions is such deception acceptable? When we do deceive our subjects, what are our ethical responsibilities to them? How does Correll deal with these questions in her work?

Constraints into Preferences: Gender, Status, and Emerging Career Aspirations

By Shelley Correll

How do gender differences in career choices emerge? Understanding the gendered nature of the career choice process is important since, if men and women make different career-relevant choices throughout their lives, the labor force will continue to be segregated by gender. Gender segregation in paid work is stubbornly resilient, persisting despite changes in society such as the vast movement of women into paid work in recent decades (Jacobs 1995a; Jacobsen 1994; Reskin 1993). The distribution of men and women into different kinds of occupations, firms, and establishments is consequential, explaining the majority of the gender gap in wages (Peterson and Morgan 1995).

Many explanations of this continued segregation have examined the impact of "demand-side" processes, a phrase referring to processes that lead to a greater demand for men when filling more desirable jobs (Anker 1997; England 1992; Nelson and Bridges 1999; Reskin and Roos 1990). This paper focuses instead on the "supply side" of the issue by addressing how men and women develop preferences or aspirations for different kinds of work.

This paper presents an experimental evaluation of the constraining effects of cultural beliefs about gender on the emerging career-relevant preferences or aspirations of men and women. The main hypothesis is that cultural beliefs about gender that accord men higher status in society than women can evoke gender-differentiated standards for attributing performance to ability, which differentially biases the assessments men and women make of their own competence at career-relevant tasks. The implication is that, if individuals act on gender-differentiated evaluations of their own competence when forming aspirations for activities that lead to different careers, then status beliefs about gender will also differentially impact the career-relevant choices that men and women make. If men and women systematically make different career-relevant choices, the gender-segregated labor force is necessarily reproduced.

SUPPLY-SIDE EXPLANATIONS OF GENDER SEGREGATION

Early on the path to many careers, men and women—indeed, even boys and girls—begin to differentially commit themselves to activities that are` career relevant. As early as high school, and even more strikingly by college, young men and women elect to take different kinds of courses

Shelley Correll. 2004. "Constraints into Preferences: Gender, Status and Emerging Career Aspirations." *American Sociological Review* 69: 93–113.

and choose different college majors, which produces gender differences in the kinds of jobs that are later seen as plausible options for students (Jacobs 1995b; National Science Foundation 1994). The gender segregation of job supply networks means that, even if all gender discrimination at the point of hire and subsequent promotion were removed, considerable gender segregation would still remain in paid work due to the different and seemingly voluntary career choices men and women make.

Human Capital Explanations

Scholars studying labor market matching processes tend to downplay the issue of gender differences in job supply networks. They assume that men and women have different tastes, preferences, or ways of maximizing utility, which leads to differences in men's and women's choices in careers and/or jobs. According to these theories, women know they will likely need to take an extended absence for child birth and/or care, so they choose jobs with the above characteristics to maximize their lifetime earnings. However, England and colleagues (1984; 1988) demonstrate that, contrary to the predictions of human capital theory, women employed in male-dominated occupations actually have higher lifetime earnings.

Human capital theorists attempt to explain this by arguing that women choose jobs that maximize their ability to coordinate family and paid work responsibilities (Marini and Brinton 1984; Polachek 1976). However, Glass (1990) shows that male-dominated jobs—compared with female-dominated jobs—are actually associated with more flexibility and autonomy, thus allowing a person, for example, to more easily leave work to tend to a sick child. In sum, women maximize neither earnings nor their ability to coordinate family and paid work duties by working in female-dominated occupations, leaving the question of why women and men choose different kinds of careers unanswered by the human capital perspective.

Cultural Constraints on Choice

What is needed is a supply-side approach that recognizes that the culture in which individuals are embedded constrains or limits what these individuals deem possible or appropriate, thereby shaping the preferences and aspirations that individuals develop for activities leading to various careers. While there are undoubtedly many reasons why individuals develop preferences for one career or another, my model assumes that, as a minimum, individuals must believe they have the skills necessary for a given career in order to develop preferences for that career. I refer to a person's understanding of his or her own competence as a "self-assessment." The model explains how cultural beliefs about gender bias the formation of self-assessments of competence at career-relevant tasks. I use "career-relevant" to refer to tasks, activities, decisions, and aspirations that, when performed, enacted, or held, impact the trajectory or path of an individual's job or career history.

In a companion study, using a national probability sample of high school and college students, I measured the extent to which cultural beliefs about gender and mathematics contribute to the gender gap in careers in science, math, and engineering (Correll 2001). Research has shown that students, parents, and teachers perceive mathematical skills to be associated with masculinity, while verbal skills are not (cf. Hyde et al. 1990). Assuming that students in my sample were aware of these beliefs, I hypothesized that cultural beliefs about gender and mathematics lead men to make higher assessments of their own mathematical competence than women do. Controlling for grades and test scores in mathematics, I found that male high school students indeed rated their own mathematical ability (but not verbal ability) higher than female students did. Also, self-assessments of task competence impacted early career-relevant decisions: controlling for actual ability, the higher students assessed their own mathematical ability, the greater their odds of enrolling in a high school calculus course and choosing a college major in science, math, or engineering. Most importantly, when mathematical self-assessment levels were controlled, the previous higher enrollment of male students in a calculus course disappeared, and the gender gap in college major choice was reduced.

The results of the companion study (Correll 2001) provide evidence that is consistent with the main causal hypothesis that cultural beliefs about gender differentially bias men and women's self-assessments of task competence. The companion study also uses "real world" data to show the utility of the model: self-assessments of task competence impact career-relevant decisions. However, these results can only provide limited support for the more general theoretical model for several reasons.

First, although the results of the companion study were obtained using a probability sample, they are still specific to a very limited set of tasks and professions, thereby limiting the generality of the model. Second, while the results illustrate the *impact* of self-assessments, they do not definitively support the hypothesis that cultural beliefs about gender bias their formation. This is because we must assume that the students in the sample were aware of the cultural beliefs about gender, mathematical, and verbal abilities and this awareness caused the observed gender differences in self-assessments of competence. Since we could not isolate and manipulate students' exposure to gender beliefs associated with these abilities, we could not rule out competing explanations for the findings.

For example, the companion study could not address the possibility that mathematical self-assessments tap an additional component of "real" mathematical ability not captured by math grades and test scores that served as controls of mathematical ability. If this is correct, the higher self-assessments male students make of their mathematical ability might not be the result of cultural beliefs about gender and mathematics that exist in society, but might instead emerge because men "really are better" at mathematics. To the extent that measures of ability are imperfect, statistical controls of ability cannot rule out explanations of unmeasured actual ability.

The following social psychological experiment was designed to overcome these limitations and provide evidence that allows for a more definitive evaluation of how gender status beliefs bias self-assessments of task competence. Each type of data (i.e., the data from the experiment and data from the probability sample) has its own strengths. Therefore, my argument is best evaluated by simultaneously considering the results of these two companion studies.

STATUS BELIEFS, SELF-ASSESSMENTS, AND EMERGING ASPIRATIONS

Gender is commonly described as a *diffuse* status characteristic, meaning that widely shared cultural beliefs about gender include expectations that men are diffusely more competent or capable at most things, as well as specific assumptions that men are better at some particular tasks (e.g., mechanical tasks), while women are better at others (e.g., nurturing tasks) (Conway, Pizzamiglio, and Mount, 1996; Fiske et al. 2002; Wagner and Berger 1997; Williams and Best 1990). Beliefs about gender and competence have changed over time; however, empirical studies continue to find that men are thought to be generally more capable (Williams and Best 1990:334) and competent (Fiske et al. 2002:892) than women.

Such status beliefs often function as "cultural schemas," and their effect is potentially far reaching: even individuals who do not personally endorse beliefs that men are generally more competent than women are likely to be aware that these beliefs exist in the culture and expect that others will treat them according to these beliefs.

When individuals assess their own competence at a task, they undoubtedly rely on performance information provided by legitimate evaluators (e.g., teachers, testing agencies, and employers). More positive evaluations of performance should lead to higher self-assessments of task competence. However, if gender is salient in the setting, gender will impact the performance expectations men and women hold for themselves. As long as the task is not one for which beliefs specifically advantage women, men will have higher performance expectations for themselves than otherwise similar women will. Men will, therefore, use a more lenient standard when assessing their own task competence. *If individuals are provided with equal performance evaluations of their competence (e.g., have equal scores on a test), but men use a more lenient standard, then men will overestimate and women will underestimate their actual task ability (Hypothesis 1).* In this way, cultural beliefs about gender can lead to biased self-assessments of task competence. *If competence at the task is perceived to be necessary for*

persisting on a particular career path, then higher self-assessments of compe-
tence lead to higher aspirations for activities that are associated with that career
path (Hypothesis 2).

Although many factors influence individuals' preferences for various careers, I argue that cultural beliefs about gender differentially impact the emerging career-relevant aspirations of men and women.

THE EXPERIMENT

The experiment was designed primarily to evaluate hypothesis 1, regarding the bias that status beliefs impose on self-assessments of task competence. It will also provide some limited evidence about the effect of self-assessments on emerging aspirations. A test of the hypotheses calls for an experimental setting in which task performance can be controlled and the *relevance* of cultural beliefs about gender can be manipulated by associating or dissociating gender with task performance. The gender belief associated with the task and the gender of the subject are independent variables; self-assessment of task competence and the standard used to infer ability are the primary dependent variables. Task performance was experimentally held constant.

In one condition of the experiment, I manipulate gender belief associated with the task to advantage males (the "male advantaged" or "MA" condition). I provide subjects in this condition with evidence that males, on average, have more ability at the experimental task. This association between gender and task performance is intended to make gender salient and task relevant, leading to the prediction that men will use a more lenient standard than women when assessing their own task competence, resulting in higher male self-assessment levels. In the contrasting condition, I specifically dissociate gender beliefs from the task (the "gender dissociated" or "GD" condition) by providing subjects with evidence that there are no gender differences in task ability. The explicit dissociation of gender from the task should eliminate the task relevance of gender in the setting and, consequently, the effect of gender on self-assessments.

The subjects were male and female first-year undergraduates, who were paid for their time and randomly assigned to either the MA or GD condition. Analysis is based on a sample of 80 subjects (20 subjects per condition).

Procedures

Subjects came to the lab individually and were told that they were participating in the pretesting of a new set of graduate admissions examinations for a national testing service, purportedly measuring their "contrast sensitivity" ability. To establish that the task is socially important and would be used to legitimately rank "test-takers," as is required by the theory, subjects were informed verbally by an undergraduate experimenter and by reading a passage on their computer screen, that a national testing organization developed the contrast sensitivity exam and that both graduate schools and Fortune 500 companies have expressed interest in using this exam as a screening device. To further emphasize that individuals would be ranked based on their scores, subjects were also told that participants who scored in the top 25 percent of the scoring distribution would be entered into a drawing for a 50-dollar cash prize.

Next, the gender task belief manipulation was introduced. As a part of the initial verbal script delivered by the experimenter, participants were told either that males, on average, perform better on tests of contrast sensitivity (the MA condition) or that there is no gender difference in scores on tests of contrast sensitivity (the GD condition). To further emphasize the association or dissociation of gender with the task, subjects read more about gender and contrast sensitivity on their computer screen. In particular, the cover story described the interest of social science researchers in understanding either the gender difference or the lack of gender difference in performance on this task. This manipulation was intended to either make gender relevant to the goals of the situation (i.e., scoring high on the test) or to explicitly break the bond of relevance between gender and task performance.

Participants then completed two, 20-item rounds of the computer-administered contrast sensitivity test, in which subjects have five seconds to judge which color (black or white) predominates in each of a series of rectangles (Troyer 2001). The contrast sensitivity task is a reliable instrument commonly used in experimental social psychology. The task has no discernable right or wrong answers, yet subject suspicion in regard to the task is low. Since the amounts of white and black area are either exactly equal or very close to equal in each rectangle, it is impossible for subjects to actually derive correct solutions to the problems. All subjects were told that they correctly answered 13 of the 20 items during round one and 12 of 20 in round two. The scores were similar between rounds to convey that the test reliably measures contrast sensitivity ability. Mid-range scores, such as these, should allow for a wider range of self-assessment values than more extreme scores would (Foschi 1996). Giving all subjects identical test "scores" ensures that they assess their ability from objectively identical performance information.

After receiving their scores at the end of each round, participants answered a series of questions designed to first provide ability standard and then self-assessment measures. After the second round, they also answered a set of questions about how likely they would be to engage in activities that required high levels of task ability. They then answered questions to assess the extent to which the experimental manipulations were successful. Before leaving, they were debriefed and paid.

Confirming the success of the manipulation, subjects in the MA condition indicated that "most people" view the task as significantly more masculine compared with their same gender counterparts in the GD condition. As can be seen in Table 1.1, the mean "most people rating" for women in the MA condition was 62.1, compared with a rating of 24.4 for women in the GD condition (t = 6.68, p <.001). Likewise, the mean for males in the MA condition was 52.5, compared with a rating of 30.0 for their same gender counterparts in the GD condition (t = 3.05, p<.01). The differences between the means for males and females within condition are not significant. As with the "most people" ratings, both males and females in the MA condition found the task to be significantly more masculine *personally* compared with their same gender counterparts in the GD condition.

MEASUREMENT OF DEPENDENT VARIABLES

Self-Assessment

The main dependent variable is self-assessment of task ability, in this case contrast sensitivity ability. This variable is measured in three different ways. The primary self-assessment dependent variable is a composite variable constructed from subjects' responses to ten items on the computerized questionnaires in which they were asked to evaluate their performance on the contrast sensitivity test. The self-assessment composite has a mean of 47.7 (out of 100) and an SD of 13.0.

The second measure of self-assessment, the self-assessment "rating" variable, was constructed from an ordinal level question where participants were asked to describe their contrast sensitivity ability on a 7-point scale ranging from "considerably below average" to "considerably above

Table 1.1. Means of Gender Task Association Manipulation Variables By Condition

	MA[a]		GD[a]	
	Females	Males	Females	Males
Most people ratings[b]				
Masculine	62.1 (16.8)	52.5 (24.9)	24.4 (18.8)	30.0 (21.6)
Feminine	39.4 (10.4)	36.0 (19.1)	31.4 (26.5)	40.0 (27.5)
Personal ratings[b]				
Masculine	51.4 (16.0)	45.7 (25.9)	21.4 (20.4)	26.4 (25.3)
Feminine	43.5 (12.1)	35.3 (20.9)	29.4 (26.7)	32.5 (28.2)

Note: Data shown as mean with standard deviation in parentheses; N = 80.

[a] Task beliefs: MA = male advantaged condition; GD = gender dissociated condition.

[b] Subjects were either asked how they perceived that "most people" would rate the task or how they "personally" would rate the task on a scale from "not at all masculine" (or feminine) to "highly masculine" (or feminine).

average." This question was asked after both rounds of the study and responses were averaged. The mean of this item is 3.89 and its SD is 1.00.

The final self-assessment measure is taken from a single item in which participants were asked to assess how well they did on the contrast sensitivity test. This variable takes on a value between zero and 100 as participants moved their computer mouse between anchors of "not very well" to "very well." The mean of this item is 35.5 and the SD is 17.0. Not surprisingly, the three self-assessment variables (composite, rating, and single-item) are positively correlated with one another (Pearson correlations range from .52 to .67).

Finally, after each round, participants indicated the score they would need to have achieved on the test to be convinced that they definitely possessed high levels of contrast sensitivity ability. Responses from the two rounds were averaged. The mean of the ability standard variable is 83.4 percent and the SD is 6.62 percent.

Emerging Aspirations

To measure their emerging aspirations for activities described as career-relevant and requiring high task ability, I asked the subjects to rate (on a six-point scale ranging from "highly unlikely" to "highly likely") how likely they would be to: 1) apply to *graduate programs* requiring high levels of contrast sensitivity ability, 2) apply for a high-paying *job* requiring high levels of contrast sensitivity ability, 3) take a one-quarter *course* designed for those who possess high levels of contrast sensitivity ability in order learn more about this ability, and 4) enroll in a 3-hour *seminar* on contrast sensitivity for those with high contrast sensitivity ability.

Two composite variables were created: one that is the sum of the course and seminar items and the other, the sum of the job and graduate school items, thereby allowing the composite variables to take on values from two to twelve. The mean of the "within university" aspiration variables is 7.49, with an SD of 2.57. The mean of the "beyond university" aspiration variable is 7.70, with an SD of 2.06.

These measures are intended to evaluate whether self-assessments impact *emerging aspirations* for activities that are believed to require task competence. Since participants only learned about the experimental task and ability upon arriving at the laboratory, we should not automatically assume that the measures reflect a commitment to actual behavior. It is also important to note that many factors will impact the aspirations individuals report for these or any activity. The argument is simply that the assessment individuals make of their own competence at a particular task will increase or decrease their emerging aspirations for paths requiring competence at that task. If men and women, on average, make different assessments of their own task competence, we would expect systematic gender differences in their aspirations for paths requiring some level of task ability.

RESULTS AND DISCUSSION

The main hypothesis about the biasing effect of gender status beliefs on self-assessments of task competence leads to the empirical prediction that men in the MA condition will assess their contrast sensitivity ability higher than women will. Recall that all subjects were given the same "score," thus ensuring that men and women received equal performance feedback. Men in the MA condition are also hypothesized to use a more lenient standard in assessing their task competence compared to women performing at the same level. No gender differences in self-assessments of task competence or in the ability standard used to assess competence are predicted in the GD condition, since the relevance of gender in the setting has been explicitly disassociated.

The top half of Table 1.2 provides means and SDs of the three self-assessment variables and the ability standard variable for women and men in the MA and GD conditions. In the MA condition, men have a mean self-assessment composite rating of 55.3 on a 100-point scale, and women, a rating of 41.1. The other two self-assessment variables show a similar pattern with men in the MA condition making higher self-assessments of their task competence than women in the MA condition. Men in the MA condition indicated that they would have to score at least 79.3 percent on

Table 1.2. Comparison of Means of Self-assessment and Ability Standard Variables by Subject Gender and Task Belief

	Self-assessment		Ability	
	Composite	Rating	Single item	Standard
Means[a]				
MA Task Belief				
Female subjects	41.1 (13.5)	6.90 (1.59)	29.3 (15.2)	88.9 (4.61)
Male subjects	55.3 (14.8)	8.85 (2.43)	43.8 (20.0)	79.3 (7.70)
GD Task Belief				
Female subjects	47.1 (11.6)	7.60 (1.31)	35.5 (13.1)	82.4 (3.93)
Male subjects	47.2 (7.90)	7.75 (2.10)	33.4 (16.7)	83.1 (5.89)
F-Values[b]				
Factor				
Subject Gender	6.77*	6.05*	2.77	12.2**
Task Belief	0.146	0.220	0.331	1.09
2-way interaction	6.71*	4.45*	4.98*	16.6**

Note: N = 80.
[a] Data shown as mean, with SD in parentheses; MA = male advantaged condition; GD = gender dissociated condition.
[b] F-values from the 2-way (gender X task belief) ANOVA.
*$p < .05$; **$p < .01$

a test of contrast sensitivity to be convinced that they had high task ability. Women reported that they would need a higher score of at least 88.9 percent correct to be certain they possessed high task ability. The gender differences in the means of these variables are smaller in the GD condition.

The results of a two-way (gender of subject and task belief) analysis of variance are shown in the lower half of Table 1.2. While no significant main effect is predicted for either the subject gender or the task belief factor, a significant interaction between the two factors is hypothesized since the interaction tests whether the effect of gender on self-assessments of task competence varies with the gender belief associated with the task. The interaction term, then, provides for a test of the status belief and biased self-assessment hypothesis. As can be seen in Table 1.2, the two-way interaction is significant for all four dependent variables, providing strong support for the main causal hypothesis.

Note that the gender main effect is also significant for three of the four dependent variables. This result is due to the magnitude of the experimental effect as can be seen in Table 1.3, which contains the results of a series of planned contrast t-tests for pairs of conditions for each of the four dependent variables. Contrast 1 compares the means of the dependent variables for men and women in the MA condition and shows that men make significantly higher self-assessments of their task competence and use significantly lower ability standards than women when a task belief advantages men. In the gender-dissociated condition, however, the gender differences in self-assessments and ability standards are insignificant (see contrast number 2).

Consistent with the first hypothesis, when males are believed to be more competent at a task, men using a more lenient standard than women for assessing their own task competence, and consequently, men assess their own task ability higher than women performing at the same level. No significant gender difference was found in the GD condition, which suggests that men do not globally assess their task competence higher regardless of the task's gender association. Instead, when gender is made relevant in the setting, status beliefs about gender differentially bias the assessments men and women make.

The results presented thus far demonstrate: 1) when a task belief advantages men a gender gap in self-assessment of task competence emerges that favors men, and 2) no gender gap appears when gender is specifically dissociated from the task. But, what is the source of the gender difference in the self-assessment in the male-advantaging condition? There are three logical ways that a gender gap in self-assessments can emerge. One is that men and women are both influenced, albeit in different directions and perhaps to differing degrees, by a male-advantaging task belief. In this scenario, confronted with a male-advantaging task belief men inflate their self-assessments and women deflate theirs, compared to the assessments they would have made if gender was explicitly defined as irrelevant to the task. The second possibility is that men ignore the male-advantaging task belief, but women attend to it. The final possibility is that women ignore the task belief, but men attend to it. To evaluate these possibilities, I compare mean self-assessments and ability standards for men and women in the MA condition with their same gender counterparts in the GD condition. These results are presented as the third and fourth set of contrasts for each dependent variable in Table 1.3.

For both the main dependent variable—the composite self-assessment variable—and the single-item self-assessment variable, men in the MA condition made significantly higher assessments of their own task competence than did men in the GD condition. Furthermore, men in the MA condition were found to use a significantly more lenient standard for assessing their task ability than men in the GD condition (79.3 percent versus 83.1 percent). Taken together, these results suggest that men inflate their self-assessments of task competence when a task belief advantages them.

The results for women were less consistent. Compared with women in the GD condition, women in the MA condition indicate that they would need higher scores to be certain they possessed high levels of task competence (i.e., their ability standard is higher). However, the differences between the means of the three self-assessment variables do not differ

Table 1.3. Planned Contrast T-tests Comparing Means of Self-assessment and Ability Standard Variables Between Conditions

Dependent		Contrast	
Variable	Number	Task Belief Contrast[a]	Self-assessment
Composite	1	Female MA vs. Male MA	−3.17*
	2	Female GD vs. Male GD	−0.10
	3	Female MA vs. Female GD	−1.52
	4	Male MA vs. Male GD	2.17*
Rating	1	Female MA vs. Male MA	−2.73*
	2	Female GD vs. Male GD	−0.27
	3	Female MA vs. Female GD	−1.52
	4	Male MA vs. Male GD	1.18
Single item	1	Female MA vs. Male MA	−2.55*
	2	Female GD vs. Male GD	0.44
	3	Female MA vs. Female GD	−1.35
	4	Male MA vs. Male GD	1.78*
Ability standard	1	Female MA vs. Male MA	4.82**
	2	Female GD vs. Male GD	−0.47
	3	Female MA vs. Female GD	4.83**
–	4	Male MA vs. Male GD	−1.78*

Note: N = 80.
[a] MA = male advantaged condition; GD = gender dissociated condition.
*p <.05; **p <.01 (one-tailed, variances not assumed to be equal)

significantly between conditions for women. Taken together, the male and female results provide some evidence that both men and women are influenced by male-advantaging beliefs, although the results are more reliable for men.

Summary of Results

The main hypothesis was strongly supported. Men use a more lenient standard to infer ability and assess their task competence higher than women when exposed to a belief about male superiority, but no gender differences in self-assessments or ability standards were found when gender was defined as irrelevant to the task. Further, these differences were produced relatively easily. Although subjects had not heard of the task before participating in the study, after minimal exposure to a belief about male superiority and two rounds of testing, significant gender differences in self-assessments of task competence emerged.

The results from the experimental are consistent with those found in the analysis of the probability sample described earlier where male students assessed their own mathematical, but not verbal, competence higher than their equal ability female counterparts did. Therefore, the survey results suggest that the causal mechanism evaluated with experimental data operates in a similar way in a "real world" (i.e., non-laboratory) setting.

The experimental data also rule out the alternative explanation described earlier for higher male self-assessments. Recall that, according to this alternative logic, self-assessments tap an additional component of unmeasured "real" ability, leading to the explanation that, in the case of mathematics, men make higher assessments of their mathematical ability, not because of the biasing effect of cultural beliefs about gender and mathematics, but because men "really are better" at mathematics. However, because correct solutions to the experimental task are impossible to derive, men cannot "really" be better at the experimental task. Nevertheless, when subjects, who were all given the same score on the task, were told that, on average, men perform better on the test, male subjects rated their task ability higher than female subjects did, consistent with the hypothesis advanced in this study.

In sum, both kinds of data support the hypothesis that status beliefs about gender bias the assessments men and women make of their own task competence. But, do gender differences in self-assessments influence emerging aspirations for activities that require task ability? The second hypothesis is that higher self-assessments of competence at a particular task lead to higher aspirations for activities that require some level of competence at that task. Therefore, higher self-assessments of contrast sensitivity ability should be associated with higher levels of aspirations for future activities that are thought to require this ability, regardless of experimental condition. However, because men in the MA condition were found to assess their contrast sensitivity ability higher than women in this condition, these men should also have higher aspiration levels.

In Table 1.4, I provide a comparison of means and SDs of the two future aspiration variables by subject gender and task belief. The top portion of the table contains the means and SDs, and the lower portion provides results from two different 2-factor analysis of variance models. As expected, the means for the two future aspirations variables are higher for men in the MA condition than for women. However, women in the GD condition have higher mean aspirations than men. The two-way interaction between gender and task belief is significant for both aspiration variables in the 2-factor analysis of variance presented in the middle portion of Table 1.4. Consistent with theoretical predictions, the significant interaction term indicates the effect of gender on emerging aspirations does differ with the gender belief associated with the task. When a belief exists

Table 1.4. Comparison of Means of Emerging Aspiration Variables by Subject Gender and Task Belief

	Within University Aspirations	Beyond University Aspirations
Means[a]		
MA Task Belief		
Female subjects	5.75 (1.89)	5.90 (1.62)
Male subjects	7.55 (3.19)	6.75 (2.47)
GD Task Belief		
Female subjects	6.75 (2.00)	7.65 (1.69)
Male subjects	5.90 (2.73)	6.70 (1.66)
F-Values[b]		
Factor		
Subject Gender	0.717	0.014
Task Belief	0.336	4.03*
2-way interaction	5.58*	4.52*
R-squared	.08	.10
F-Values[c]		
Factor		
Gender	0.040	0.620
Task Belief	0.251	4.69*
2-way interaction	2.83	2.05
Self-assess (beta)	0.052*	0.040*
R-squared	.14	.16

Note: N = 80.
[a] Data shown as mean, with SD in parentheses; MA = male advantaged condition; GD = gender dissociated condition.
[b] F-values for baseline 2-factor ANOVA (gender X task belief) with no covariates.
[c] F-values for 2-factor ANCOVA (gender X task belief) with self-assessment covariate added.
*p <.05; **p <.01

that men are better at a task, men have higher aspirations than women for paths requiring some level of task ability.

But, is the interactive effect the result of the gender difference in self-assessments found in the MA condition? To answer this question, I added the self-assessment composite variable as a covariate to the baseline model above (see bottom portion of Table 1.4). The self-assessment composite variable has a significant positive effect on both aspiration variables, and the model fit improves significantly with the addition of this variable. Higher self-assessments of task competence do increase individuals' reported aspirations to continue on a path requiring high levels of task competence.

Importantly, the two-way interaction is no longer significant once the model is conditioned on level of self-assessment. This result is consistent with the mechanism advanced in this study: gender differences in self-assessments of task competence play a mediating role in producing gender differences in emerging aspirations. While many factors undoubtedly influence the formation of aspirations for activities thought to be career-relevant, the experimental data suggest that status beliefs about gender bias individual self-assessments and differentially influence the emerging aspirations of men and women.

CONCLUSION AND IMPLICATIONS

Gender differences in self-assessment of mathematical competence, which are biased by cultural beliefs about gender and mathematics, influence actual commitment to paths leading to careers in science, math, and engineering, thereby contributing to the continued dearth of women in the quantitative professions. Taken together, the experimental and survey results illustrate that gender-differentiated self-assessments of task competence impact emerging aspirations and early career-relevant decisions.

The motivation for this study was to better understand how gender segregation in paid labor persists over other structural changes in society by focusing on the supply-side of the issue, examining how cultural beliefs about gender differentially constrain the emerging career-relevant aspirations or preferences of men and women. The implication of the theory is that if gender differences in aspirations emerge, men and women will likely make different career-relevant choices, which will funnel them into supply networks for different types of jobs. Rather than examining how men and women's aspirations emerge, many previous supply-side explanations simply document or assume that men and women *have* different aspirations or different career-relevant preferences. However, as I have shown, individuals form aspirations by drawing on perceptions of their own competence at career-relevant tasks, and the perceptions men and women form are differentially biased by cultural beliefs about gender. In this way, macro belief structures constrain emerging preferences and aspirations and, to the extent that individuals act on their aspirations, individual choice. The failure to recognize the constrained aspect of choice obscures some of the processes by which gender inequality is perpetuated. It either defines the problem away or locates its source in the individualistic actions of those already disadvantaged by their position in the labor market.

REFLECTION

Causal Claims and Ethical Concern: The Why and When of Laboratory Experiments

By Shelley Correll

The purpose of the experimental method is to assess whether one thing causes another. For example, educational researchers have long been interested in whether smaller class sizes might cause an increase in student learning. An experiment is an ideal method with which to answer this question: place some students in a classroom with a small number of students and others in a classroom with a larger number of students, and then compare the academic performance of the two groups over the course of the school year. We would want the two groups of students to be as identical as possible before the study started, and we would want the large and small classrooms to be as similar as possible, except of course for the difference in the number students. We would then be poised to answer the question of whether small classroom size causes an increase in learning.

Two key features differentiate experiments from other methods. First, the researcher manipulates the independent variable of interest to create "conditions," or levels, of the independent variable. In our classroom example, the two conditions are the small- and large-size classrooms. Second, the researcher randomly assigns participants to each condition. In our example, the researcher might draw names out of a hat in order to determine which students are placed in each condition. Random assignment ensures that the students who were assigned to the small-size classrooms do not differ in some important way from students assigned to the large classrooms.

In the study that you just read, "Constraints into Preferences," I used a laboratory experiment to assess whether gender beliefs (also called gender stereotypes) cause men and women to assess their task performance differently and, consequently, to develop different career aspirations. In the paragraphs below, I'll discuss why I chose to use an experiment to answer this question and point out the advantages of the experimental method and also some of the drawbacks. I'll also reflect on the ethical issues that I grappled with when designing this study. In the end, I hope to leave you with an appreciation for laboratory experiments and how they might effectively be used in social research.

My Research Question (and How I Came to Conduct an Experiment)

When I entered graduate school to become a sociology professor, I was interested in studying how gender affects the kinds of careers that men and women decide to enter. I knew that men were more likely to be in careers, like engineering, that paid relatively well, while women were more likely to be in careers, like elementary school teaching, whose salaries were considerably lower. I wanted to understand how these differences emerged and wondered whether gender stereotypes about careers might funnel women and men along different career paths rather than innate personal preferences. At this early stage in my career, I had no intention of conducting experiments to answer this question.

In fact, my first research project on this topic used survey data to analyze why there are so few women in math, science, and engineering professions. To enter these professions, students must take an extensive number of mathematics classes. Research has shown that mathematics is stereotyped as masculine, meaning that large numbers of people believe that men are better than women at math. (There is very little evidence that this stereotype is accurate, but it exists nonetheless.) Because mathematics is stereotyped as masculine, I hypothesized that men would be more likely than women to think they were good at math and thus, I reasoned, men might also be more likely than women to aspire to careers requiring high levels of mathematical ability.

Using a large, nationally representative survey of American high school students, I compared how young men and women with the same math grades and math test scores assessed their own mathematical ability. Consistent with my hypothesis, the data showed that boys thought they were better at math than girls did. Importantly, the higher self-assessments boys made of their own mathematical ability led boys to be more likely than girls to select majors in science, math, and engineering when they enrolled in college.

I was initially delighted with this result since it was consistent with my argument about how gender stereotypes shape career aspirations. The data were from a large, representative, and highly regarded survey of students, so the results had high external validity, meaning we could confidently expect that these results would generalize to the larger population of U.S. students. Yet at the same time, I was unsatisfied. The study did not actually show that gender stereotypes caused gender differences in career aspirations. The survey had not asked students about their knowledge of gender stereotypes. Instead, I had to assume that the boys and girls in my sample had a sense of the stereotypes about mathematics and that this affected how they assessed their mathematical ability. So while the result was consistent with my hypothesis, I had not definitively established that negative stereotypes cause lower self-assessments.

I also could not rule out the possibility that some other difference between the boys and girls in my sample caused the differences in self-assessments of mathematical ability. I made sure they had equivalent math grades and math test scores, that they had taken the same number of mathematics classes, and that they were from similar family backgrounds. But what if some other factor differentiated the boys from the girls? And what if it was this factor (and not gender stereotypes) that caused the differences in self-assessments?

One critic even suggested to me that the boys in my sample might actually be better at mathematics and that their (supposed) higher ability is what caused them make higher self-assessments. While I had ensured that the boys and girls had equal math grades and math test scores, the critic suggested that perhaps there was some other aspect of math ability that differentiated the boys from the girls. It was at this point that I knew I had to conduct the experiment that you read about. It was the only way that I could silence the critic and convince myself that negative stereotypes cause lower self-assessments. Only experiments can show that a given factor, not some other factor, is the cause of an outcome.

At a more abstract level, my argument asserts that individuals exposed to a negative stereotype or belief that their group lacks some important ability will use a stricter standard when evaluating themselves. Consequently, they will make lower assessments of their ability. A laboratory experiment allows the researcher to be able to create just the situations she needs to evaluate this sort of abstract argument. My plan was to create two conditions where I expose some participants to a negative form of a stereotype and other participants to a neutral form of a stereotype. I would hold all other factors in the environment constant. I would then randomly assign individuals to the two conditions and measure what affect the different types of stereotypes had on their assessments of their ability.

Evaluating the Argument

Creating an experiment to test my argument required several steps. First, I needed to create different kinds of stereotypes about some ability. That ability needed to be unfamiliar to individuals since familiar abilities already have stereotypes attached to them. I decided to use "contrast sensitivity" ability, which, unbeknownst to participants, is not actually a real ability. As you read, I told participants that contrast sensitivity ability is "an ability to quickly and accurately detect subtle differences in visual images." They were further told that preliminary research indicates that tests of contrast sensitivity are highly correlated with both graduate school success and early career success.

Participants were given a test where they judged the relative amount of white and black area in a series of images. They were told that this test measured their contrast sensitivity ability. In actuality, there were no right or wrong answers—the images were generated such that they contained equal amounts of black and white. Since there were no right or wrong answers, I was able to give participants whatever score I wished. I gave all participants the same score, so they all had the same performance information from which to assess their ability. And with no right or wrong answers, men could not actually be better at the task. I was on my way to silencing that critic.

Before participants took the test, I need to create a "cover story," a false rationale for why they are being asked to participate in the study. Without some sense of a plausible purpose, I worried that participants might become disengaged or distracted trying to figure out the experiment's real aim. I told participants, "the primary goal of this study is to evaluate a new set of tests that has been developed to be included in some graduate school admissions exams." At this point, you may be understandably concerned about all of the deception—I lied to participants about the purpose of the study, exposed them to false stereotypes, and gave them false feedback about a fake ability. I'll discuss how I grappled with issues of deception shortly.

Recall that the two main features of an experiment are manipulation of the independent variable and random assignment to conditions. My independent variable was the gender stereotype attached to the task. To manipulate this variable, I created two conditions: the male advantaging (MA) condition and the gender dissociated (GD) condition. In the male advantaging condition, participants were informed that men, on average, score higher than women on tests of contrast sensitivity ability. In the gender dissociated condition, participants were informed that researchers have found no gender differences in contrast sensitivity ability.

Participants were then randomly assigned to one of these two conditions. I created a stack of folders for participants in each condition—40 folders for the MA condition and 40 for the GD condition—and shuffled these 80 folders so that they were in a random order. As participants showed up for the study, I took the top folder from the stack, thereby assigning participants to a condition based on a random process.

Random assignment is often called "the great equalizer." By randomly assigning participants to conditions, any differences that exist between them are evenly distributed across conditions. Imagine, for example, that some participants simply have higher confidence levels overall. If so, they might be more likely to make high assessments of their contrast sensitivity ability just because they are very confident. With random assignment, differences in confidence levels will be equally distributed across the two conditions. Equal numbers of highly confident people will be in each condition.

Finally, I needed measures of my three dependent variables: 1) the ability standard that participants used to judge their performance, 2) the self-assessments they made of their ability, and 3) their aspirations for career paths that required contrast sensitivity ability. We asked participants to state the number of the test items they would need to answer correctly to be sure they had contrast sensitivity ability. We expected women would set a higher standard than men in the MA condition (because they heard that men had more ability in that condition) but not in the GD condition. We then asked them to rate how much contrast sensitivity ability they felt they had on a scale from 0 (no ability) to 100 (very high ability). We expected that men would assess their ability higher than women in the MA condition but not in the GD condition. Finally, we asked participants to state how likely they would be to apply for a graduate school program or job that required high contrast sensitivity ability. We expected that men would have higher aspirations than women in the MA condition but not in the GD condition.

All of these hypotheses were supported. Since men and women were given the exact same test scores, since there were no actual differences in their abilities, and since they were randomly assigned to condition, thereby equalizing other differences between participants in the two conditions, I felt confident in claiming that the gender stereotypes caused the differences we found.

Limits to the Experimental Method

Laboratory experiments are often said to be the "gold standard" for establishing causality. In a well-designed, highly controlled laboratory setting, we can ensure that the only difference between conditions is the independent variable of interest. However, highly controlled situations are necessarily artificial. Who sits in a cubicle by herself taking tests of fake abilities? Furthermore, experiments are often conducted on convenience samples, usually undergraduate students who participate in the experiment in exchange for pay or credit in a course. Because of the artificiality of the setting and the use of convenience samples, results of experiments do not generalize directly to larger populations. That is, experimental data often lack external validity even though they have high levels of internal validity.

By contrast, the study I described earlier, which used survey data to evaluate how students assess their mathematical ability, had high levels of external validity (since the data came from a random sample of US high school students) but lacked internal validity, since we could not rule out the possibility that some other factor besides stereotypes caused gender differences in self-assessments. As these examples illustrate, external validity and internal validity are often in tension with one another. In the "Constraints into Preferences" study , I chose an experimental method, because my main goal was to convince my critic and myself that negative stereotypes cause individuals to make lower assessments of their abilities. I was willing to sacrifice the power to generalize from the data so that I could gain strong evidence about the underlying causal process.

But external validity is important. We would like to know whether negative stereotypes have similar effects on people outside the laboratory. We'd like to know whether people of different ages, ethnicities, and educational levels react similarly to negative stereotypes. One way to increase the external validity of the study is to repeat the experiment with participants from populations different from those found on college campuses. The experiment could be repeated, for example, at a shopping mall.

A second way to achieve more external validity is to evaluate the same hypothesis with different research methods. This was my approach. "Constraints into Preferences" was designed to complement my earlier research that relied on survey data from a random sample of US students. Taken together, the results of these two studies maximize the strength of each research method: the experiment provides strong evidence about the causal process involving stereotypes, while the survey data illustrates that the causal process operates similarly outside the laboratory. By combining results from more than one research method, we can produce more well rounded knowledge, knowledge that sheds light on different aspects of the same problem and that minimizes the limits associated with any particular research method.

Ethical Issues

While experiments are well suited for assessing causal processes, not all research questions can be ethically answered with experimental methods. For example, we might be interested in whether insufficient nutrition causes students to perform more poorly in school. It would clearly be unethical to randomly assign some children to a condition where they were given insufficient nutrition so we could observe how poor nutrition affects their school performance.

Even when research questions are suitable for experiments, experiments raise other unique ethical issues. In particular, laboratory experiments often involve deception. In the study you just read, I told participants, falsely, that the test they were taking was going to be included on future graduate admission exams. They were also given false feedback about their performance and exposed to false stereotypes about the task. Why lie to participants? The answer is that deception allows researchers to evaluate hypotheses that would be hard or even impossible to evaluate if participants knew a study's true purpose.

Imagine if I had simply told participants the truth: "You are going to take a test that has no right or wrong answers, and I will give you a made-up score. I will then ask you to assess your ability at the task while you pretend that the task is one where men generally perform better." Participants would likely react very differently under these situations and their behavior would not realistically reflect how they might behave in more "real world" situations.

While deceiving participants allowed me to more accurately evaluate my hypothesis, I still had to grapple with whether I was justified in lying to participants. With any research project, researchers should ask the fundamental question of whether the gains in knowledge that their study is likely to produce outweigh the costs to participants who participate in the study. Deception increases the cost to participants.

Since researchers have a deep interest in their own work, they are not the ones to answer the question of whether the benefits of a study outweigh the cost to participants. Instead, an impartial oversight board, called an institutional review board (IRB), makes this decision. For an IRB's members to approve a study that involves deception, they must be convinced that the knowledge produced is sufficiently important and that deception was necessary to produce that knowledge. Furthermore, they insist that researchers use the minimal amount of deception necessary.

In my case, the IRB felt that knowledge about the disadvantaging effects of stereotypes was sufficiently important to approve the study. However, the IRB did insist, as it frequently does when experiments involve deception, that participants be fully "debriefed" at the conclusion of the study. Debriefing involves telling participants the true details about the study once the study is over. Most importantly, I had to be sure that participants knew that contrast sensitivity was not a real ability and that their "score" did not reflect their ability in any domain. It was very important to me (and to the IRB) that participants not leave the laboratory thinking they lacked some important ability. To be sure this did not happen, I had participants repeat to me a statement about contrast sensitivity being a fake ability.

While experiments often raise unique ethical concerns, it is important to keep in mind that there are costs to participants whenever they are part of any research study. Even a short survey takes up time that a participant could have been using for some other purpose. No knowledge is free. This is why we must carefully consider whether the value of the knowledge obtained in any particular study outweighs the costs to participants.

PARTING THOUGHTS

In the years since I started on the path to becoming a college professor, I have used a variety of research methods, including surveys, interviews, ethnography, and experiments. Deciding what method to use as I embark on a new project requires me to think hard about what question I am trying to answer and what sorts of data will provide the most compelling answer to that question. This is never an easy decision, because all research methods have their particular strengths and corresponding weaknesses. Since my main challenge in the study you read was determining whether my hypothesis about the causal role of stereotypes was correct, I decided to conduct an experiment. I hope my personal reflection has helped you to see the unique value of experiments for assessing causal processes like these.

NOTES

1. An "independent variable" is something that has an effect on a dependent variable. So, if we think there is a relationship between gender stereotypes and whether or not you work in a math/science field, the "independent variable" would be gender stereotypes, as it might possibly explain the field where you work.
2. Experiments can get more complicated, adding several treatment groups. But their basic logic remains the same.

REFERENCES

American Association of University Women. 1992. *How Schools Shortchange Girls.* Washington, DC: American Association of University Women Educational Foundation.

Anker, Richard. 1997. "Theories of Occupational Segregation by Sex: An Overview." *International Labour Review* 136: 315–39.

Biernat, Monica, and Diane D. Kobrynowicz. 1997. "Gender and Race-Based Standards of Competence: Lower Minimum Standards but Higher Ability Standards for Devalued Groups." *Journal of Personality and Social Psychology* 72: 544–57.

Bourdieu, Pierre. 1984 [o]1979[c]. *Distinction. A Social Critique of the Judgment of Taste,* translated by Richard Nice. Cambridge, MA: Harvard University Press.

Browne, Irene, and Paula England. 1997. "Oppression from Within and Without in Sociological Theories: An Application to Gender." *Current Perspectives in Social Theory* 17: 77–104.

Conway, Michael, M. Teresa Pizzamiglio, and Lauren Mount. 1996. "Status, Communality and Agency: Implications for Stereotypes of Gender and Other Groups." *Journal of Personality and Social Psychology* 71: 25–38.

Correll, Shelley J. 2001. "Gender and the Career Choice Process: The Role of Biased Self-assessments." *American Journal of Sociology* 106: 1691–730.

England, Paula. 1981. "Assessing Trends in Occupational Sex Segregation, 1900–1976." In I. Berg (ed.), *Sociological Perspectives on the Labor Market,* 273–95. New York: Academic Press.

———. 1984. "Wage Appreciation and Depreciation: A Test of Neoclassical Economic Explanations of Occupational Sex Segregation." *Social Forces* 62: 726–49.

———. 1992. *Comparable Worth: Theories and Evidence.* New York: Aldine.

England, Paula, George Farkas, Barbara Stanek Kilbourne, and Thomas Dou. 1988. "Explaining Occupational Sex Segregation and Wages: Findings from a Model with Fixed Effects." *American Sociological Review* 53: 544–558.

Fiske, Susan T. 1998. "Stereotyping, Prejudice, and Discrimination." In D. T. Gilbert, S. T. Fiske, and G. Lindsey (eds.), *The Handbook of Social Psychology,* 4th ed., vol. 2, 357–411. Boston: McGraw-Hill.

Fiske, Susan T., Amy J. C. Cuddy, Peter Glick, and Jun Xu. 2002. "A Model of (Often Mixed) Stereotype Content: Competence and Warmth Respectively Follow from Perceived Status and Competition. *Journal of Personality and Social Psychology* 82: 878–902.

Foschi, Martha. 1996. "Double Standards in the Evaluation of Men and Women." *Social Psychology Quarterly* 59: 237–54.

Glass, Jennifer. 1990. "The Impact of Occupational Segregation on Working Conditions." *Social Forces* 68:779–96.

Hyde, Janet Shibley, Elizabeth Fennema, Marilyn Ryan, Laurie A. Frost, and Carolyn Hoop. 1990. "Gender Comparisons of Mathematics Attitudes and Affect: A Meta Analysis." *Psychology of Women Quarterly*, Volume 14, Issue 4299–324.

Jacobs, Jerry A. 1995a. "Trends in Occupational and Industrial Sex Segregation in 56 Countries, 1960–1980." In Jerry A. Jacobs (ed.), *Gender Inequality at Work*, 259–93. Thousand Oaks, CA: Sage.

———. 1995b. "Gender and Academic Specialties: Trends among Recipients of College Degrees in the 1980s." *Sociology of Education* 68: 81–98.

Jacobsen, Joyce P. 1994. "Trends in Work Force Segregation, 1960–1990." *Social Science Quarterly* 75 (1): 204–11.

Marini, Margaret Mooney, and Mary C. Briton. 1984. "Sex Typing in Occupational Socialization." In Barbara Reskin (ed.), *Sex Segregation in the Workplace*, 192–232. Washington, DC: National Academy Press.

Markus, Hazel R., and Elissa Wurf. 1987. "The Dynamic Self-Concept: A Social Psychological Perspective." *Annual Review of Psychology* 38: 299–337.

National Science Foundation. 1994. *Women, Minorities and Persons with Disabilities in Science and Engineering: 1994*. Arlington, VA: National Science Foundation (NSF 94–333HL).

Nelson, Robert L., and William P. Bridges. 1999. *Legalizing Inequality: Courts, Markets and Unequal Pay for Women in America*. Cambridge, MA: Cambridge University Press.

Peterson, Trond, and Laurie A. Morgan. 1995. "Separate and Unequal: Occupation-Establishment Sex Segregation and the Gender Wage Gap." *American Journal of Sociology* 101: 329–65.

Polachek, Solomon. 1976. "Occupational Segregation: An Alternative Hypothesis." *Journal of Contemporary Business* 5: 1–12.

Reskin, Barbara. 1993. "Sex Segregation in the Workplace." *Annual Review of Sociology* 19: 241–70.

Reskin, Barbara, and Patricia A. Roos. 1990. *Job Queues, Gender Queues: Explaining Women's Inroads into Male Occupations*. Philadelphia: Temple University Press.

Troyer, Lisa, 2001. *SES v 7.2: A Computerized Version of the Expectation States Research Program's Standardized Experimental Setting*.

Wagner, David G., and Joseph Berger. 1997. "Gender and Interpersonal Task Behaviors: Status Expectation Accounts." *Sociological Perspectives* 40: 1–32.

Williams, John E., and Deborah L. Best. 1990. *Measuring Sex Stereotypes: A Multinational Study*. Newbury Park, CA: Sage.

CHAPTER 2

Survey Research

In contrast to experimental research, which focuses on manipulation of the independent variable into treatment and control conditions to determine causality, survey research involves describing the frequency of certain characteristics among groups of people. In this research method, a large group of people is asked a series of structured questions. The group is selected (or sampled) to represent the population of interest. And so researchers administering surveys focus much of their attention on making sure that their sampling frame represents the people about whom they want to acquire information. For a quick primer on sampling, we encourage you to look at the introduction to this book.

Survey research permeates life today—with public opinion polls and product surveys, as well as the census—it is extremely common and one of the most widely recognizable social science research methods. Surveys can be administered in person, over the phone, or through the mail. In recent years, researchers have begun administering surveys through computer-mediated forms of communication, like e-mail and over the World Wide Web. Interestingly, as the author discusses in detail in her paper, even though the research paper you are about to read studies Internet use, the author explicitly chooses not to conduct her survey over the Internet.

ABOUT SURVEYS

There are two main challenges in survey research: developing a strong survey instrument and developing a sampling frame that adequately represents the population of interest. First, attention is devoted to making sure that the questions are **internally valid**. In other words, the questions must measure what the researcher wants to measure. For example, if a researcher uses a survey to study citizen participation in democracy, then he or she must decide on a variable that represents "civic participation" (picking a variable to represent your concept is also called "**operationalization**"). In one famous case, a researcher asked about participation in bowling leagues to measure an aspect of civic participation (Putnam 2000), and this study resulted in considerable debate about whether or not such information really measured what the researcher claimed it did.

Second, **sampling** refers to how the researcher decides who is actually asked the questions. In a perfect world, research would always be conducted directly on the population of interest—so if you wanted to understand how and why college students decide to apply to graduate school, you would ask ALL college students their opinions. In that case, the data collected from the survey would be generalizable to the population—because everyone in the population was included in the study. However, it is frequently not possible to include everyone in a study because it would take too long and be too expensive. Sampling is a technique where the researcher identifies a smaller group of subjects to study. This small group is meant to represent the population of interest. The quality and characteristics of the sampling technique determine how generalizable the results are to the broader population.

Once a survey instrument is designed and a sampling frame is determined, then the survey is conducted and data are collected from the respondents. The data from the survey are then coded and analyzed using a variety of methods. The next two research excerpts represent two very different examples of survey research. In both cases, the data were collected by the researchers themselves; in other papers in this volume, we will see researchers analyze survey data from an existing source—where a large agency gathered the data. The first reading, "Digital Na(t)ives," analyzes survey data that were collected from college students using a paper-and-pencil survey during a required college class for all first-year students. As Eszter Hargittai discusses in her piece, by sampling from this required class, she hopes to avoid any biases that would have emerged if she had included just students from a class that was required only for sociology students. She argues that her sampling technique allows her to draw conclusions about all the students at the university under study, even if she did not ask her questions to all the students enrolled.

THE BIG QUESTION OF "DIGITAL NA(T)IVES"

Hargittai's excerpt focuses on testing the assumption that exists in both the academic literature and in the popular media that young people are very adept at using information and communication technologies. This assumption builds on the general notion that young people are "digital natives" because the Internet has been around their entire lives. To test this assumption empirically, she studies the ways a diverse group of young people use the Internet. The research is based on data collected through a written survey. Hargittai chose not to collect the data online, her explanation of why she made this decision is an important part of her article. As she is interested in questions of whether or not young people have a range of online skills, from being very comfortable online to being unfamiliar with online technologies, an online survey would have been more challenging for respondents who are less comfortable with the

Internet. This issue may have influenced their responses or the likelihood of their taking the survey in the first place. It is very important to keep this point in mind as we consider and develop our own research, and it goes well beyond research on Internet use: we must all be careful that our data collection method does not affect the results of the research. This issue is sometimes called "selecting on the dependent variable." In her reflection Hargittai also raises this issue. We would encourage students to pay particular attention to this concern.

Using data collected through the written survey, Hargittai is able to give us a sense of how various young people use and are comfortable with information and communication technologies; this study teaches us a lot more about Internet usage than if she asked people these questions over the medium of the Internet. Finally, students might pay particular attention to the variables Hargittai controls for in her research and why.

ISSUES TO CONSIDER

As you read Hargittai's piece and her reflection on doing such survey research, we suggest that you keep a number of points in mind. First, think about the author's method. She discusses why she chose to use a pen-and-paper survey instead of an Internet-based survey. For what populations and what questions might an Internet-based survey be the best method to use? What does Hargittai's research project tell us about the concerns of using such a collection technique? What part of the population might we miss with this data-gathering technique, and how might this technique influence the quality of answers that we receive? Also, when would a pen-and-paper survey be problematic for data collection? Second, consider Hargittai's sampling method and why the author chose to construct her sample from first-year college students at an urban public research university. She discusses why her sample makes sense to answer her big question. Can you think when this sampling method would not work and why? In a situation where her sampling would not work, what would a better method of sampling be and why? Finally, what are the implications for her sampling method on the overall generalizability of her study (e.g., its external validity)? How broadly can we draw conclusions based upon her sampling techniques?

Digital Na(t)ives? Variation in Internet Skills and Uses among Members of the "Net Generation"

By Eszter Hargittai

Soon after the Internet started spreading across the mass population, concerns about its unequal distribution were voiced both in academic as well as policy circles (see, for example, Compaine 2001; Hoffman and Novak 1998; National Telecommunications and Information Administration 1995). The initial focus of investigation and discussion was the so-called "digital divide" or the differences between the connected versus those not online at all. Undoubtedly, this was and remains an important area of inquiry given that a sizeable portion of the population even in the United States continues to be disconnected (Jones and Fox 2009; Zhang, Callegaro and Thomas 2008) and since lack of Internet access excludes people from many important resources. Nonetheless, an underlying assumption permeates such a concentration of attention on the single question of connectivity: that once people go online issues of inequality are no longer a concern.

This approach seems to be especially strong when it comes to looking at young people's information and communication technology (ICT) uses. Both in popular media and elsewhere, assumptions prevail about their inherent savvy with technologies (Prensky 2001, Tapscott 1998) simply due to the idea that they have had exposure to digital media throughout their lives. This perspective has led to a whole cohort of people being labeled "digital natives" (as opposed to "digital immigrants") (Prensky 2001) or the "Net generation" (Tapscott 1998) with the implication that differences in ICT uses is not a concern among the young given their widespread exposure and a supposed resulting comfort with and expert knowledge of digital media.

However, critiques have warned that such assumptions about widespread digital skills among youth have not been backed up with empirical evidence (Bennett, Maton and Kervin 2008). If anything, the more general scholarly literature on Internet use suggests that even once people cross the initial connectivity divide, numerous differences remain among them when it comes to how they incorporate the Internet into their lives (e.g., Barzilai-Nahon 2006; DiMaggio et al. 2004). Consequently, it is important for research in this area to investigate differentiated uses among those online so we have a better understanding of the contours of digital inequality and what processes underlie them even once the majority of Americans have crossed over to the connected side of the "digital divide". Focusing on young people, in particular, has the added benefit of also

Eszter Hargittai. 2010. "Digital Na(t)ives? Variation in Internet Skills and Uses among Members of the 'Net Generation.'" *Sociological Inquiry* 80 (1): 92–113.

providing an empirical test of assumptions about the supposed inherent savvy of the so-called "digital natives".

In his address on December 6, 2008, then President-Elect Barack Obama talked about the relatively bad condition of broadband adoption in the United States (see comparisons with other countries in Organization for Economic Cooperation and Development 2008) and suggested that improving the state of affairs in this domain would be an important part of his public works construction program (Office of the President-Elect 2008). Indeed, the American Recovery and Reinvestment Act of 2009 allocated billions of dollars for such efforts (Committee on Appropriations 2009). While increasing broadband access is a necessary step toward making sure that Americans from diverse backgrounds have the potential to take advantage of all that the Internet has to offer, as sociologists of technology know (e.g., Bijker, Hughes and Pinch 1987; and for communication technologies in particular: Starr 2004), the social implications of technologies are dependent on much more than inherent characteristics of technologies alone. Accordingly, achieving a knowledgeable Internet citizenry is unlikely to be resolved through a solely technical approach that focuses only on infrastructure without any consideration of the social processes and institutions in which people's Internet uses are embedded. To offer evidence of this proposition, this paper analyzes data on the Internet uses of a diverse group of young adults who are all connected. By controlling for basic Internet access and use, it is possible to examine whether variation remains among users once basic connectivity has been achieved and whether divergent uses are randomly distributed or are systematically related to certain social factors.

DATA AND METHODS

Consistent in the literature is that both age (e.g., Jones and Fox 2009; Loges and Jung 2001) and education (e.g., Hargittai and Hinnant 2008; Howard, Rainie, and Jones 2001) are important predictors of varied Internet usage. By working with a population where these two factors are held constant, it is possible to investigate in more depth what other factors might matter in differentiated Web uses. Consequently, this paper is based on a population where level of education is held constant and there is only small variation in age among participants, namely, all respondents are young adults and they all have equal levels of education.

The study's population is the entire first-year college class of an urban public research university that is not the flagship campus of the state's university system.[1] In winter, 2007, a paper-pencil survey was administered in class to students in the one course on campus that is required for everybody thereby avoiding any selection bias as to who is enrolled in the class. There were 87 sections in this course out of which 85 took part in the project for a 98 percent section participation rate. Students who were absent on the day of the survey administered in their respective sections were excluded yielding an overall 82 percent response rate from among those enrolled in the course. The survey was administered on paper rather than online so as not to bias against those who spend less time using the Internet or who may feel less comfortable filling out forms online. Since both time spent online and level of Web-user skill are variables of interest in the study, it was important not to use a data-collection method that might be related to these variables.

While a nationally representative sample would be the most ideal for testing the hypotheses, no such data set exists to date with sufficiently nuanced information about the variables of interest here. Worthy of note is the fact that some other results published from this data set (Hargittai 2007) have been replicated in subsequent research on a national scale (Nielsen Wire 2009) suggesting that certain findings may well be generalizable well beyond the population covered in the study. Nonetheless, it is important to stay conscious of the fact that the sample is not representative especially on age and education. Since existing literature has identified both of these variables with higher levels of Internet use, if anything, this suggests that findings from this group about the potential role of factors such as socioeconomic status are likely to be conservative compared to a more diverse sample that also included people of all ages and those with lower educational backgrounds.

[. . .]

MEASURES: INDEPENDENT VARIABLES

Students were asked their year of birth to calculate age. Parental education is used as a proxy for socioeconomic status.[2] Respondents are asked to report the level of education of both their mother and their father using the following categories: (a) less than high school degree; (b) high school degree; (c) some college; (d) college degree (for example: B.A., B.S., B.S.E); (e) advanced graduate (for example: master's, professional, Ph.D., M.D., Ed.D.). Using information from these two questions, I created a parental education variable that is assigned the value of the highest education by either parent, e.g., if a student has a mother with a high school degree and a father with a college degree, the parental education variable for that student is coded as "college degree". To measure race and ethnicity, students were first asked if they were Hispanic or of Latino origin. Then they were asked their race including the following categories: (a) White/Anglo/Caucasian/Middle Eastern; (b) Black/ African American; (c) Asian; (d) American Indian or Alaskan Native; (e) Other. Most responses in the "Other" category indicated Hispanic origin and were recoded accordingly. The final categories are: Hispanic, non-Hispanic African American, non-Hispanic Asian American, non-Hispanic Native American, and non-Hispanic White.

In order to be able to identify the importance of technological context of use, participants were asked some questions about the availability of computer and Internet-related resources in their everyday lives. Respondents were asked whether they own a laptop, measured as a dichotomous variable. The survey asked about different locations where participants have access to the Internet (as opposed to actually using it regularly at various locations) by having the choice to check off all applicable locations from a list of eleven options. I created a summary variable from these; the final measure ranges from zero to eleven locations. Two measures are used to assess experience with the Internet: number of use years and hours spent on the Web weekly. The former measure is calculated using information from survey questions that ask about the stage in one's academic career when the student first became an Internet user (i.e., during elementary school, middle school, or a particular year in high school). User years is capped at 10 (a response given by just under 20 percent of the sample) and is logged in the analyses due to the idea that there are diminishing returns to additional years as the number of years increases. Time spent on the Web weekly (excluding email, chat and voice services) is derived from answers to two questions asking about hours spent on the Web on an average day; one inquiring about weekdays, the other about an average Saturday or Sunday. This measure ranges from 0–42 hours and is also logged in the analyses for reasons similar to logging number of use years. Table 2.1 presents these figures in detail.

[. . .]

METHODS OF ANALYSIS

First, I present bivariate analyses of the data to illustrate the relationship between the variables of most interest, namely, the relationship of parental education, gender and race/ethnicity to the technical context of people's online experiences as well as skills and use diversity. Then, I use ordinary least squares regression to look at predictors of skill level and diversity of Web usage while controlling for various social and use context factors. Since both outcome variables (skill score and number of types of Web sites visited weekly) are interval level and meet the requirement of normal distribution, this method is most appropriate. The correlations among the independent variables are not so high as to cause a concern of multicollinearity.

[. . .]

THE RELATIONSHIP OF USER BACKGROUND, TECHNOLOGICAL CONTEXT OF USE AND EXPERIENCES

I consider the relationship of user characteristics and several measures of technology use in an attempt to identify where exactly the contours of inequality lie in the domain of Internet usage. Figures 2.1 and 2.2, and Table 2.1 look at the binary relationship of parental education, race/ethnicity and gender to measures of technical context of Internet uses, skill and Web use diversity, respectively. In Figure 2.1, parental education is broken into five categories depicted on the x-axis ranging from students coming from families where both parents have less than a high school degree to students who have at least one parent with a graduate degree. The six graphs each look at one aspect of use: laptop ownership, number of access locations, number of use years, weekly Web hours, skill score and number of types of sites visited. In all of these cases, there is an upward trajectory as we move from students with parents having lower levels of education to students from more educated parental backgrounds. For example, while just over half (55.1 percent) of students from the lowest parental education category—less than high school education—own laptops, four out of five (81.2 percent) among the highest parental education group have such a resource at their disposal. The graph showing number of use years is the only one where there is no clear relationship between the two variables as the values level off among those students whose parents have at least some college education. Even there, however, those in the two lowest parental education categories have fewer experiences with the Internet.

As the graphs in Figure 2.2 suggest, the relationship of race/ethnicity to various Internet use measures is mixed. For the most part, African American and Hispanic students score lower on the resource and experience measures than Whites and Asian Americans. Students in the latter two categories tend to be similar regarding resources and experiences. This relationship does not hold, however, in the case of autonomy (as measured by number of access locations) and weekly hours spent online. Regarding the former measure, Whites have the most autonomy followed by Hispanic students and then Asian Americans. Concerning time spent online, African Americans claim to be surfing the Web more than their peers in any other category.

Table 2.1. Descriptive Statistics of Internet Use Variables Used in the Analyses

	Project Participants		
	Mean	St. Dev.	N
Owns laptop (0 = no, 1 = yes)	.72	.45	1060
Number of access locations (0–11)	6.16	2.11	1060
Number of use years (0–10)	6.35	2.02	1051
Weekly Web hours (0–42)	15.54	10.04	1056
Summary skill item score (0–108)*	54.32	22.64	1060
Diversity of sites visited (0–25)*	9.58	3.98	1060

* Possible range in parentheses

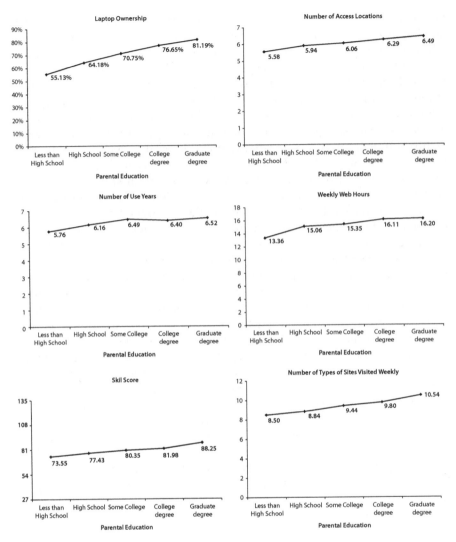

Figure 2.1. Relationship of Parental Education to Computer and Internet Use Variables

As regards gender (Table 2.2), we find statistically significant differences among the young men and women in this sample when it comes to their Web use autonomy and experiences on all, but one of the measures. Men are slightly more likely to own a laptop than women although this difference is not statistically significant. Men report, on average, about half an access location more than women. Male respondents have been online for longer than female participants and also spend more hours on the Web weekly. The difference in their reported skill scores is the starkest and we also observe variation in their diversity of online activities.

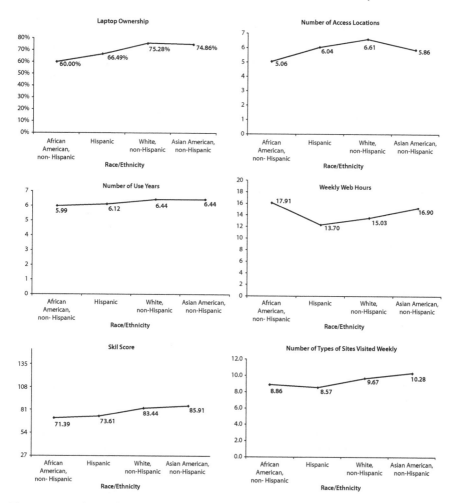

Figure 2.2. Relationship of Race/Ethnicity to Computer and Internet Use Variables

EXPLAINING DIFFERENCES IN SKILL

I consider the relationship of user characteristics and several measures of technology use in an attempt to identify where exactly the contours of inequality lie in this domain. Bivariate statistics help us understand basic trends, but it is important to look at the relationship of various user characteristics while controlling for other factors to get a better sense of what factors—demographic, socioeconomic and contextual—are mainly responsible for variations in skill. Accordingly, I use multiple regression analyses to examine predictors of skill level. Table 2.3 presents the findings from two OLS regression models with skill as the outcome variable. First, I simply look at how age, gender, parental education and race/ethnicity relate

Table 2.2. Relationship of Gender and Computer and Internet Use Variables*

	Laptop Ownership	Number of Access Locations	Number of Use Years	Weekly Web Hours	Skill Score	Number of Types of Sites Visited
Men	73.99%	6.41	6.56	16.58	65.15	10.73
Women	71.07%	5.95	6.19	14.72	45.73	8.68

*All differences are statistically significant except for Laptop Ownership

Table 2.3. OLS Regression Predicting Skill

Variable	B		B	
Age	.57	(.79)	.80	(.74)
Female (= 1)	−17.94***	(1.30)	−15.98***	(1.22)
Parental Education				
Less than high school	−7.84**	(2.92)	−4.45	(2.76)
High school	−5.31*	(2.09)	−3.78#	(1.98)
Some college	−3.37	(2.07)	−2.44	(1.94)
College	−4.33*	(1.81)	−3.79*	(1.70)
Race/Ethnicity				
African American, non-Hispanic	−6.12*	(2.51)	−5.14*	(2.39)
Asian American, non-Hispanic	2.01	(1.51)	1.92	(1.44)
Hispanic	−6.26***	(1.87)	−5.61***	(1.75)
Owns laptop			−.542	(1.37)
Number of access locations			1.59***	(.30)
Number of use years (logged)			10.16***	(2.13)
Weekly Web hours (logged)			8.21***	(.91)
Intercept	58.70	(14.75)	1.45	(14.87)
N	1,032		1,020	
R²	.217		.325	
Adjusted R²	.210		.316	

Note. Standard Errors are in parentheses. For Parental Education, Graduate degree is the omitted category, for race it is White, non-Hispanic.

= <.1, *p = <.05, **p = <.01, ***p = <.001

to skill. Then, I supplement the model with information about autonomy (laptop ownership, number of access locations) and experience (years of use, weekly Web hours).

Results show that women claim lower levels of know-how regarding Internet-related terms. Regarding parental educational background, findings suggest that even when we hold respondents' education level constant—all respondents in the sample are in their first year of college—parental education nonetheless matters in explaining variation in user skill. Those from families with at least one parent holding a graduate degree (the baseline category) exhibit statistically significantly higher level know-how about the Web than others even when we control for other background characteristics. Regarding race and ethnicity, compared to Whites (the omitted category), African Americans and Hispanic students report knowing less about the Internet. These findings hold even when we control for Internet resources and experiences as per the second model. That is, while number of access locations, number of use years and weekly Web use hours are all positively related to online skills, they do not account fully for the relationship of gender, education and race/ethnicity to skills. Rather, there is an independent relationship among these variables suggesting that user background relates to online know-how beyond the technical context of use.

CONCLUSION

Certain differences in Americans' Internet uses have been widely documented over the years, including the importance of age and education in whether people are online. These investigations may lead one to believe that once we control for such factors, differences in usage will no longer remain. By looking at a universally wired group of first-year college students and thereby largely controlling for two of the most important variables—age and education—found to be important in the literature on differentiated Internet uses, this study is able to examine whether factors beyond these user characteristics contribute to digital inequality.

[. . .]

Regarding diverse types of Internet uses, results suggest that those from a lower socioeconomic background, women, and students of Hispanic origin tend to engage in fewer information-seeking activities online on a regular basis than others. When controlling for user context, however, many of these associations no longer hold. Rather, autonomy of use (both laptop ownership and number of access locations) and amount of time spent online (although not number of years a student has been a user) matter in predicting diversity of Web usage. Parental education and ethnicity no longer explain differentiated uses although women report doing fewer things online even when we control for user context. Additionally, Asian American students engage in more activities on the Web regardless of resources and experience. As for the unique variable whose significance most studies are unable to consider, Internet user skill turns out to be strongly associated with diverse types of uses. Students with higher-level know-how engage in more activities online than those who understand the Web less. Of course, these two factors likely have a reinforcing relationship. More diverse types of uses probably feed back into increased user savvy. Nonetheless, recognizing this relationship is important in understanding what factors explain differentiated uses among people, especially among young people who are commonly perceived and assumed to be universally knowledgeable about and generally comfortable with all facets of the Web.

Overall, the results of this study show support for the importance of taking a more nuanced approach to studying the relationship of Internet use to social inequality. Far from being simply dependent on mere access, systematic differences are present in how people incorporate digital media into their lives even when we control for basic connectivity. Moreover, these differences hold even among a group of college students, precisely the type of population that popular rhetoric assumes to be universally wired and digitally savvy. These assumptions are not supported by the evidence, however. The particular societal positions that people inhabit are reflected in their Internet uses. Those who are already more privileged tend to have more Internet use autonomy and resources, more online experiences, higher levels of know-how and report engaging in more diverse types of uses than the less privileged, precisely the group that would stand a better chance of benefitting from these activities if they were more engaged with them.

REFLECTION

The Potential—and Potential Pitfalls—of Survey Research

By Eszter Hargittai

Surveys seem ubiquitous in today's world. It is hard not to stumble upon forms asking us to divulge information about ourselves—our gender, our age, our zip code, our opinions, our experiences and so on. Whether a multinational corporation or a local business, whether a political candidate or your health care provider, whether your favorite charitable organization or your alma mater, everybody wants to know more about their users, their customers, their constituents, their members. A seemingly easy way to learn about people is to ask them questions about themselves: their characteristics, their behavior, their thoughts, wants and needs. But just as with most other things, doing a good job collecting data about people through self-reports requires a careful undertaking.

Perhaps it is the ubiquity of surveys in everyday life that makes many people think that it is a simple method of data collection and all that it takes is a few quick questions on a form to gather informative data. Good survey research, however, takes much time and effort. It is both an art and a science. Doing it well, as with anything else, takes careful thought, dedication, and detailed preparation. Not only could bad surveys be meaningless if not done carefully, they could lead to outright misleading conclusions. The goal of this reflection is to help you recognize and reflect upon some of the most essential considerations when embarking on a survey project. In addition to making some general points, I will draw on the specifics of a survey study I conducted on a group of college students' Internet uses and skills, which is excerpted here (Hargittai 2010).

MOTIVATING RESEARCH QUESTIONS

Before it makes sense to think about what method to use for a study, it is important to have a research question. I went to college and graduate school as the Internet was starting to spread to an increasing portion of the population. At first heralded as the great equalizer, soon enough academics and policymakers started realizing that its benefits may not be available equally to people from all walks of life (e.g., Hoffman and Novak 1998, Norris 2001, Wilson 2000). At the most basic level, not everybody had access to the Internet. But even once people gained access to it, I speculated, people would have different levels of online skills resulting in differentiated opportunities provided by the medium (Hargittai 2003). The first study I conducted to test this supposition empirically involved in-person observations and interviews focusing on people's Web-use skills; that is, their ability to use the Internet effectively and efficiently (Hargittai 2002). One of my findings was that, on average, older people were less skilled than their younger counterparts. While this result confirmed conventional wisdom, I was not convinced that it necessarily meant universal Web savvy among youth despite the ubiquity of such assumptions in the popular press and among some commentators (Prensky 2001). Reflecting on how people acquire Web know-how and having read other research in the field, I decided that it would be important to test whether we would observe variation in skill when looking at young adults only. While the one hundred in-person observations and interviews I had administered earlier were helpful for learning in depth about people's online abilities, they were extremely time intensive and prohibitive to do on a larger scale that would allow more generalization of the results. I needed a method that would allow me to collect data on a larger number of people in a systematic way and would lend itself to comparison across them and beyond. I opted for administering a survey.

WHEN IS A SURVEY A GOOD IDEA?

As the other chapters in this book attest, there are numerous methods at your disposal for doing empirical social science research. They each have strengths and weaknesses. If you can draw on prior work—your own or others'—to inform your study and you would like to be able to identify patterns across a larger group of cases (whether individuals or organizations) than you would be able to observe in depth on a case-by-case basis, then surveys may be a helpful tool. If done right, survey data can allow you to generalize your findings to cases about which you are unable to collect information. With surveys, you rarely gather data about every unit of interest (e.g., every student in a school, all Internet users in the United States, all nonprofit organizations in a city); rather, you collect information about a sample of the population. Here, the population refers to the entirety of the units that are your focus; for example, all students enrolled at a university, all Internet users in a country, all nonprofit organizations in a geographic area. This sample cannot simply be made up of a convenience sample of volunteer respondents, however. Every member of the population has to have a measurable chance of being included in the study, so that once you have your data, you can figure out how your findings from just a portion of the population apply to the rest of that larger group. Most helpful is if you can sample respondents randomly, so that each case has an equal chance of ending up in your study. With a random sample you can infer findings about a portion of the group to the group as a whole, even for units about which you did not collect data directly.

The reason it is helpful to be able to draw on prior work when constructing a survey is that creating questions to ask respondents often requires some prior knowledge about your topic of interest. If you are interested in measuring how people tend to spend their time online but have absolutely no idea about the matter going into the project, then you are left with too many possible questions and answer options. But if you have some sense of how people spend their time on the Web, then that can help you craft questions in a way that allows you to home in on what is of most interest to you in a way that results in meaningful responses. Also, it ensures that you are not asking about things that nobody does or everybody does similarly, which would yield data difficult to analyze. That is, if you end up with no variation in what people report, then there are no differences among your respondents to try to explain, and the most you can do is state that nobody or everybody engages in what you are studying.

When I first started studying Internet skill, no one had developed measures for it yet, and it was not clear what one or two questions could get at people's online skills in a way that would accurately reflect their online abilities. As I mentioned above, at that stage of my research I conducted in-person observations and in-depth interviews with people to get a sense of people's actual Web-use skills through monitoring their online actions. In conjunction with that study, I tested different survey questions to see which ones would be good proxy measures for Web-use skill in the future (Hargittai 2005). That is, I wanted to know which survey measures corresponded best to people's online abilities based on their actual abilities and thus could stand in for skill on future questionnaires when it would not be possible to observe the actual online actions of every study participant individually. Since such survey measures of skill were thus available to me later, thanks to this prior work, I had a list of questions upon which to draw for a survey study. Questions developed through prior work do not always map onto the specific needs of a study, and thus you may be left designing your own questions. It is beyond the scope of this chapter to teach you the details of actual survey construction. You should consult literature to help you avoid some very basic mistakes, such as those that many newbies to survey research seem to make, mistakes that can be avoided rather quickly as long as people are aware of them (e.g., ensuring mutually exclusive answer categories and neutral phrasing, avoiding double-barreled questions).

USING OFFLINE METHODS TO STUDY ONLINE EXPERIENCES

Digital technologies make it possible to reach more people more quickly than using other types of communication media such as postal mail or phone calls, two modes often used traditionally to collect responses to questionnaires. Nonetheless, I opted against surveying my respondents online. Why would I not take advantage of this convenient method?

In short, I would be sampling on the dependent variable. Sampling on the dependent variable means that you are picking cases on the outcome of interest, thereby resulting in a biased sample and thus problematic results. In the case of this particular study, the concern would be that people who (a) spend more time online, (b) have more private time online, and (c) are more skilled with the Internet would be more likely to take the survey in the first place. In a similar vein, people who do not spend a lot of time online, who have to share machines with others or are in a situation where their online actions can easily be seen by others, and who are less knowledgeable about using the Web would be less likely to participate. Accordingly, in the end I would have a sample biased on measures central to my research questions having to do with people's Internet skills and uses. The data set would result in biased estimates about how much time the average person in the group spends online, how free this person is to do whatever he or she wants to do online, and how skilled he or she is at using the medium, since all of those factors may well have contributed to participation in the study in the first place. Additionally, I likely would not have the level of variance on those measures as is otherwise reflected in the population, making it more difficult to identify how other factors (e.g., gender, race/ethnicity, socioeconomic status) relate to the Internet experience outcomes of interest. In sum, it is extremely important to use a data-collection method that is not related to the substantive questions of interest in your study.

SELECTING A RELEVANT POPULATION

I knew I was not going to rely on online sampling for my study. This still left open numerous possibilities for what population to survey. A nationally representative random sample would have been ideal, but such methods can be cost prohibitive. To give you an idea, in 2003 I contracted with a survey firm to administer a 15-minute phone survey of a nationally representative group of young adults in the 18–26 age range, and that study cost approximately $20,000 for a sample of 270 respondents (Hargittai and Hinnant 2008). You can quickly do the math for what a longer survey would cost with more details about Internet uses. I decided to study college students, as that is precisely the population that is assumed by some literature (Prensky 2001; Tapscott 1998) to be universally savvy with digital media, an assumption heretofore untested empirically despite the claims. There are dozens of higher-education institutions in the Chicago area—my home base—that could have served as a population for my project. Easiest would have been to choose my own university (Northwestern), yet I ended up doing the study at the University of Illinois, Chicago (UIC). Again, I opted for the less-than-convenient option, not because I like giving myself extra work. Why then? As before, it had to do with the importance of decoupling the substantive questions of interest in my study from the research methods used to study said questions.

Motivated by findings from prior work (Hargittai and Hinnant 2008; Bonfadelli 2002), I hypothesized that user background, such as demographic characteristics and socioeconomic status, would be related to Internet skills, so it was important to gather data about a population that varies considerably on such factors. The University of Illinois, Chicago is one of the most ethnically and racially diverse research universities in the United States (US News and World Report 2006), with about half of the students coming from families where neither parent has a college degree, thus constituting a diverse population on variables of key concern in my study (i.e., race, ethnicity, socioeconomic status).

Additionally, UIC has a course requirement for all first-year students—the First-Year Writing Program—and this program was willing to work with me on the project. Were I to survey students who happened to be enrolled in a particular course, the study would bias toward people interested in particular subjects, which may itself be related to the focus of the project and was thus best avoided. Also, thanks to the support of the program, my team was able to administer the survey during class sessions, boosting the likelihood that students would participate. Indeed, the only people who were not part of the sample were students who happened not to show up on the day when we administered the survey, resulting in an overall response rate of 82 percent, impressively high for a survey project.

PRETESTING THE INSTRUMENT

Assuming that you have followed the advice outlined above and have built on prior tested work to develop your instrument, then you likely have a sound list of questions and answer options on your hands. However, before launching the actual data collection, it is imperative first to pretest the survey. Pretesting refers to having people take your survey with the purpose of getting their feedback on the questions and answer options. You should start by filling out the survey yourself. Do this before working on special formatting and layout, and do it before you transfer the survey to an online tool if it will be administered digitally. At the first stage, simply print it out on paper. Take notes on the side about things that are not clear, signal any typographical or spelling mistakes, make note of any confusing ordering of items. And of course, try to answer the questions to the best of your abilities. If something is confusing to you, then you can be sure that it will be confusing to your study participants as well, and you will need to revise it. Once you have gone through the survey, update the survey document with your changes. Do not do this as you go along. Take the entire survey in one sitting, just as your future respondents will. You want to emulate their experience as much as possible.

Repeat this process until you reach a point where you find yourself making little to no changes anymore. As you do this, put the starting time on the first page so that you can time how long it takes. This process will give you an estimate of how long the survey will take others, although this estimate will not be perfect. You will be very familiar with the questions and will likely read through them more quickly than someone who is encountering the text for the first time. Keep that in mind and try to slow your pace. At this point, you will start getting sick of reading the same questions over and over again, but given the amount of time you have already put into the project, these extra few minutes are worth the effort. You will reach a point when you are no longer making notations about either content or layout and the length is about right. This is the point when you know that you are ready to share the instrument with others. But wait! It is not ready for prime time just yet.

Next you should transfer the content to whatever format you will be using for data collection (e.g., special layout, online form) and then ask some friends and mentors to test the full instrument for you using that mode of presentation. You want to get a sense of how the list of questions as a whole will read to someone who encounters them for the first time (i.e., your future study participants) and how the final layout will work. Ask your pretesters to take note of anything on the survey that is not clear to them—whether the instructions, the questions, the answer options, the sequence of items—and after they are done, ask them to explain these to you. Make any necessary final changes to the instrument to address these concerns. Take the full survey one more time, and once it no longer requires any changes, it is ready to go.

PARTING WORDS

Due to space constraints, there is only so much that this reflection can cover. As you gear up for data collection, you will need to think about the best method of contacting your respondents, depending on the mode of data collection and any potential peculiarities of your population. You should also think about how you will organize your data once you have collected them and how you will transfer them to a format you can then analyze.

Survey data can help you figure out the characteristics of a population by providing some basic descriptive statistics about the group (e.g., what percentage of people do one or another thing). More importantly, they can help you identify patterns across the population by looking at the systematic relationship of two or more variables. Be sure to think about what research questions are of most interest to you throughout the process of constructing your survey. Make sure that you have items on your instrument that will help you answer those questions as directly as possible. While it is tempting to keep adding questions to a survey, remember that respondents get tired after a certain number, and so the survey cannot be too long. Make sure that the items you have will allow you to address your original questions as precisely as possible.

While surveys are a lot of work, some of it very tedious, they can be a fun and satisfying way of doing research. They often lead to results that are straightforward to explain to others; which can be an advantage. Keeping the recommendations of this piece in mind should help you develop a survey study that is methodologically sound and thus leads to results that will stand up to scrutiny.

NOTES

1. The author of this piece is not now nor has ever been affiliated with this school. Selection of the campus was due to the diverse composition of the student body and the importance of that factor to the questions of interest in the study.
2. Although measures of income would be ideal for a study examining the relationship of Internet use and socioeconomic status, reliable information of this sort is nearly impossible to collect from a college population for several reasons. For one, students rarely know the income of their parents. Also, students' own incomes are not indicative of their financial resources since many are still dependent on parental support. Additionally, asking students about household income is problematic since many live with roommates about whose financial situation they may know little.

REFERENCES

Barzilai-Nahon, Karine. 2006. "Gaps and Bits: Conceptualizing Measurements for Digital Divide/s." *Information Society* 22:269–78.

Bennett, Sue, Karl Maton, and Lisa Kervin. 2008. "The "Digital Natives" Debate: A Critical Review of Evidence." *British Journal of Educational Technology* 39: 775–86.

Bijker, W., T. Hughes, and T. Pinch, eds. 1987. *The Social Construction of Technological Systems: New Directions in the Sociology and History of Technology.* Cambridge, MA: MIT Press.

Bonfadelli, Heinz. 2002. "The Internet and Knowledge Gaps: A Theoretical and Empirical Investigation." *European Journal of Communication* 17: 65–84.

Hargittai, E. 2002. "Second-Level Digital Divide: Differences in People's Online Skills." *First Monday* 7 (4)

———. 2003. "The Digital Divide and What to Do about It." In D. C. Jones (ed.), *New Economy Handbook*, 822–41. San Diego, CA: Academic Press.

———. 2005. "Survey Measures of Web-Oriented Digital Literacy." *Social Science Computer Review* 23 (3), 371–9.

———. 2009. "An Update on Survey Measures of Web-Oriented Digital Literacy." *Social Science Computer Review* 27 (1): 130–7.

———. 2010. "Digital Na(t)ives? Variation in Internet Skills and Uses among Members of the 'Net Generation.'" *Sociological Inquiry* 80 (1): 92–113.

Committee on Appropriations. 2009. *The American Recovery and Reinvestment Act of 2009.* Washington, DC: US House of Representatives.

Compaine, Benjamin M., ed. 2001. *The Digital Divide: Facing a Crisis or Creating a Myth?* Cambridge, MA: MIT Press.

DiMaggio, Paul, Eszter Hargittai, Coral Celeste, and Steven Shafer. 2004. "Digital Inequality: From Unequal Access to Differentiated Use." In Kathryn Neckerman (ed.), *Social Inequality*, 355–400. New York: Russell Sage Foundation.

Hargittai, Eszter. 2007. "Whose Space? Differences among Users and Non-users of Social Network Sites." *Journal of Computer-Mediated Communication* 13: 276–97.

Hargittai, E., and A. Hinnant. 2008. "Digital Inequality: Differences in Young Adults' Use of the Internet." *Communication Research* 35 (5): 602–21.

Hoffman, D. L., and T. P. Novak. 1998. "Bridging the Racial Divide on the Internet." *Science* (5362): 390–1.

Howard, Philip N., Lee Rainie, and Steve Jones. 2001. "Days and Nights on the Internet: The Impact of a Diffusing Technology." *American Behavioral Scientist* 45: 383–404.

Jones, S., and S. Fox. 2009. *Generations Online in 2009.* Washington, DC: Pew Internet and American Life Project.

Loges, William E. and Joo-Young Jung. 2001. "Exploring the Digital Divide: Internet Connectedness and Age." *Communications Research* 28: 536–62.

Mossberger, Karen, Caroline J. Tolbert, and Mary Stansbury. 2003. *Virtual Inequality: Beyond the Digital Divide.* Washington DC: Georgetown University Press.

National Telecommunications and Information Administration. 1995. *Falling through the Net: A Survey of the "Have Nots" in Rural and Urban America.* Washington, DC: NTIA.

Nielsen Wire. 2009. *The More Affluent and More Urban Are More Likely to Use Social Networks.* Retrieved December 12, 2009. http://blog.nielsen.com/nielsenwire/

online_mobile/the-moreaffluent-and-more-urban-are-more-likely-to-use-social-networks/.

Office of the President-Elect. 2008. President-Elect Barack Obama Lays Out Key Parts of the Economic Recovery Plan. Washington, DC: Office of the President-Elect.

Organization for Economic Cooperation and Development. 2008. *Broadband Growth and Policies in OECD Countries*. Paris: Organization for Economic Cooperation and Development.

Prensky, M. 2001. "Digital Natives, Digital Immigrants." *On the Horizon* 9: 1–6.

Putnam, Robert. 2000. *Bowling Alone: The Collapse and Revival of American Community*. New York: Simon and Schuster.

Starr, Paul. 2004. *The Creation of the Media: Political Origins of Modern Communications*. New York: Basic Books.

Tapscott, D. 1998. *Growing Up Digital: The Rise of the Net Generation*. New York: McGraw Hill.

US News and World Report. 2006. "Campus Ethnic Diversity: National Universities." *America's Best Colleges 2007*.

Zhang, C., M. Callegaro, and M. Thomas. 2008. "More Than the Digital Divide?: Investigating the Differences between Internet and Non-Internet Users." In *Midwest Association of Public Opinion Research*. Chicago.

CHAPTER 3

Survey Research, Analyzing Social Networks

Like Hargittai's study of young people's Internet usage, Michael T. Heaney and Fabio Rojas's paper is based on data collected from a written survey. "Partisans, Nonpartisans, and the Antiwar Movement" uses data collected from a sample of antiwar protesters who are participating in legally permitted demonstrations out in the streets. Although the authors note that they collect what is called a **nonprobability sample** of participants at these protest events, which means that the subjects are not randomly selected, they go through a series of steps to minimize potential biases due to nonrandomness. The method they employ is innovative and tries to ensure the best possible sample. In other words, it makes it less likely that the protesters that are selected into their sample do not represent just those people who wanted to participate and ignores those who were unlikely to volunteer to be part of their research project.

This piece also provides an example of a type of analysis that is becoming increasingly popular in the social sciences: social network analysis. **Social network analysis** focuses on the *connections* between the individuals or organizations that are the subject of the research. In many cases, social network analysts are interested in explaining how and why people are connected. Scholars then analyze flows within these networks, as well as how the structure of the network creates opportunities and constraints for social processes. For example, research has explored how people get jobs by studying how they are socially connected to other people. Often it is those connections, not an individual's qualifications, that explain the likelihood of getting a job. Such research suggests that we can explain many social outcomes by a subject's connections and interconnections with others (without ever knowing other properties or variables about those subjects).

Other social network analysis looks at the traits of people or organizations to explain specific connections or types of connections. For example, social network analysis can be used to study a local community and how members of the community are connected, seeing if age, race, or other traits explain their connections. So if you think about the people at a college, what traits explain why some people are connected to one another? Is race particularly important (if two people are Asian, are they more likely to know each other)? Does religious affiliation matter for predicting a social tie? This kind of work is different than that mentioned above, in that individual-level traits are central to the analysis. And it helps us understand what traits are salient, or important, in certain communities.

Social network analysis also allows the researcher to explore the strength of the relationship among respondents. The strength of a tie is defined by the number of connections that respondents have in common. In the example above, two respondents would have a stronger tie if they went to the same school, played soccer, and lived on the same block. Two respondents who only went to the same school would have a weaker relationship. While common sense often tells us that strong ties are the building block of society, social research, going back over a century to the work of Émile Durkheim often argues differently. Social network analysis has shown the "strength of weak ties"—that social relationships marked by weak ties are often more robust than those of strong ties. Though this finding may seem counterintuitive, think about two different groups of friends, one with strong ties, where everyone knows each other (and is friends with everyone else), and another with weak ties, where people know each other somewhat but often through other people. If there is a big fight between two people in the group with strong ties, everyone is affected, and the entire friendship community could break down. But if the same kind of fight happens in the weak ties community, then the impacts of this fight are somewhat isolated. This kind of finding provides a quick glimpse of the insights produced by social network analysis.

THE BIG QUESTION OF "PARTISANS, NONPARTISANS, AND THE ANTIWAR MOVEMENT"

Heaney and Rojas's paper aims to understand the ways that social movements and American political parties interact. This paper represents one of the few empirical studies that explore the relationship between activism and partisan politics in the United States. In most research, people who engage in social movement activities, like protesting, and people who participate in electoral politics by volunteering for political campaigns tend to be studied separately. By combining them, we get a better sense of how the whole political process works. The authors study this interaction by focusing on participants in the antiwar movement in 2004 and 2005. The article itself has three components: first, it looks at the relationship between political party affiliation and organizational membership of activists in the network; second, it explores the types of activities activists participate in based on their political affiliations; and third, it assesses the relationship between access to a congressperson and the partisan identity of congressional representatives. In the excerpt that follows, we have included only the first section of the paper. This excerpt focuses specifically on the relationship between partisanship and the social movement by using social network analysis.

ISSUES TO CONSIDER

While you are reading Heaney and Rojas's excerpt and Michael T. Heaney's reflection on how they conducted their research, we suggest you think about the method and sampling procedure that the authors employed. When would this procedure yield good data, and when might it not be usable? What kind of **reliability** would we expect from their data gathering technique? And how **externally valid** are their results beyond the movements studied? There are a number of times when a face-to-face survey of crowd participants would not work or would be successful only for a specific subsample of the population, yielding biased data. How confident are you that the sampling technique they chose allows them to generalize beyond their participants to a broader population of interest? You might also think about what kinds of questions would not be answered by research subjects in a face-to-face survey in a public place. Finally, what was the added benefit of looking at social networks within these data? How did Heaney and Rojas gather network data? And is there anything missing from the network data they collected?

Partisans, Nonpartisans, and the Antiwar Movement in the United States

By Michael T. Heaney and Fabio Rojas

W̄e argue that social movements and American political parties often interact in significant and consequential ways. Although many issue activists prefer to work outside of the party system or to turn to third parties, others recognize the potential to achieve their objectives through one or both of the major parties. Considering the case of the contemporary antiwar movement, we investigate three types of inter-action. First, we examine whether partisan loyalties and nonpartisan attitudes help to structure the network of movement activists and orga-nizations. Second, we consider whether partisan loyalties and nonparti-san attitudes affect the ways that activists participate in the movement. Third, we test whether partisan organization within Congress affects the access that movement activists have (or fail to have) to decision makers. Our observation of antiwar events and surveys of antiwar activists at major protests held between August 2004 and September 2005 leads us to answer each of these questions in the affirmative. We conclude that the intersecting network of parties and social movements is a "party in the street," which shapes the strategies of social movements and politi-cal parties.

[. . .]

DATA COLLECTION

We began to observe the antiwar movement systematically in August 2004, after it had reached a point of organizational maturity. For a 1-year period, we (or our surrogates) conducted surveys of participants at all of the large-scale antiwar protests held in the United States. We attended five events: (a) the protest outside the Republican National Convention in New York City on August 29, 2004, which drew an estimated crowd of more than 500,000 people (McFadden, 2004); (b) the counter-inaugural protest in Washington, DC, on January 20, 2005; (c) antiwar rallies held to commemorate the second anniversary of the Iraq War on March 19–20, 2005, in New York City, Washington, DC, Fayetteville, NC, Indianapolis, IN, Chicago, IL, San Diego, CA, and San Francisco, CA; (d) May Day ral-lies held in New York City on May 1, 2005; and (e) antiwar protests in Washington, DC, on September 24, 2005, which drew an estimated crowd of more than 300,000 people (Dvorak, 2005).

Michael T. Heaney and Fabio Rojas. 2007. "Partisans, Nonpartisans, and the Antiwar Movement in the United States." *American Politics Research* (July) 35 (4): 431–64.

We administered a 1-page survey at each event, with the exception of the September 24–26, 2005, event, where we also administered a second page of questions. The one-page survey gathered data on age, sex, race, place of residence, partisan identification, electoral participation, organizational memberships and contacts, source of information, and reasons for participating in the event. The second page focused on respondent involvement with, and attitudes toward, political parties.

We drew nonprobability samples of participants at each event while taking aggressive measures to minimize sampling biases because of nonrandomness. We hired teams of surveyors, who spanned out geographically across the crowds. Each surveyor was instructed first to choose an individual from the crowd to serve as an "anchor" for selection. The anchor was not approached by the surveyor or invited to participate in the study. Second, the surveyor counted five individuals in a line from the anchor and invited the fifth person to participate in the survey. The surveyor then counted five persons from that individual and made another invitation. The process continued until three respondents accepted surveys. The surveyor allowed all three persons to complete the surveys and then moved forward in the crowd to identify a new anchor. Although there may be biases in our initial selection of the anchors because of the spatial grouping of activists, we expect that these biases are reduced substantially by selecting only individuals close to the anchors (rather than the anchors themselves) and by distributing the surveyors widely throughout the crowd. The response rate to the survey was a favorably high 89%.

We examine responses to two questions. First, respondents were asked, "Do you consider yourself to be a member of a political party? If 'yes', which parties are you a member of?" and "Were you contacted to attend today by any particular organization? If 'yes,' which organizations? (List as many as contacted you.)" The answers to these questions in 2,529 surveys compose our data on the organizations that contacted people to attend antiwar protests and the partisan identifications of those contacted individuals.

DATA ANALYSIS

The survey data reveal the partisan identifications of individuals attending protest events, along with the organizations that contacted them. We find that 40% of the activists within the antiwar movement describe themselves as Democrats, 39% identify as independents (i.e., they list no party affiliation), 20% claim membership in a third party, and only 2% belong to the Republican Party. These results reflect a high degree of loyalty to the Democratic Party, a willingness to embrace alternative political parties, and a nearly complete rejection of the Republican Party.

We examine the relationship between individual partisanship and the structure of the antiwar movement in Table 3.1, which lists the 20 leading

Table 3.1. Partisan Bias of the Most Active Antiwar Organizations

Rank	Organization Name (Abbreviation)	Total Contacts	% Democrats	% Republicans	% Third Party	% Independents (No Party)	Pro-Democratic Bias T-Score	Partisan Bias
	Entire Antiwar Movement	**1,000**	**40**	**2**	**20**	**39**	—	
1	United for Peace & Justice (UFPJ)	181	42	0	22	37	0.06	
2	International ANSWER (Answer)	73	40	0	22	39	-0.07	
3	MoveOn.org (MoveOn)	62	65	0	10	26	4.08 *	Democratic
4	Code Pink: Women for Peace (CP)	40	70	3	8	20	3.97 *	Democratic
5	International Socialist Organization (ISO)	18	17	0	28	56	-2.05 *	Independent
6	International Action Center (IAC)	17	24	0	41	35	-1.41	
6	Peace Action (PA)	17	41	0	18	41	-0.09	
8	Not in our Name (NION)	15	40	0	20	40	0.01	
8	Troops Out Now (TON)	15	13	0	13	73	-2.13 *	Independent
10	Military Families Speak Out (MFSO)	14	71	0	0	29	2.41 *	Democratic
11	AFL-CIO (AFLCIO)	10	40	0	0	60	0.01	
11	American Friends Service Committee (AFSC)	10	40	10	10	40	0.01	
11	Progressive Democrats of America (PDA)	10	90	0	0	10	3.25 *	Democratic
11	Veterans for Peace (VFP)	10	60	0	20	20	-1.29	
15	Brooklyn Parents for Peace (BPP)	9	22	0	44	33	1.10	
15	Democratic Party Organization (Dem)	9	89	0	0	11	3.01 *	Democratic
15	North Carolina Peace & Justice Coalition (NCJPC)	9	78	0	0	22	2.32 *	Democratic
18	Professional Staff Congress (PSC)	8	50	0	0	50	-0.57	
19	Billionaires for Bush (B4B)	7	29	0	43	29	0.62	
19	Communist Party Organization (Comm)	7	0	0	86	14	-2.18 *	Communist

Notes: * denotes statistical significance at the .05 level.

Percentages may not add up to 100% due to rounding. Independents are defined as having no party. ANSWER = Act now to Stop War and End Racism.

Source: Surveys of 2,529 activists at major antiwar protests conducted August 29, 2004 through September 26, 2005 in Washington, DC; New York, NY; Fayetteville, NC; Indianapolis, IN; Chicago, IL; San Diego, CA; and San Francisco, CA.

organizations in the movement, along with the partisan identifications of those they contacted. Our 2,529 respondents received exactly 1,000 contacts from organizations, with 31% of respondents being contacted by at least one organization.[1] Only a handful of national organizations contact a large number of people, with UFPJ (United for Peace and Justice), International ANSWER (Act Now to Stop War and End Racism), MoveOn.org, and Code Pink topping the list. Many of the smaller contacting organizations were local peace groups that forwarded on the information they received from national organizations.

For the largest organizations in the movement, we are able to ascertain the partisan leanings of their adherents. We conducted t tests to determine whether the percentage of Democrats in the organization differed from the percentage in the movement as a whole. The two leading organizations, UFPJ and ANSWER, closely approximated the partisan composition of the movement as a whole, with 42% and 40% Democrats, respectively. The third and fourth most active organizations, MoveOn.org and Code Pink, exhibited a clear bias toward mobilizing Democrats. Other Democratic-leaning organizations included Military Families Speak Out (MFSO), the Progressive Democrats of America (PDA), the North Carolina Peace and Justice Coalition (NCJPC), and the Democratic Party itself.[2] These organizations all have constituencies who support the Democratic Party, enabling them to slant their work toward explicitly partisan causes. MoveOn.org, for example, openly works with Democratic organizations and politicians, such as former Vice President Al Gore and Senator Russ Feingold (MoveOn.org, 2007). PDA aims to "create local 'homes,' chapters, and caucuses inside existing Democratic Party structures at the state and local level" (PDA, 2007, p. 2). The partisan goals of these organizations are reflected both in their adherents and in their activities.

Adherents to other leading organizations categorically reject the Democratic Party, including the International Social Organization (ISO), Troops Out Now (TON), and the Communist Party. These organizations actively promote alternatives to the Democratic Party in the political system. At the same time, organizations like Peace Action (PA), Not in Our Name (NION), and the American Friends Service Committee (AFSC) contact individuals who are roughly similar to the movement as a whole in terms of their partisan orientations. These organizations are most likely to experience internal struggles about whether their organizations should pursue partisan or nonpartisan means to ending the war (Blee & Currier, 2006).

We derive the network of antiwar activists, reported in Figure 3.1, from the co-contacts by organizations in our data. Each shape (or "node") represents an organization that contacted individuals to attend antiwar protest events. Two organizations are connected with a line (or "link") in this network if they contacted the same individual to attend a protest event, with

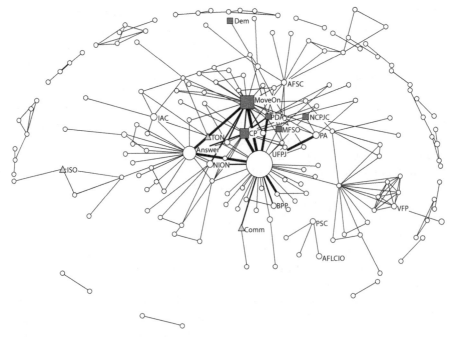

Figure 3.1. Network of Antiwar Activists, 2004–2005

Notes: Each shape represents one organization. Lines are co-contacts between organizations with thicker lines representing more contacts. Squares are organizations that lean Democratic, triangles lean toward a third party, and circles have no statistically significant lean.

Source: Surveys of 2,529 activists conducted between August 29, 2004, and September 26, 2005.

thicker lines denoting more co-contacts. We use the spring-embedding algorithm in Netdraw 2.046 to position organizations close to one another in the network if they have a similar pattern of contacts with activists. Nodes are scaled in size to the number of contacts that they have with activists; larger nodes reflect more contacts. For the 20 most active organizations, we indicate the name of the organization to the right of the node and depict the partisan leaning with shape and color.[3] Organizations that are not connected to the main component of the network are placed on the periphery of the network. Black squares represent Democratic-leaning organizations, gray triangles favor third parties, and white circles have no significant partisan bias.

Examination of Figure 3.1 reveals that organizations cluster in the network based on their partisan leanings. Strongly Democratic-leaning organizations cluster in the north central part of the network, with MoveOn. org, PDA, MFSO, and Code Pink grouped closely together. Nonpartisan organizations—notably, ANSWER, NION, and UFPJ—occupy the center of the network. Third party-leaning organizations are positioned to the left of center. These findings support our hypothesis that partisanship plays a role in structuring the network of antiwar activists. Organizations are drawn close to one another in the network in part based on the partisan or nonpartisan leanings of their activists. These networks provide the basis for collective actions that define the nature of the movement's activities (McAdam, 1986).

[. . .]

A PARTY IN THE STREET

Although a social movement as a whole may not pursue a partisan course, this research establishes that a sizeable percentage of social movement activists maintain dual loyalties to the movement and to a major political party. These loyalties are neither coincidental nor unrelated to one another. Rather, they are both integral to the way these "movement-partisans" participate in politics. The movement-partisans tend to join organizations with others who share their leanings and are more likely to choose institutionalized modes of participation, such as lobbying, whereby they gain access to elected officials who share their partisan identification. An important question is whether these actors play any special role either in the social movement or in the political party.

The role of the movement-partisans can be conceptualized as that of a "party in the street." We define a party in the street as a coordinated, though informal, network of activists and organizations that simultaneously maintain loyalty to and involvement within a major political party and a social movement. We represent this idea in Figure 3.2. The intersecting circles contain three regions: (a) on the right, the mainstream political party that rejects the social movement; (b) on the left, the radical social movement that rejects party politics; and (c) in the center, the party in the street that embraces both the social movement and the political party. In the case of the contemporary antiwar movement, the party in the street is

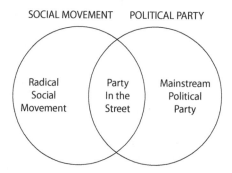

Figure 3.2. The Party in the Street

the set of black squares clustered in the north central region of Figure 3.2. Within this space, organizations like MoveOn.org, PDA, MFSO, and Code Pink are the primary points of connection between the antiwar movement and the Democratic Party.

Rather than attempt to create a movement party—as would be a likely strategy in Europe—the party in the street is an informal way to bring movement politics into a major party. This strategy is potentially viable because, as Sorauf (1968, pp. 11–12) explains, American party structures are "mixed, varied, and even contradictory" and operate according to the principles of an "open, inclusive, semi-public political organization." Access to the party is not only attained formally through elected officials and paid employees of party organizations but also through informal networks of campaign consultants, lobbyists, financial contributors, and activists (Monroe, 2001; Schwartz, 1990). Movement-partisans have opportunities to join party networks, although they depend on grassroots networks for influence rather than on financial prowess. MoveOn.org, PDA, and like-minded organizations start by connecting to the periphery of these networks. If they remain well organized and attract enthusiastic young activists, then the mainstream political party is unable to ignore them for long.

We do not claim that the party in the street has equal standing with the party in government, the party in the electorate, or the party as organization, as they have been traditionally conceptualized (Key, 1964). We are not asserting that the formal party organization is coordinating these activities. The party in the street lacks the stability possessed by other parts of the party because it is not supported by enduring institutions. Furthermore, it is small relative to other parts of the party and at times may be virtually nonexistent. However, at certain moments in history, the party in the street may be a critical element in the paths taken by a political party and a social movement.

The 2006 congressional elections and their aftermath afford an example of the party in the street in action. Movement-partisans were highly involved in supporting antiwar candidates, such as Jim Webb of Virginia, now a member of the Senate who is expected to be a public face for the antiwar movement (Craig & Shear, 2006). During the campaign, movement-partisans worked closely with antiwar members of Congress, such as Barbara Lee, Jim McGovern, John Murtha, and Lynn Woolsey, in crafting positions and planning strategies. When the election returns came in and the Democrats reclaimed control of the House and Senate, media accounts widely attributed the victory to public dissatisfaction with the Iraq War (Grunwald, 2006). Speaker-Elect Nancy Pelosi took these interpretations to heart, naming John Murtha as her choice for House Majority Leader (over next-in-line Steny Hoyer) because of his opposition to the war and work with the antiwar movement (Wiseman, 2006). Murtha was defeated for the post, in part because of questions about his reputation on ethics issues. Yet the fact that the Speaker-Elect pushed Murtha for the slot reflected a major turnabout in the fortunes of antiwar activists. Their radical position had quickly become mainstream as prominent members of Congress now lined up to denounce the war (Levey, 2007). We expect that movement-partisans will enjoy increased access to Democratic leaders throughout the 110th Congress. When the Democratic National Convention opens in Denver in 2008, we suspect that movement-partisans will find their place as convention delegates, in caucuses, and in informal gatherings sponsored by organizations like PDA.

The success of Democrats in the 2006 midterm elections has important implications for the organizations within the antiwar movement. With the Democrats in power again and a changed climate of debate on the war, some formerly partisan activists may be willing to reengage with the Democratic Party through the party in the street. This willingness may shift the energy of the movement toward greater lobbying and away from the preferred tactics of many nonpartisans and third-party adherents.

CONCLUSION

As a group, antiwar activists are neither wholehearted supporters of the Democratic Party nor skeptics who categorically reject the instrumental value of partisan organizations. They are a heterogeneous mix of activists who disagree, often passionately, about the best means of advocating for the end of the American occupation of Iraq. Individuals and organizations tend to segregate into segments of the movement that share their political views. This segregation allows some parts of the movement to undertake highly partisan activities, whereas other parts of the movement pursue an unabashedly nonpartisan or third-party course. The partisans are likely to adopt different tactics, such as lobbying, than are the nonpartisans. Democratic congressional offices see enough partisan value in the antiwar movement that they are beginning to recognize it as an organized constituency interest within the party (cf. Greenstone, 1969).

The findings of this research suggest that the current separation between the study of political parties and social movements comes at a cost. Social movements are key points of political involvement for many individuals who identify with a major political party. They see the movement as a way of achieving their partisan goals, whether they relate to defeating the other major party at the ballot box or to molding the agenda of their home party to their taste. Political leaders recognize the potential value of the movement to their goals and, thus, are willing to grant access to activists on the basis of partisanship. Likewise, political parties are a factor in the dynamics of social movements. When some leading organizations in a movement have a clear partisan bias and other leading organizations unambiguously reject partisanship, the seeds of strategic and tactical disagreements are sown.

Our research establishes that the intersection between parties and social movements is a significant space, which we have labeled the party in the street. Future research might fruitfully address several additional questions about this phenomenon. First, is the party in the street limited to the Democratic Party, or is it also an important part of Republican politics?

Although there are significant cultural and organizational differences between the formal and informal structures of the two major parties (J. Freeman, 1986), we believe that the party in the street matters to the Republican Party too. The activities of the Christian Right movement may provide at least one significant example of a party in the street within the Republican Party, even if its organizational processes and tactics differ from those of the antiwar movement. Second, how does the party in the street grow and shrink over time? What are the mechanisms that select some movement partisans as party leaders—like John F. Kerry from the anti-Vietnam-War movement or Ralph Reed from the Christian Right movement—while rejecting others? Third, is the development of the social movement advanced or stymied by its intersection with the party? What factors explain whether movements tend to be co-opted quickly or whether they substantially promote their objectives through the party? Further research along these lines would go a long way toward deepening our understanding of the dynamic intersection between political parties and social movements.

REFLECTION

Finding the Party in the Street

By Michael T. Heaney

Social networks have captured the world's imagination in recent years with the emergence of online social networks such as MySpace, Facebook, LinkedIn, and Google+. These days, ordinary people think about and talk about how to "build their social network." One potential downside of this craze is that it may lead us to believe that online social networks are the only important social networks and, thus, distract us from the myriad other ways in which the social world is connected through networks. Networks have been a vital part of human existence since the beginning of time. Families are the world's most basic social network, with networks emerging in all other dimensions of our lives through work, professions, hobbies, and more. Networks are everywhere. An important question for social scientists to ask is whether, when, and how these networks influence human behavior and shape social outcomes.

This reflection is a story of how my research partner, Fabio Rojas, and I sought to understand the structure and consequences of social networks for the antiwar movement within the United States. We found that a seemingly amorphous blob of protesters is connected through networks in ways that help to explain its place in the political world. Specifically, we examined how grassroots organizational networks intersected with political party loyalties to influence the behavior of activists. However, this story is also—if not more so—the tale of the beginnings and evolution of a research project. Research ideas and projects sometimes come from unlikely places. They have a self-reinforcing logic that can lead researchers in unexpected directions. Part of the craft of research is knowing when and how to recognize and embrace serendipity when it presents itself.

PROJECT ORIGINS

The germ of the idea for this project was born in the fall of 2002, while I was working on my dissertation in Washington, DC. Unrelated to my dissertation, I attended a few protests that were held downtown, including protests against International Monetary Fund and the Iraq War. What struck me about these events was that they were not composed of a homogenous group of people that all wanted the same thing. Rather, the crowds appeared to be carefully differentiated into well organized subgroups: anarchists, union members, Catholics, Episcopalians, women, Democrats, environmentalists, socialists, Palestinian rights activists, and so on. Some people were not explicitly affiliated with any group, of course, but the ones that were conveyed a common ethos indicated by dress (e.g., black bandannas, green T-shirts), signs, and chants. I suspected that something interesting was going on here. My first thought was that I should start conducting surveys of the people attending these rallies. My second thought was that I should probably, instead, focus on completing my PhD dissertation; otherwise I was going to find myself unemployed and without a place to live.

Having passed upon the impulse to begin studying protest, I returned to writing my PhD dissertation, which examined the social networks of interest groups working on health policy in the United States. Through this project, I identified the leading interest groups in health policy and conducted interviews with their lobbyists to assess the nature of the networks that connected them. As part of this research, I observed that these networks had a partisan dimension that had not been explored closely by previous scholars (Heaney 2006).

It occurred to me that a logical next step for the research—after completing the dissertation—would be to look more closely at how interest groups networked with political parties. One possible research design for this study would be to attend both the Democratic and Republican National Conventions to see how interest groups participated in these conventions. For example, which interest groups sponsored receptions? Which groups gave money? Which delegates were affiliated with interest groups? As the opportunity to conduct a comparative study of interest groups at the Democratic and Republican National Conventions drew near in 2004, I found that I still had to put the final touches on my PhD dissertation. By the time I finished that, it was August 4. I had missed the Democratic National Convention entirely. And there was no time to obtain the credentials needed to get inside the Republican National Convention. It seemed that I had blown my chance, for this election cycle at least.

As I was planning to start a postdoctoral fellowship that fall at Yale University, I heard that a coalition of organizations was planning a series of protests outside the Republican National Convention in New York City, only two hours away, by train. Then I got a crazy idea: perhaps the Republican National Convention protests would be an opportunity to seize upon my interest in studying protests while unifying it with my insight that the relationship between parties and groups deserved greater attention. I decided to call Fabio Rojas, my graduate school colleague from the University of Chicago, who had recently joined the faculty of Indiana University, Bloomington, as assistant professor of sociology. Fabio and I had worked together in developing a survey of Africana studies professors for his book *From Black Power to Black Studies: How a Radical Social Movement Became an Academic Discipline* (Rojas 2007). Since we had previously collaborated, it seemed natural that we would try another project together. So we agreed that we would jointly conduct a survey of protesters outside the convention.

DEVELOPING THE RESEARCH

Fabio and I began the research with a loosely defined research question: What is the relationship between social networks, social movement organizations, and political parties in mobilizing protests? We did not have a clear hypothesis or mechanism in mind when we began the research. What we did have was confidence in a research method. We designed a one-page survey that elicited network data by asking people about their memberships in organizations and which organizations contacted them to attend the protest. We also requested information on party identification, reasons for attending the protest, and basic demographic information. Fabio suggested that we adapt the method of sampling using in exit polling, which required the selection of every nth person coming out of a polling station. Because the crowd that we wished to survey was mobile, we devised a method of selecting "anchors," which allowed us to draw a sample as we moved through the crowd.

The protests at the Republican National Convention were organized by different groups on different days. We conducted surveys at an antiwar protest that was held on August 29, two poor people's marches on August 30, and a labor rally that was held on September 1. At the labor rally, I noticed how the setup of the event—with large-screen televisions and people standing, not marching—resembled a political convention, only outside the convention hall rather than inside it. I noted that this scene seemed like a political "party in the street." Fabio seized upon this idea and suggested that we make "the party in the street" a theme in the research.

After collecting and coding over five hundred surveys from the week of the convention, Fabio and I began our efforts to write a paper based on the research. We were able to derive networks from the data by looking at which protesters had organizational memberships in common with one another. If two protesters were members of the same organization, then we considered them to have a common link in their social network. Likewise, if two organizations had a protester in common (e.g., a single protester was a member of United for Peace and Justice, as well as Code Pink: Women for Peace), then we considered the organizations to have a common link in their social network.

We titled our manuscript "The Party in the Street," presented it at two conferences, and submitted it to two journals. Readers liked the essence of what we were up to but were uncomfortable with our party in the street idea. We seemed to be suggesting that the protests were merely an arm of the Democratic Party, which was in tension with the finding that many of the protesters did not ally with any political party, even though Democratic Party membership was the overwhelming choice of those who did identify with a political party. To our frustration, our manuscript was rejected sequentially by the two journals to which we submitted it.

Fabio and I were convinced that we were on to something interesting, even though our work was not receiving the reception that we had hoped. Fabio was adamant that if we would just keep at it—keep collecting data—then we would eventually solve the problem that we were having. We corralled a team of our friends in Washington, DC, to conduct surveys at the 2005 presidential inauguration protests. When nationwide protests were scheduled for the second anniversary of the Iraq War in March, we decided to narrow our focus from "protest in general" to the antiwar movement in particular. This narrowing made sense, since both the Republican National Convention and inauguration protests had included marches with an antiwar focus. We conducted surveys in seven different cities on the weekend of the second anniversary protests. We kept going with surveys at a May Day rally in New York City and a massive antiwar rally in Washington, DC, in September 2005. Before we knew it, we had systematically conducted surveys of demonstrators at all the major antiwar rallies in the United States for a one-year period. We were able to graph an organizational network of the antiwar movement.

Despite having conducted over 2,000 surveys, our work was still lacking the focus that we needed to say something definitive. Luckily, we were aided by the institutional development of the antiwar movement itself. As the antiwar movement grew, its leaders became more ambitious with their hope for political influence. In conjunction with the massive protest planned for Saturday, September 24, in Washington, DC, organizers decided to hold a lobby day on Capitol Hill on Monday, September 26. To prepare citizen lobbyists for the lobby day, a training session was held on Sunday, September 25. These events helped us to meet many of the leading organizers and activists in the antiwar movement. We became a part of their dialogue. After contributing some of our time to the movement's work, Fabio and I were soon trusted activists within the movement.

Through our conversations with movement leaders, we gained a greater understanding of what was motivating the behavior of the activists in our data and why some of the reviewers were unpersuaded by the manuscripts that we had written to date. We came to discover that many of the activists who had indicated that they had no party affiliation in response to our surveys were not simply passively avoiding party membership. Instead, they were actively antagonistic to parties. In fact, we learned that there was a huge divide within the antiwar movement between those that thought that the Democratic Party could advance the antiwar cause and those who thought that the Democrats were just as bad as the Republicans. Our simple observation about a party in the street had overlooked what proved to be one of the central conflicts within the movement.

After participating in these conversations, we returned to our data. We determined the partisan bias of every organization that contacted protesters in our sample and then graphed these biases in our network. Sure enough, the Democratic-leaning organizations clustered together. One part of the network was definitively Democratic. The party in the street *was* a part of the antiwar movement, but it was only a *part*. We realized that we could gain leverage from looking at how partisans and nonpartisans acted differently within the movement, as well as how they were positioned differently within the movement's networks. Ultimately, we were able to transform the central criticism of our work into its central point.

LESSONS LEARNED

The experience of studying networks of activists in the antiwar movement has transformed the way that I think about research. The following lessons are among the most important ones that I learned.

First, it is not always possible to have a clear research question, hypothesis, or research design at the beginning of a project. Sometimes it is possible to know these key elements in advance. But sometimes the phenomenon you are observing is too new or fluid to devise a sufficient plan based on reading the previous literature alone. Fabio and I found ourselves in the midst of an emerging antiwar movement. In August 2004, we could not possibly have known that we would be conducting antiwar surveys in March 2005. Indeed, it seemed possible that John Kerry would be elected president in November 2004, that he would change the direction of the war in Iraq, and that antiwar protests would then dissipate. In order to understand what was going on, we had to go with the flow of events. Our questions, hypotheses, and research design evolved with the movement. For example, we could not have planned to study the people who showed up at a grassroots lobby day until movement leaders decided that they needed to hold a lobby day in the first place.

Second, a great amount of time at universities is devoted to teaching students how to perform statistical methods correctly. However, in an actual research project, the process of collecting, cleaning, and coding the data is much more time intensive than is the process of analyzing them. It is essential to think systematically about methods for recording data, not just methods for analyzing them. The network data that we collected, for example—the names of organizations that contacted people to attend a protest—contained a substantial amount of ambiguity. We needed to develop a good system for resolving that ambiguity. Overall, the amount of effort that we spent managing the data far outstripped the amount of effort that we spent collecting it in the field or analyzing it on the computer.

Third, if you collaborate with others, whom you choose as your collaborators is critical. A good collaborator is more than just someone with whom you have common intellectual interests. A good collaborator is someone who has skills that complement yours, who shares your vision of the project, and with whom you can get along well during the months or years that it will take to complete the research. I am lucky to have had Fabio to work with. The research would have been different in innumerable ways if I had worked with someone else.

Fourth, good research usually motivates more research. Indeed, one of the most satisfying parts of looking back on the "Partisans, Nonpartisans" article is to see how it led to a larger, long-term project. Fabio and I did not envision a long-term project at the start. We thought, perhaps, we would publish one or two journal articles. As of this writing, however, Fabio and I have authored seven different articles on the antiwar movement. We currently have several more articles and a book manuscript in progress. Ironically, if our first manuscript had been quickly accepted, we might have quit working on the project. Rejection seemed to motivate us to keep deepening and extending the research.

Each piece we write raises new questions for us. For example, "Partisans, Nonpartisans" looked at the party in the street at one point in time. But is it possible that the party expands and contracts in size? To answer this question, we followed the antiwar movement for three more years, from 2007 to 2009 (Heaney and Rojas 2011). We found that participation of Democrats in the movement plummeted in conjunction with Democratic electoral success. Without the threat of Republican government, it became difficult for the antiwar movement to achieve critical mass.

Finally, this research project testifies both to the power of research methods to help us understand the world and to the insufficiency of quantitative methods alone in this quest. The mass of protesters that we observed were connected by social network ties that would have been invisible to us without survey methods. The survey data would have made little sense without network analysis to help us visualize the connections among organizations created by the protesters' organizational comemberships. However, the ultimate insight of our research—about the critical division between partisans and nonpartisans—came through ethnography. Qualitative research guided our quantitative analysis. Unless we had spent some time talking to antiwar activists and becoming a part of their community, we never would have understood what to look for in the network analysis. We had to combine quantitative and qualitative methods to find our answer .

Our approach to studying social networks in the antiwar movement differed considerably from studies of social networks in other areas. Networks based on friendship, alumni connections, or interlocking corporate board memberships, for example, must be approached in a different fashion. We determined our approach based on the nature of the phenomena at hand—dynamic protests flowing through the streets—and adapted our research design along with the evolution of the movement. Even though we did not really know what we were getting into at the inception of the project, we developed a fruitful line of research that continues to keep us busy today.

NOTES

1. Individuals who were not contacted by a specific organization may have learned about the protest through friends, the mass media, flyers, the Internet, or another source. In these cases, the organizational sponsors of the protest are the ultimate sources of information, although it is communicated through a multistep chain, rather than directly through organizational contact.
2. The Democratic Party did not undertake any official effort to mobilize participants for the antiwar movement. We believe that the cases in which we observe the Democratic Party listed as a contacting organization are the result of informal efforts by individual party officials and activists, rather than a campaign by the formal party apparatus.
3. Billionaires for Bush contacted 7 respondents in our sample and ranked 19th for frequency of contact. However, the Billionaires did not contact any individuals who also reported a contact from another organization, so they had

zero co-contacts. As a result, they are an isolated group and are not connected within the network in Figure 3.1. We deleted all isolates from the diagram, including Billionaires for Bush.

REFERENCES

Blee, K. M., and Currier, A. 2006. "How Local Social Movement Groups Handle a Presidential Election." *Qualitative Sociology* 29: 261–80.

Craig, T., and Shear, M. D. 2006. "Webb May Be Senate Maverick: Newest Member Expected to Take Antiwar Lead." *Washington Post*, November 12, C1.

Dvorak, P. 2005. "Antiwar Fervor Fills the Streets; Demonstration Is Largest in Capital since U.S. Military Invaded Iraq." *Washington Post*, September 25, A1.

Freeman, J. 1986. "The Political Culture of the Democratic and Republican Parties." *Political Science Quarterly* 101: 327–56.

Greenstone, J. D. 1969. *Labor in American Politics*. New York: Knopf.

Grunwald, M. 2006. "Opposition to War Buoys Democrats." *Washington Post*, November 8, A31.

Heaney, Michael T. 2006. "Brokering Health Policy: Coalitions, Parties, and Interest Group Influence." *Journal of Health Politics, Policy and Law* 31, no. 5 (October): 887–944.

Heaney, Michael T., and Fabio Rojas. 2011. "The Partisan Dynamics of Contention: Demobilization of the Antiwar Movement in the United States, 2007–2009." *Mobilization: An International Journal* 16, no. 1 (March): 45–64.

Key, V. O. 1964. *Politics, Parties, and Pressure Groups*. 5th ed. New York: Thomas Y. Crowell.

Levey, N. N. 2007. "Democrats No Longer Fearful of Anti-war Reputation." *Los Angeles Times*, January 13, A1.

McAdam, D. 1986. "Recruitment to High-Risk Activism: The Case of Freedom Summer." *American Journal of Sociology*, 92, 64–90.

Monroe, J. P. 2001. *The Political Party Matrix: The Persistence of Organization*. Albany: State University of New York Press.

MoveOn.org. 2007. "Current Campaigns." Retrieved January 4, 2007, http://moveon.org/campaigns.html.

Progressive Democrats of America (PDA). 2007. "A Progressive Plan to Change America." Retrieved January 2, 2007, http://pdamerica.org/org/plan.php.

Rojas, Fabio. 2007. *From Black Power to Black Studies: How a Radical Social Movement Became an Academic Discipline*. Baltimore: Johns Hopkins University Press.

Schwartz, M. A. 1990. *The Party Network: The Robust Organization of Illinois Republicans*. Madison: University of Wisconsin Press.

Sorauf, F. J. 1968. *Party Politics in America*. Boston: Little, Brown.

Wiseman, J. 2006. "In Backing Murtha, Pelosi Draws Fire." *Washington Post*, November 14, A1.

CHAPTER 4

Field Observation/Ethnography

Ethnography goes by lots of names. Sometimes people call it "field observation" or "field research" and sometimes "participant observation." But regardless of what we call it, this method is consistent: it explores how people manage their day-to-day lives by observing their lives.

ABOUT ETHNOGRAPHY

Whereas most methods take people outside their lives and into a research situation—sitting in a room answering questions in an interview or on a survey, going through an experiment in a laboratory setting, and the like—ethnography's research situation *is* the day-to-day lives of research subjects. And while ethnographers do talk to their subjects in interview-like ways, a great emphasis is placed, not on what people say, but on what they do.

Researchers have used this method for a long time, and it is strongly tied to a research tradition in anthropology. The classic view of anthropology is that the researcher goes to some faraway land (say, a village on remote island in the South Pacific), observes the life of those people, and brings back basic lessons about the structure, culture, and functioning of human societies.

This kind of work is still done today by social scientists, but more often than not it is done in miniature. So instead of looking at an entire society, scholars might look at life in a neighborhood, in a school, or among a particular group of people. Often the observations are just outside the door of a researcher's home.

Some ethnographers use **inductive** techniques. In other words, instead of starting with a theory about how the world works and testing it, researchers will try to keep as open a mind as possible and use their observations to generate a theory or an account that is generalizable beyond the particular observations made. Other ethnographers use more **deductive** techniques. This process involves starting with a general idea of how the world works and using their observations to "test" this idea—not just whether it is right or wrong but also what its limits are and how it might be amended.

Regardless of what approach ethnographers take, a primary concern is the **reliability** of their observations. "Reliability" is that idea that empirical observations are not conditional on the observer. If two people observe the same situation, will they generate the same account? If they will not, then the researcher might be concerned that the account of the situation is not accurate and therefore cannot be used as the basis of an empirical claim.

In some ethnographic projects—particularly "team ethnographies," which use more than one observer—researchers can directly test reliability. But in most instances, ethnographers are single researchers. So how can they trust their data? There are several ways ethnographers ensure reliability. First, ethnographers take a scientific stance to their observations: skepticism. Once they have observed something, their aim is to critically evaluate this observation. This process involves making sure that the observation is part of a pattern; this means making sure that more, similar observations are made. But it also means taking a more scientific approach. We know something is likely to be true, not by providing lots of evidence confirming it,[1] but instead by trying to provide lots of evidence that it is false but being unable to do so. And so the ethnographer does just this: exploring the limits of their observations and seeing of the conclusions drawn can be disconfirmed. Second, ethnographers have others who also observe what they have observed: their research subjects. These subjects can help the ethnographer evaluate whether or not their observations are consistent with their subjects' observations. If they are not, it does not necessarily mean that the ethnographer is wrong. But it means the researcher must more critically evaluate his or her observations.

Finally, researchers can use two data recording methods. The first is that they take detailed notes, every day, of what they observe. These are called **field notes**. These notes serve as an archive of observations, or the ethnographer's data. When taking such notes ethnographers make a distinction between their accounts of situations and their impressions of a situation. The former are meant to be a strict account of what happened. The latter are the researcher's sense of what happened. The second data recording technique is that ethnographers often mechanically record their data on tapes or other devices. These recordings help ethnographers return to situations and compare their accounts in field notes to what subjects actually said on tape.

Since ethnographers usually write their scholarly work after leaving the field, the quality of their data collection is paramount. Researchers usually cannot remember what happened months or years ago, nor can they trust the accuracy of their memory. And so field notes and recordings are essential. The capacity of an ethnographer to **generalize** from her observations beyond her site is a subject of great debate. Some scholars maintain that the uniqueness of situations makes generalizability almost impossible. Ethnographers have a "sample size of 1" from which they cannot make claims. But many ethnographers claim that their sample size is much larger. Every situation they are in counts as an observation. And minute-by-minute they are gathering more and more data. Ethnographers typically spend a year or more in the field. And so these constant observations mean a mass of data from which to draw generalizations.

THE BIG QUESTION OF "PRIVILEGE"

The excerpt you are about to read is from a yearlong ethnography done at one of the most elite high schools in the nation. The school costs close to $50,000 a year (2012), and the school spends nearly 10 times what most high schools spend on each student. Shamus Khan, himself a graduate of the school, sought to study "The American Elite" and its relationship to rising inequality.

In the book, Khan argues that students from elite schools use the language of meritocracy to explain their success. Students claim that if you work hard, you get ahead. But Khan observes that most of the students at elite schools are from wealthy families and that students do not always work very hard but they often get ahead anyway. So he uses another group of people on campus who are "locked in place"—the staff—to explore how students make sense of a group of people who are working hard but not getting ahead.

ISSUES TO CONSIDER

As you read Khan's piece and his reflection, return to the basic questions of **reliability** and **validity**. Are his observations conditional on the fact that *he* made them? If someone else had done the study, would they have found something else? If they would have found something else, how big a problem is this for Khan's claims? Does it matter that he is a graduate of the school he's studying? You might also think about the overall generalizability of his study. He spent one year at a small school. How much can be said on the basis of these observations? And you should consider Khan's research technique. Is he more **inductive**, using small-scale observations to make general points? Or is he **deductive**, testing a general idea with particular observations? Finally, what are the ethical considerations to this kind of research? Khan is spending time with teenagers, observing their everyday interactions and talking to them about their lives. What kind of steps should be taken to make sure that these young men and women have their privacy respected?

How Elite Students Think about "The Staff"

By Shamus Khan

At St. Paul's there are many people who work very hard and experience none of the promise of the students. Indeed, there are many people who stay at the school for far longer than four years. These people are the staff, the men and women who make the school function day in and day out. They are some of the most intriguing and most overlooked people on campus, and they offer a radically different vision of what entitlement, privilege, and experience mean in our country.

Though these individuals are often invisible, the school runs on the work performed by those behind the Gothic doorways and the immaculate campus grounds. So we must ask: How does the St. Paul's community bridge the interactions of people who seem to come from two different worlds—on the one hand, the American elite, and on the other, those who feed and pick up after them? While living at St. Paul's one is disciplined into recognizing the hard work of the staff. Staff members are celebrated in the Chapel after every five years of service to the school, and students in dorms are regularly reminded of the hard work that staff members do to keep their spaces clean. Each year the seniors coordinate the purchase of a Christmas gift for the custodial staff in their dorm. And these seniors typically demand payments from every student in accordance with their ability to pay.

Many of us probably assume that these students, like most impudent teenagers, would be utterly oblivious of the staff. However, the reality is far more nuanced. With some surprise, I found what Alexis de Tocqueville had seen a century and half ago as he traveled across our then new nation. Rather than act like European aristocrats, who maintained what seemed to be immutable distinctions between classes, Americans seemed to be striving for the removal of such distinctions: "In the United States the more opulent citizens take great care not to stand aloof from the people; on the contrary they constantly keep on easy terms with the lower classes: they listen to them, and speak to them every day." Yet these observations were in part due to the shock Tocqueville, himself an aristocrat, experienced and in part a kind of wishful thinking. As I asked students and staff alike about the gap between elites and the workers around them, I identified some of the crucial distinctions that mark elites and that differentiate them from all others. We commonly assume that the gap between the wealthy and the rest of us is due to differences in cultural knowledge, or perhaps we simply cannot get over the differences in wealth. Or maybe interactions between these groups are doomed to fail—people are unable

Shamus Khan. 2011. *Privilege: The Making of an Adolescent Elite at St. Paul's School.* Princeton, NJ: Princeton University Press.

to cross that enormous chasm and interact with one another in meaning-ful ways. But after my time at St. Paul's, I believe that it is none of these things.

Joyce is getting close to retirement. She is no longer middle-aged but an older woman, with rough hands from cleaning with chemicals day after day. She must still have the considerable physical stamina required to clean day in and day out. But to look at her is to look at someone who seems tired from a lifetime of work. She had cleaned the Schoolhouse during all my years as a student, and I was saddened to see that she was still at work when I returned. I was embarrassed that I did not remember her. This isn't unique. While some of the people students are fondest of are staff members who clean their houses, serve them food, or deliver their mail, the majority of the staff recess to the background of students' awareness. In fact, many students interact with most staff by ignoring them.

Yet members of the staff know things about the school that few oth-ers do. They find condom wrappers and alert faculty to where students are having sex; they clean up vomit from bathrooms after students are sick (or, more likely, have been drinking too much); they notice what stu-dents eat or, more important, who is not eating. Sometimes they protect students' secrets, sometimes they reveal them, and most of the time they just do their jobs and go home at the end of the day. Home is in the sur-rounding towns; as they get into their cars to leave at the end of the day, their departure and separate lives from the school help construct a sym-bolic boundary between students and faculty who live on campus and staff who have lives somewhere else.

Joyce was rather happy to talk to me (and proved to be so through-out the year). She arrives every morning at 4:30 a.m.; she works until 12:30. She has to do most of her cleaning before the students arrive in the building at 8:30. The job is clearly a difficult one and harder, she tells me, as she gets older. The Schoolhouse is the largest building on campus, housing dozens of offices, classrooms, bathrooms, and hall-ways. During class times about a third of the school, or some two hun-dred people, are in the building. Joyce is close to her seventies. I cannot imagine doing her job. Yet for all its difficulties, Joyce expresses pride in her work and none of the sadness (and perhaps bourgeois guilt) that I felt.

"I've been working at St. Paul's for twenty-three years," she tells me. "My old boss was having trouble with this person before me. She took a lot of time off. With a building like this you can't be like that. So he asked me if I'd do the job. And I've been doing it for fifteen years." She is clearly proud of her continued capacity for one of the most difficult custodial jobs on campus. "I don't know what they're going to do when I retire. When I take off people all tell me and my boss, 'I wouldn't want to do that building.'" Joyce smiles at me. She could do a job others couldn't imagine. "But it's getting harder." Six days a week classes are held in this building; she arrives hours before any of the rest of us just to deal with the aftermath of five hundred students, one hundred faculty members, and many staff.

Like Stan, [a student at the school] she talks about just how hard she's worked at the school. Like Stan, she expresses pride in the work she has done. Yet unlike Stan, she has not advanced. She never had the same opportunities. After finishing public high school she soon married and began a life of work and family. The job she had at St. Paul's was a good, steady one. They pay was not high, but it was reliable. Jobs that might pay more were largely unavailable to Joyce. She had not attended college, and the manufacturing jobs that had once paid higher wages had long ago left the Northeast.

I thought of her as stuck. But Joyce thought differently. She is proud of her work, her family (whom I never met but heard much about), and herself. And she is proud that she works at a school around students who are being given chances she never had. Her pride in this work is not connected to advancement, as Stan's is. While students consistently employ the language of hard work, so do staff. The difference is that for students, this work got them somewhere; for the staff, like Joyce, the hard work gave them something: a sense of pride. Though both employ the codes of hard work, the meanings of those codes are quite different. For one, it is work hard, get ahead. For the other it is pride in a job well done and being part of a school that is one of the best in the world.

Yet it would be foolish of me to suggest that the staff were blissfully happy, duped into thinking their lives were like the elite around them. They saw the inequalities walking by on campus and knew what their life chances were. Most staff rarely chose to interact with me (or with any other faculty or students). I continually and clumsily asked about this; in one of my less admirable moments I inquired, "Why is it that we don't know your name? That we don't ever interact?" These questions were avoided, except on one occasion, late in the year, when a cleaning woman said to me, coldly, "Because you don't have to, *Shamus*; and we know not to." As she said my name, she pointed forcefully to the upper left-hand area of her shirt. Suzanne wears a nametag. The message was clear: she knows and is expected to know my name; no such expectation exists for me. I am provided a tag to look at when needed. Suzanne's terse statement seemed a painfully accurate summary of relations between staff and the "real" people at the school. Students learn from the distance created around the staff; they realize whom they need to know and interact with and those who can be invisible to them.

During my years as a student, if one of us broke a major school rule—if we were caught using alcohol or drugs or out of the dorm after check-in, or if we engaged in academic dishonesty—we were assigned "work duty." This meant that the student had to perform manual labor with the staff. Yet the school recently eliminated work duty because it was perceived as demeaning to the staff—when students acted poorly they were punished by doing the work that staff did every day as a job. The change struck me simultaneously as an intriguing instance of enlightened thinking and as yet another means for the students to avoid interacting with those who serve them. When I asked staff, they understood the school's decision but didn't think the issue was particularly important. As one janitor, James, said to me, "When my kid gets in trouble I make him work around the house. That work is good for him. He learns a lesson. Same with these kids. But the thing is, my wife and me do that work every day. It's not demeaning to us to make him do the work that we would otherwise do. It teaches him a lesson he needs. I mean, when those kids worked with us, I didn't care. This is just my job." James looked me up and down quickly, eyeing me. I suspect he was trying to assess whether I could be trusted. "Want to show me you respect my work?" he asked. "Give me a raise."

The faculty and students' disregard of the staff and the administration's willingness to cut staff positions to save money often made the staff feel underappreciated. In the years before I arrived, the new rector, Craig Anderson, had worried that the school was relying too heavily on its endowment. And so he proposed that the school begin tightening its belt. Among other things, this meant cutting staff positions. As custodial and service staff members were fired, those who remained picked up the slack. This is an old and common story in organizations, where the worst paid are often asked to bear the brunt of sacrifices. What made it particularly hurtful to the staff—and what helped accelerate the eventual departure of Anderson—was that as staff positions were cut to save money, Anderson enriched himself, raising his salary from around $180,000 to $530,000. In addition to these riches, he had a mansion, a custodial staff, and a personal chef, none of whom was sacrificed to help save money.

Yet even amid this relative lack of appreciation or recognition, staff often found meaning in their jobs, and this meaning was similar to that of teachers; many staff expressed to me the importance of the fact that they worked at a school. "I used to work in this office," Cindy, a server in the cafeteria, told me, "and the work was fine. It actually wasn't that hard. And I even got paid more. But the job didn't do anything for me but pay the rent. I like the kids here. I like seeing them, being part of their day. I can tell when they're down and know how to make them smile. That makes it worth it."

Cindy was not alone in such sentiments. Tom, who maintained the Chapel, won a million-dollar lottery when I was a student. Yet he kept his job. As he explained it, "I like working here. I like the kids. And I know how to take care of this place. It's a big responsibility, but it's important. . . . Sometimes it's really hard and I think about quitting. But then something happens and I realize I'm a part of something." I would regularly see Cindy do emotional work for students, lifting their spirits, listening to them complain about the latest adolescent debacle, counseling them about a breakup or an overeager parent. She regularly did the same for me.

Though James points to a raise as the sign of an institution's "respect" for its workers, in one way or another almost all the staff did the unpaid— and often unacknowledged—work of helping care for and raise teenage boys and girls. And all of them placed value upon this experience. Many staff members are like Joyce: stuck in an area of the country where high-paying manufacturing jobs are long gone and a high school diploma provides little but low-wage employment. And so this care work also helps create meaning in a world where rewards are unlikely to come through wages. When telling me about her office job, Cindy remarked that it was much easier than her present job at St. Paul's. But for her the harder work is worth it. Students, faculty, and staff share not only a common belief in the value of hard work. They also share a commitment to the importance of the place where they work and the enterprise they are involved in. From this vantage point, staff and students would seem to have a lot in common. And yet for every moving interaction between student and staff member, there were a thousand moments where the two groups seemed to exist in parallel but utterly separate universes.

I have argued that part of the work done by American elites is to preserve hierarchies while making them invisible. If so, then how do young members of the elite deal with persistent, visible reminders of hierarchy around them and of the obvious inequality that emerges from such hierarchy? The most common way was to simply ignore the staff. When I asked students about the staff, few were able to actually name those who served them food on a daily basis or continually cleaned the buildings they inhabited, or any of those with whom they interacted on a regular basis.

And yet every student I spoke with objected to any suggestion of aloofness and mentioned a personal relationship with a staff member. These personal relationships were offered as examples of how staff were not simply ignored. Jessica, a junior from a wealthy New England family, argued that just because she did not know the names of cafeteria workers it did not mean that she did not know the staff. In fact, a few were a central part of her life. Speaking about one of the women who cleaned her dorm, she said, "I mean, actually, Gretchen is someone I really look forward to seeing every day. She's really sweet. Like an older aunt or something. And she'll remember something. If I tell her I'm stressed about a test on Thursday, she'll ask me about it on Friday. We talk. And I can talk to her in a way that I don't really talk to anyone else here. . . . Part of it is that she's just not caught up in it all. Honestly, I don't know how I'd get through it all without Gretchen. She's really important to my time here." As she said this, she turned away from me, looking away into nothing, as if to have a personal moment of reflection.

Jessica was not unique. The stories I heard were often very touching; for one student it was clear that the small birthday present from a staff member meant an enormous amount to her—as much as her far more expensive present from her parents. And Cindy was not unique in arguing that the students similarly brought meaning to her work: unlike her office job, her work at St. Paul's was important—she helped educate students. This education was far more practical than what students learned in the classroom. But these everyday life lessons were seen as important by both the staff and the students. On an occasion where a new student sat down in the cafeteria and had a cafeteria worker come out from the kitchen to "serve" breakfast, an older student scolded her. When I asked the older student about this, she told me she had done the same thing when she was a new student, and the worker who brought her plate had lightly joked that it wasn't his job to wait on her hand and foot. It was a valuable lesson she had been instilled with and one that we both revisited with students throughout the year.

Yet there are important differences between how students interact with staff and how they interact with faculty. Jessica referred to the woman who cleaned her dorm as "Gretchen." I never heard a student call a faculty member by his or her first name. I was always "Mr. Khan," even as students were sobbing in my office or telling me things that they would never tell their parents. Though there is enormous intimacy between students and faculty—they live together, after all—there are still symbolic boundaries of respect that are never breached. And as I pushed Jessica about Gretchen's life, it quickly became clear that she knew almost nothing about her life outside of the school.

When I asked Gretchen about why she knew about students' lives and why students didn't know about hers, she quickly argued that it was not because the students didn't care. "I don't want to bring my home to work. I like to keep that part of my life separate. These kids are . . . well . . . kids. It may seem like they're not. Because they're more independent than most kids. They live away from their parents. And they have a lot weighing on them. But it's part of being an adult. Kids don't know about your life. It isn't that they don't care. I don't talk about it. And how many sixteen-year-olds do you know who take an active interest in your life?"

I did not answer Gretchen's question. But during my year at St. Paul's, the answer was "a lot." Students often had a near pathological fascination with faculty lives. On countless occasions I heard students talking about faculty and their families, speculating about the ins and outs of their lives. Students were also eager to pump me for information about other teachers and were unafraid to ask me about my own life. For unmarried faculty, our romantic lives were the source of endless speculation. And for faculty alumni, of which there were many, students spent considerable time in the library, poring over yearbooks to find out details of their lives while they had been students at the school. Knowing about faculty was important to students; knowing about staff was not. In part this was because students did not "share" the relationships they had with staff; such relationships were far from the collective bonds that formed in a classroom.

If students had any relationships at all with staff members, such bonds revolved around small intimacies, such as saying hi every morning in the hallway or chatting in the corner of the dining hall—moments that did not involve other students. But the lack of knowledge about staff was also simply because of the huge gulf that separated their lives. Staff and students were from different worlds, headed in radically different directions. The staff were likely to remain working at a school in Concord, or a place like it, for much of their lives. The students could reasonably expect the rewards of wealth and power in their future.

As I pushed students to think about the careers of the school's staff and why these men and women were in what many people (including the students' parents) would likely consider dead-end jobs, many initially expressed surprise at the idea. It seemed as though these students had never thought about the quality of the jobs performed all around them, their possibilities (or lack thereof) and their pitfalls. The obliviousness struck me as perfectly adolescent. And then, more often than not, the students began to relate stories about the staff that they had relationships with. These stories tended to emphasize the way in which staff were unlucky, had different values, or were from a past generation where opportunities weren't as available—or some combination of the three. Jessica suggested that Gretchen was clearly competent, as she "remembered things I never would," but that she was probably unlucky. "I mean, I've been really lucky to have so many opportunities. Some people don't get those. They've had really bad luck." Jason talked to me about Mike, a groundskeeper he had developed a relationship with, noting that Mike simply made different choices. "He really likes hunting. We talk about it. He's happy. Nearby he can hunt and fish. That's what Mike loves in life. And I totally get that. I mean, it actually makes sense. He's happier than a lot of people I know." And in thinking about Justine, an older cafeteria worker, another student argued that she probably wasn't afforded the same opportunities. "Forty years ago, women weren't allowed into places like this. We've come a long way. Things are different now." In each instance we see students constructing particular stories to explain a lack of mobility. The attendant difficulties in each staff member's life are unique. A result of this is that the students don't have to acknowledge how the staff as a whole is comparatively immobile. The durability of inequality is obscured, chalked up to individual difficulties rather than structural inequalities (or past inequalities that have been transcended).

As I asked students about the staff, I noticed that every student talked to me about two particular staff members: "Big Guy" and the "Milk Gnome." I was often asked if these two staff fixtures had been at the school when I was a student. Students seemed pleased when I told them yes, as if the longevity of these staff members proved a kind of universality and centrality of these two figures to the school. "Big Guy" is actually Bradley Mason; he has worked in the St. Paul's cafeteria for at least twenty-five years. All students know him because he makes an effort to know every student. He learns almost all the students' names each year and regularly talks to students. He also attends every student dance, and dances the entire night. He happily will tell you, "I'm the best dancer on campus!" Mason is called "Big Guy" because that's what he calls himself. He trains new students to interact with him in a very particular way. During the afternoon he will often walk through campus. As students approach, he will say, "Hey [student name], who's number one?" Students will almost always answer, "You are, Big Guy!" to which Mason will reply, "Woo!" and put his hand in the air, holding up his index finger. This makes most students smile. In talking to Mason about these interactions, he told me how he enjoys interacting with the kids on campus, having fun with them at dances, and making them happy. Mason is developmentally disabled; as a result, some students are uncomfortable around him and avoid interacting with him. Still others will interact with him in ways that are condescending, getting a laugh out of him.

By contrast, the "Milk Gnome" rarely interacts with students. Faculty are less tolerant of students referring to George Stevens as the "Milk Gnome" since, unlike Mason, it is not a self-given nickname. I am not even sure that Stevens knows of his given nickname. I was too embarrassed to ask him about it. Students have given Stevens this name because he is short and one of his many jobs in the cafeteria is to replace the milk as it runs out. The nickname has endured and has been passed down since at least my time as a student over a decade ago.

Unlike Mason's indulgent kindness, Stevens is far less gregarious and cheerful. He tends to interact in a much more gruff manner, demanding that students move immediately so that he can replace the milk or perform his other tasks at work. He is a hard and efficient worker, and seems to have no time to waste on the students. Like Mason, Stevens is also developmentally disabled. The students all know him, yet very few know his real name.

If Mason were the only staff member that most students knew, I would attribute his unique presence among the student body to his dynamic personality and continued interaction with and interest in students. But Stevens is the other staff member that all students know. Stevens shares none of Mason's personality and I never saw him interact with students other than to ask them to get out of his way. Their common features are two: they both work in the cafeteria, where every student goes two or three times a day, and they are both developmentally disabled. And as there are many other people who work in the cafeteria whom students do not all know or notice, the explanatory feature of both is their disability.

In the students' eyes, the staff members they individually know—and the fact that they may be "stuck" in their job at the school—are exceptions to the students' general faith in the American creed that anyone can make it. They are unlucky, have different values, or are unfortunate victims of past unfairness. The two members of the staff whom all students know, the two who do not recess into the background of students' daily lives and who are collectively acknowledged by the students, are the two who provide the least challenge to the way students frame their experiences. While staff could serve as a persistent reminder that there are other processes that might explain how some in society acquire privileges and others do not, the staff students notice do not. In short, students can comfortably notice Mason and Stevens and collectively share in their relationships with them because their disability offers an obvious explanation for why they don't advance.

The awkward position of staff members in the lives of St. Paul's students becomes even more interesting when you consider that a few of the students may actually have parents who are housecleaners, dishwashers, or office workers. About a third of St. Paul's students receive substantial scholarship, and the school makes a very conscious effort to recruit students from the lower rungs of the socioeconomic ladder. I assumed that these middle- and working-class students would have an easier time interacting with these overlooked members of the community, as their earlier lives would have been spent among the working and middle classes. I reasoned that wealthy students, by contrast, would be uncomfortable interacting with staff, as their privileged position would have prevented them from knowing what the lives of staff members were like. I was wrong.

It was actually the wealthy kids who "noticed" staff more frequently than did the middle-class kids; they were also more likely to build relationships with them. At first this observation struck me as improbable. I suspected that the students I spoke to were simply gregarious (perhaps because they were more comfortable at the school) and therefore more likely to strike up conversations with anyone. Yet as I pushed this idea I found that it was the wealthy students who worked much harder to argue with me about the importance of their relationships with staff members and the depth and shared quality of the connection. Wealthy students, it seemed, were intentionally developing the capacity to interact with those "below" them. This development is a useful and necessary tool within our democratized America; elite students will be required to interact with nonelites throughout their professional lives. And they will be held to account for these interactions. Learning to successfully negotiate them was an important skill to develop.

Nonwealthy students, by contrast, were much more concerned with developing a set of interactional tools that would aid them in navigating upward, through elite institutions and networks. Further, wealthy students could more comfortably recognize and interact with staff members, as their own status and position were clear. For the wealthy, already ensconced in their place, the staff's presence did not highlight the tensions inherent in the efforts to transition into the elite. For middle- and working-class students, the presence of the staff members brought into relief the distinction between their present lives at St. Paul's and their past lives at home. Nonwealthy students had to learn to manage the contradictions between their "exceptional" experience at the school and their former, "everyday" experience at a home that was very different from St. Paul's. For wealthy students, no such contradiction management was necessary. For middle-class kids, the staff were a daily reminder that the space at St. Paul's—with its opulent, wood-paneled rooms, its gorgeous buildings and sacred spaces, and its immaculately manicured grounds—was not where they came from or what they were used to. The staff were reminders of this contradiction, of the seeming foreignness of their presence; the staff made more difficult the essential task of displaying ease and knowledge of the place.

In learning to construct intimacy with staff members—those permanently below them—students developed the capacity to interact across the social boundaries of class. By learning these interactions, elites prepared for a future where dealing with the lower classes would be inevitable, and at the same time they made such boundaries seem artificial or unimportant. If you can chat with the cashier or trade jokes with the janitor, then you obscure the categorical distinctions essential for durable forms of inequality. There is no need to harp on class differences or the stark limits of the American Dream. Instead, students viewed the small slices of inequality, or the lack of social mobility, that they observed as "exceptional" cases—Mason and Stevens, as we saw, could not possibly advance—or through creating personal narratives, as with the other workers who were good people and were at the school as a result of bad luck, different choices, or past inequality. The lack of mobility, then, is not a systemic feature of social life; it is an exception, particularly among those who value the same kinds of things that students do: belonging to an educational institution and working hard.

REFLECTION

The Science of Everyday Life

By Shamus Khan

The purpose of ethnography is to provide a sense of how people live their lives in particular places. This means studying three things: (1) people, (2) places, and (3) people in places. Ethnography often seems the most natural and obvious of methods, as navigating our lives requires that we make sense of people and situations. We are all ethnographers. And yet there is something very different between living one's own life and making sense of the lives of others. Its seemingly natural and everyday quality is part of what makes doing ethnographic work so challenging.

Ethnography is a method wherein the scholar embeds himself in the relations under study, spending long periods of time with research subjects. For me it meant getting a job at St. Paul's School, one of the most elite boarding schools in the country. St. Paul's costs almost as much as the most expensive colleges in the nation; the most common college that students from this high school attend is Harvard. For my research I moved into an apartment on campus, coached the tennis and squash teams, taught, advised students in a dorm, and most important, observed the daily life of the school. After my year at St. Paul's I returned many times, and I sought out alumni to interview and discuss some of the things I'd learned. Collected, these observations and discussions make up my data. It is important to remember ethnography is not interviewing. It relies more on watching people do things in the world than asking their accounts about the world. In this sense, ethnography should show us how people negotiate everyday situations.

As students read through my personal reflection I would encourage them to remember that my approach is not *the definitive approach* to doing ethnography. There are various ways in which social scientists work—and we often argue about the best way. What this memo will reveal is, not how ethnography is done, but instead how the ethnography you have just read was done. And hopefully it will inspire you to think of the advantages to doing work in this way and the disadvantages that might push you to think of doing work in your own way.

MY BASIC QUESTION

In choosing to study St. Paul's, I was motivated by the desire to explain how the experience of going to an elite school provided advantages for students. Certain questions are ideally suited for ethnography, and certain ones are better addressed by other methods. If we're interested in explaining causes or comparing outcomes—as we often are in the social sciences—then experiments or large-scale representative data are ideal. So if I were to ask, "Do students who go to elite schools do better than those who do not?" I would not be well served by doing ethnographic work for a host of reasons: I am able to observe people only for a short period of time in their overall lives, I have no idea if the people I'm observing are representative of the population as a whole, and it would be almost impossible to construct comparison cases wherein I was confident that I could explain the outcome by elite schooling rather than some other factor.

However, while it is not ideally suited at answering these kind of comparative outcome questions, ethnography is the method, par excellence, at answering *how* questions. From other studies of large-scale data sets, I had learned that students from elite private high schools had higher earnings later in life than similarly qualified students who didn't go to such schools. Though these survey studies could tell us about different outcomes, they were ill equipped to answer the how and why questions. What is it that students learn at these schools? How do they learn those things? Why would this matter? I position my work in relationship to other sociological work on stratification—work that often draws upon analyzing surveys. And I use the ethnographic method to answer the how questions that these surveys have difficulty answering.

In short, my method and my question were closely tied to one another. For students, I think the match of question and method is one of the most important aspects of any research project. If choosing ethnography, one should ideally be studying how people (or groups of people) live their lives, make sense of their experiences, generate meaning and aspects of their self, how they interact with others, and how all of this happens within particular settings. The method is naturally a descriptive one. And such rich description is the advantage of the method. Though other methods can be far more explanatory, particularly of causal outcomes, ethnography enables us to get closer to the how and why of social life.

SELECTING A SETTING, GAINING ACCESS, AND PRESENTING ONESELF TO RESEARCH SUBJECTS

For me, the selection of a setting was rather straightforward. I attended St. Paul's School as a student. I approached members of the administration I previously knew in order to negotiate access. This is not uncommon. Ethnographers often know and are known in the communities they study. This is not to say that you should study only a place you know. But as the task of the ethnographer is to become part of the community under study, feeling comfortable within that community is essential to the craft. Does this mean, in my case, that you have to be an elite to study elites? Or that you have to have experienced poverty to study the poor?

Certainly not. Sometimes "outsider" status can be beneficial when studying the social world, particularly when as an outsider you recognize the taken-for-granted principles of a social group. But the task of the ethnographer is to know the lives of one's subjects. And the best way to know about someone's life is to be a part of it. So when selecting a setting, it is imperative that you select a setting you know you can live within. If you are unable to live the relations under study, you will be largely unable to complete your work. This doesn't just mean knowing about your subjects, it means knowing about yourself and what you are capable of.

When I entered St. Paul's I was completely honest about my research project. I told the school my aim, "to understand the American elite," and how I would achieve it—by living at the school, observing its workings, and talking to people. During my year of research I continually conveyed this purpose to the community. Such honesty is essential to ethnographic projects. This goes beyond the moral obligation to the people we are studying. Acting, obscuring, tricking, or hiding things from subjects works against the trust required to become part of people's lives. And maintaining such a false facade makes observations less about how people negotiate their lives in an everyday context and more about how they do so within the game that you have set up for them. The advantage of ethnography is in its capacity to reveal situated action. Manipulating the situation with deception can be enormously problematic.

Further, to receive the informed consent of participants it is essential to inform them of your purposes. Some might worry that this compromises your data—that in telling subjects what you want to see, they respond in ways that produce what you are looking for. But I have found that though subjects certainly can do this over the short term, in the long term it becomes an arduous task. As an ethnographer you are there for the long term. And in observing the day-to-day practices of your research subjects, when all the operative constraints and opportunities of their lives are in play, such artificial production of relations is not sustainable. As you become deeply embedded in the situation and the lives of your subjects, they soon fall back into the patterns of their lives—those patterns which you are there to understand.

THE SCIENTIFIC STANCE OF THE ETHNOGRAPHER

No doubt some readers may worry about such deep embedding into real world scenarios. In my case, readers may worry that as an alumnus of St. Paul's I would be too close to the object of study to truly engage in serious ethnographic work. How can the ethnographer be an objective observer? The simple answer is that the ethnographer cannot be objective, but to insist on objectivity is often to miss the strength of the ethnographic method. Objectivity is often a false mask that researchers hide behind in order to assert their scientific authority. To stand outside people, looking in at their lives as if they were in some laboratory or snow globe is to not understand them. During my first weeks at St. Paul's I had an incredibly hard time learning anything. People were mistrustful. Interactions were awkward. I had tried not to position myself anywhere in the school, feeling that being inside would leave large blind spots. But I found that from my attempts at an objective stance I could see almost nothing.

Luckily, I inadvertently positioned myself within the relations of the school. Early in the year, as we prepared for a faculty meeting to discuss a recent hazing crisis on campus, a report was circulated by the school's lawyers to help us understand the research on hazing. The research was terrible; I sent an e-mail denouncing it and arguing that it should not be the basis of any policy. I soon received e-mails from fellow faculty members, joking that my firing was only a matter of time and that they would help me pack my things. I was surprised by the reaction and worried about the consequences. Though I was yelled at by the administration for undermining their lawyers, people soon began talking to me. They knew where I stood, and this made connections possible. Though my relationship with the administration suffered somewhat, even they began to discuss things with me that they never had before. It was in becoming positioned in the overall relations of the school that I could be a successful ethnographer, not in being somehow "outside" or "objective." This is not to say that I believe in a postmodern epistemology. I am a realist and an empiricist at heart. I simply feel that the study of human relations is necessarily an embedded one; to pretend otherwise obscures more than it illuminates.

The reason for this position is rather simple: we reveal and become ourselves among people we know. The task of the ethnographer can be achieved only through insinuating oneself into the lives of the people under study. Only from this position, not from a stance of the distant observer, can we see people as they truly are themselves in situations of their choosing. Most of us can see this point when we look at our own lives: we are ourselves around the people we know, not around those people who are purposefully distant or removed from us.

This may worry readers. If ethnography is not objective, how do we know that what we are can count as knowledge? How is it part of a social science academic enterprise? I have several different answers to these questions. The first is that ethnography is a *how* method, one that provides a rich description of the lives of human communities. As such, its power is not always in generating causal explanations. We could compare ethnography to the experimental method. Experiments are quite good at establishing causal claims. But they are often plagued by the fact that their external validity—their capacity to explain the real world experience of actors—can be quite low. Further, they often cannot speak about much beyond the independent variable they have manipulated. But the weakness of experiments is exactly the strength of ethnography. It can help the researcher think through a broad set of relations in contexts that are as close to real world experiences as possible.

This is not to say that ethnography is "better than" the experimental method. Rather than competing methods, I prefer to think of methods as complementary. And so while ethnographers might not be particularly objective, they do not exist in a world of their own. Instead, we work alongside other scholars who employ different research methods. The importance of knowing a variety of methods is that scholars can understand how their peers have answered certain questions and how one's own method can aid in helping a community of scholars understanding things they otherwise don't. What experimental work can't do, ethnography can. And vice versa. Taken together, they help a community of scholars better understand the world.

Finally, a good ethnographer may stand inside rather than outside her observations, but this does not mean that observations are taken for granted or at face value. Good ethnographers have internalized the logic of scientific investigation. That logic is not one of confirmation. Instead, science works by the logic of negation. So the job of the scientist is to always be skeptical, to attempt to disconfirm findings. The section of my book that you have just read engages in such skepticism. It takes what students say—that if you work hard you will get ahead—and evaluates it relative to "the staff" on campus. In this sense, ethnography is not simply the reporting of what people tell the ethnographer. Instead, it is the interrogation of it, and the skeptical stance both to subjects themselves and to each claim that the ethnographer himself tries to make. This points to an enormous difference between, on the one hand, one's time in the field and analyzing one's data and, on the other, the time writing. When we write we seek to make a case for our argument. But when we gather data and analyze it, our task is something quite different: to work to negate rather than to confirm. This healthy skepticism (both of one's own arguments and of what our subjects tell us), more than objectivity, is essential to the ethnographic enterprise. And when combined with conversations with other scholars, who themselves have worked hard to make sense of the social world, such ethnographic work can serve as part of a firm basis for understanding human communities.

ETHICAL CONSIDERATIONS

I feel it important for ethnographers to think of informed consent as a process and not an event. Situations change quite rapidly as we do ethnographic work. I went from being an outsider at St. Paul's to a friend, coach, mentor, confidant, and regular member of the community. This is exactly what I wanted from a methods point of view. But it also meant that members of the community began to treat me differently. They thought of me less as an ethnographer and more as their friend or just a regular teacher on campus. They told me things and acted in ways they never would have had they remembered that I was a social scientist who went home at night and dutifully wrote out field notes on what they said and did.

The ethical question here is "Does the consent that was granted to the stranger-social scientist on the first day extend to the friend and confidant five months later?" My feeling is that it does not and that ethnographers should be responsible in revisiting their role with their subjects throughout their time in the field. This is what I mean by informed consent being a process rather than an event—a one-time event.

In my case I reminded subjects (friends) of my role in different ways. First, I would talk about my work—things I was observing and trying to make sense of in contexts that my interlocutor was not a part of. So with a fellow teacher I might talk about the dynamics on my tennis team. With a student I might talk about an interaction I had with a staff member. This served a dual purpose. On the one hand, it reminded the subject that he or she was a subject. And on the other, it helped me make sense of things from the point of view of the community I was studying. Similarly, I often "checked" my field notes against the community member I was writing about. Quite often I would write to a subject, providing my field notes of our encounter to insure that my account was accurate. Again, this served the purpose of reminding subjects of my role. But it also helped me check my recollection and information.

There were times where subjects asked me not to reveal information that they had told me. I respected these requests. Though at times this was disappointing—particularly if a juicy detail or compelling example was lost—I forced myself to remember two things. First, ethnography is only possible insofar as people consent to allowing ethnographers into their lives. That consent can always be revoked, and it is conditional on the ethnographer's respect for his subjects. This does not mean that we always write in ways that are flattering—indeed, my own work should reveal that that is not always the case. But it does mean providing a degree of respect to subjects in terms of what can and cannot be reported. Second, though I might lose an ideal piece of information by being asked by a subject not to report it, the task of an ethnographer is to discover patterns to social life. And so if an example is exemplary of a pattern to be discussed, by definition other such examples exist.

I hope that from this reflection and my work, students take away the lesson that ethnography is an exciting and dynamic method and one particularly good at making sense of how people live their lives in everyday situations.

I close by reminding the reader that approaches to ethnography are varied. If students are interested in learning more about the varieties of approaches to ethnography, I would encourage them to begin by exploring very different approaches (different both from my own and from one another). They are listed below.

NOTE

1. Scholars often call this error "**confirmation bias.**"

REFERENCES

Burawoy, Michael. "The Extended Case Method." *Sociological Theory* 16(1): 4–33.
Duneier, Mitchell. 1999. "Appendix: A Statement on Method." In *Sidewalk*, 333–58. New York: Farrar Straus Giroux.

CHAPTER 5

Field Interviewing

There are a number of ways to do interview research that range from more to less structured. In some cases, interviews are similar to an ethnography and are very unstructured and do not require a formal script. During such interviews, researchers ask a series of questions that are adjusted based on the subject and his or her responses to the questions. With this type of interview, responses tend to be open-ended, and analysis looks at similarities and differences in the responses across subjects. In other cases, interviews are completely scripted, with researchers reading the text of a survey verbatim to the subject. Responses to this type of interview are usually classified into categories and they tend to take the form of survey responses with limited options (like yes/no or male/female). Since more structured interviews follow very similar methods to that of survey research, here we focus on open-ended semistructured interviews.

ABOUT OPEN-ENDED SEMISTRUCTURED INTERVIEWS

Open-ended semistructured interviews are frequently conducted at a field site with research subjects. Many researchers feel it is important to conduct research "in the field" because it is a natural setting where the subjects participate in the practices that the researcher is interested in understanding. While conducting interviews, researchers also collect observational information about the field site. Like ethnographic research, one of the major challenges of doing this type of interview research involves gaining access to the research site. Although some field sites, like the US Congress, are public places, most sites (including the offices of elected officials) are private places—like companies, schools or organizations—where a researcher cannot just loiter trying to recruit research subjects. As a result, doing this type of research involves a lot of set-up, in the form of contacting people who might be able to grant access to the field site.

Once a researcher has gotten access to the field site, he must determine how he will structure his interviews. This step involves deciding on the general questions to ask as well as where they will be asked. Some types of questions, such as those that ask subjects if they engage in any behaviors that are seen as socially deviant, will yield better responses if the researcher finds a private place. People will be less likely to admit to lying or stealing and to discuss their motivations, for example, if they can be heard by colleagues or others. Also, the researcher must determine the order of his questions. Since questions and their responses may influence subsequent responses, highly charged questions are often put later in the interview protocol or even asked last so as to minimize these effects.

Even though this type of research is semistructured, there is a structure that involves the researcher having a sense of what the research questions are that he hopes to answer. In most cases, researchers develop a basic interview guide, or what some call an "interview protocol," for the questions that they want to ask. This step has become increasingly common, as universities now require researchers to submit their questions for review by an **institutional review board** before they are approved to conduct their research. Moreover, having such a protocol to follow contributes to the **reliability** of the data that are being collected, because all respondents answer the same questions. And if there are multiple interviewers on a project, the protocol lists common questions that all subjects answer and provides the general order in which the questions should be asked.

Since the interviews are semistructured, however, the researcher is able to follow any theme that emerges in an interview that may be relevant to the research project. For example, in Dana Fisher's study of canvassers, her interview guide included a question about whether the canvassers felt they were "making a difference." If the respondent answered the general question by discussing his or her family background or previous activist experience, Fisher probed the respondent for more information about how this experience was related to a sense of making a difference and impressions of the work of canvassing.

In most cases, interviews are recorded so that they can be transcribed; the content of the interview is typed for further analysis. Having all subjects' verbatim responses provides a data set that can be analyzed and coded to answer the research questions. Because the researcher asks the same question of everyone in the sample, analysis involves comparing and contrasting responses across the subjects.

To ensure that the findings from open-ended semistructured interviews are **generalizable**, interview research must also develop a sample that is representative of the population to whom the researcher wants to generalize. Although it is very common for researchers to conduct interviews with a convenience sample of respondents, this type of sampling will limit the generalizability of the findings significantly. The strongest interview research is that which employs a sampling frame that either aims to include everyone in the population of interest or randomly selects respondents from the population.

THE BIG QUESTION OF "ACTIVISM, INC."

In *Activism, Inc.*, Dana Fisher studies the experience that young people have working as canvassers. Canvassers are predominantly young people who work as paid activists raising money and/or memberships for a social movement organization. The excerpt below specifically looks at how the canvassing organization (which Fisher calls the "People's Project" in the book) works and how it coordinates campaigns for a handful of other organizations. The findings from this study are based on open-ended semi-structured interviews and follow-up interviews conducted with 116 canvassers, as well as interviews with representatives of organizations that have hired the People's Project to run their campaigns.

In the book, Fisher finds that although the People's Project aims to train and empower a cohort of young activists, the experience of canvassing has unintended consequences for the canvassers. Instead of staying engaged in the campaigns that the canvassers work on, the majority of young people in her sample ended up burned out and turned off by the experiences they had working for the People's Project. She traces these consequences beyond this one organization and into the 2004 presidential election in the United States.

ISSUES TO CONSIDER

While reading Fisher's piece and her reflection, think about the steps she took to make the findings as **generalizable** as possible given her research method. To what degree does it work? Are there aspects of her design that limit her generalizability? Also, she discusses how data were collected with a team of researchers. What are the strengths and weakness of having multiple individuals collect interview data? Fisher spent one week in each of the six randomly selected field sites under study. What are the advantages of doing so? In what ways would the research be stronger if Fisher and her team had spent more time in fewer field sites talking to a smaller number of canvassers?

Finally, Fisher discusses in her reflection how the organization threatened to sue her when the book was coming out. What steps did she take to protect herself and her research subjects? What else could she have done? What is the appropriate balance between the obligation to convey what her research found and the interests of her research subjects (both individuals and organizations)?

Running an Outsourced Canvass

By Dana R. Fisher

The standardized canvassing model of the People's Project assumes that "anybody who can walk, talk, and carry a clipboard" can become an effective activist (Mike, 33, Atlanta canvass). It makes it possible for the organization to get canvassers trained quickly and out on the streets raising money and support for their grassroots campaigns within hours. Although most posters and flyers for the People's Project advertise jobs for the environment, with the consolidation of canvassing the campaigns that are being run out of the Project's local offices do not necessarily focus on environmental protection. Each campaign is different, and the organization runs canvasses of varying lengths. The canvassers I spoke to in the summer of 2003 had worked on issues as diverse as child welfare, same-sex marriage initiatives, urban sprawl, drinking water protection, international toxic-chemical usage, and deforestation. A director in the Portland office, Will, who had started working for the organization as a canvasser in 2000, recalled that, since joining the organization: "I've probably worked on twenty or thirty different issues in two-and-a-half years." Not only did Will work on many campaigns but, during his time in the Portland office, he had also canvassed on behalf of numerous groups.[1]

Smaller canvass offices, such as the 2003 Baltimore and Ann Arbor offices, run only one campaign at a time.[2] As a result, the young people who respond to the organization's standardized job flyers, which are posted around town during the summer and on college campuses when the organization is recruiting in the spring, end up working on whatever campaign the national and regional offices have decided to run out of that canvassing office when they start. Eileen, who had just finished her junior year of college and worked for the Ann Arbor office of the People's Project, for example, was not particularly inspired by the campaign under way when she worked there. Originally attracted by the idea of working for the environment, she had hoped to work on issues related to clean air. Instead, Eileen ended up working to protect open spaces from development for three weeks until she was let go for not making quota. "Quite honestly," she said, "I'm only doing this, or working on this issue, because that's what the office is working on. I think there are really other . . . more important issues." For Eileen, those issues were environmental, but canvassers in smaller offices are expected to work on whatever is the campaign of the day; they have no choice.

In contrast, larger offices run multiple campaigns for different national groups simultaneously. In the large Portland office of the People's Project, they were "working on anywhere from, like, three to five different issues

Dana R. Fisher. 2006. *Activism, Inc.* Stanford, CA: Stanford University Press.

at any one time" (Will, 30, Portland canvass). When an office runs more than one campaign concurrently, as is common during the summer, the directors assign a canvasser to a campaign based on the needs of the office and/or the canvasser's interests. As a result, some young people who were attracted by the idea of making money while trying to help the environment found themselves working on unrelated campaigns.

Paul had just finished his sophomore year at an elite West Coast school and was recruited during the school year to work for the People's Project. He recalled being very interested in the particular environmental campaign that the recruiters visiting his school said would be the focus of the summer's campaign: "It looked like a very, very good summer job. . . . They were concentrating especially on Arctic drilling and, considering how much of the forest has been destroyed in my country and the exploitation of my country, it really bothered me that they would be [cutting down forests to drill for oil] here in the United States." Paul's personal experience growing up in Honduras had inspired him to work on environmental protection, but when he arrived at the office he was assigned to work on child welfare issues instead. "I ended up working for Save the Children as opposed to environmental issues." Despite this change, Paul was happy with his job: "The environment is important to me, but at the same time, Save the Children was a lot closer to home and . . . you don't get a lot of the mean responses [like] you do if you come up to maybe a logger's house . . . [when you're canvassing for] the Sierra Club. . . . Most of the people are supportive, which is nice."

Other canvassers, however, did not find such a good fit. Some even recalled being asked to work on campaigns that they did not support. Tiffany in the Portland office remembered being moved from one campaign to another:

> They would just take you off of a campaign you were working on and stick you on another one, and you didn't really have discretion over that. If you're going into a job . . . because you truly believe in it, you want to be doing something that's true to your ethics and OK for you. I wasn't necessarily totally comfortable working for the Sierra Club. I'm not a huge fan of theirs. . . . I expressed discomfort about doing it and they were just, like, "Well, we need you to."

Being moved from one canvass to another was not unique to Tiffany's experience. Representatives of the national groups that were outsourcing to the People's Project were well aware that the canvassers were working on multiple campaigns for different groups simultaneously. In the words of Joe Solmonese, the president of the Human Rights Campaign, for example: "The person who is out standing on the street corner trying to sign you up to join HRC . . . they honestly, like the next day, might be doing the same thing for [a different organization]." After working for about seven months out of the Portland office of the People's Project, Jason, a 24-year-old college graduate, agreed: "In a given week, I'll canvass on three different campaigns."

For canvassers like Tiffany and Jason who were bounced from one campaign to another, sometimes without warning, keeping track of the specifics of the grassroots campaigns they were working on could be very difficult. Representatives of the national groups that hired the People's Project to run their campaigns worked with the organization to maintain a consistent message by providing information as well as running briefings for the local offices from time to time. How effective such training was, however, was unknown. During my meetings with representatives of the outsourcing groups, a number of them wondered how much information actually trickled down to the young people who were going door-to-door or standing on the streets.

Speaking about the ways that the HRC provides information to the canvassers who are fundraising on its behalf, for example, Sally Green Heaven, the deputy field director of the group, considered the limitations: "In practice, I guess I wonder how much it penetrated, like to the level of the canvasser that was out in every city. . . . The kind of training that we provided was mostly phone briefings." This national field director also recalled the group running in-person training sessions from time to time, but since the lifespan of the average canvasser is only a few weeks, it is unlikely that many canvassers benefited from such briefings. In fact, most of the young people who were canvassing on behalf of the HRC on any given day probably had neither received a phone briefing nor participated in any in-person training. Other outsourcing groups faced similar challenges. According to Jessica Hodge, the Washington, D.C., field representative for the Sierra Club: "The only real connection is [between] the canvass director in the local office [of the People's Project] and the Sierra Club office."

Perhaps in part to address the suspected limitations of the diffusion of information, the People's Project tries to maintain consistency across campaigns. As such, all campaigns rely on Scripts that are almost identical. Because the Scripts are easy to learn, canvassers can be easily moved from campaign to campaign. Beyond learning a different Script for each campaign, however, canvassers reported not receiving much additional training about the group or the campaign before being shuffled from one campaign to another.

Hailey, an 18-year-old canvasser who was working out of the Portland office, for example, had spent her first two weeks canvassing for a clean water campaign in the office. She spoke about being switched without undergoing any training: "They just sent me out there . . . I learned the [Script] and they sent me out there." Her concerns were particularly warranted as canvassers reported that each campaign had a different quota--some significantly higher than others. Although Hailey told me she was worried about meeting the quota of the new campaign, she reported: "I did well that day, so I was OK with it, I was like 'whatever.'" Without learning much about the organization or the campaign for which she was to raise funds, Hailey was able to meet the requirements of the new campaign by using her canvassing skills and the campaign's Script alone.

Even directors who had been working out of the Portland office for much longer than Hailey had limited knowledge of some of the organizations and campaigns the office was running in the summer of 2003. On the day that I interviewed him, Roy was planning to canvass on behalf of Save the Children. A representative of Save the Children had told me that, in order to maintain the integrity of her group's "brand," the group visited canvassing offices "as needed throughout the year." However, these visits did not seem particularly effective in providing information to those who were doing the actual fundraising--not even to a long-term member of the canvass like Roy. When I asked him about the group for whom he would be fundraising that evening, he replied: "Yeah I don't know too much. . . . You probably know as much as I do." Although his lack of information did not give me much confidence in the national group's "training visits," Roy did not seem too concerned about his lack of knowledge. In fact, he was confident in his ability to recruit support for Save the Children: "I read all [of the group's] literature, I can express to people at the door, and I got the [Script] to say. [I'll] smile [and they'll] write checks."

At least for Hailey and Roy, the lack of training did not seem to interfere with their ability to canvass well and recruit members. Beyond fundraising, however, it is unclear how effective canvassers can be in building grassroots support for these campaigns when they have such limited knowledge of and passion for them. Given the canvassers' inadequate understanding of the national groups and their political campaigns, it is likely that the outsourcing of canvassing has widened rather than narrowed the disconnect between these national groups and their members.

NARROWING THE LOCAL CHANNELS INTO NATIONAL POLITICS

The consolidation of canvassing has also affected the channels through which interested young people can enter progressive politics. As I learned from my former student Laura's experience, competition for even an entry-level position in a national progressive group's Washington, D.C., office is fierce. Every year, college graduates converge on the nation's capital to find jobs working in progressive politics. Many go looking for work at the national or legislative headquarters of a progressive group whose issues interest them. Unfortunately, paying jobs are limited and the majority of entry-level positions in these Washington offices are unpaid internships.[3] In the words of Jessica Hodge of the Sierra Club, many young people come to Washington "because they want to work on national policy. . . . We definitely have a lot of people that used to be interns here now . . . [Our office has] a ton of them actually." Of the forty paid staff members in the group's legislative office in Washington, D.C., she estimated that one-quarter of them began their work there as interns.[4]

There are, however, a limited number of paid jobs for recent college graduates in national progressive politics. The People's Project partners with groups that run a handful of paid programs for recent graduates to gain experience in grassroots organizing at the local, state, and national levels. These jobs have become increasingly competitive in recent years. They include a fellowship program and the campus organizer program, both of which require three months of canvass directing during the summer.[5] In addition, the organization partners with the Green Corps program, which calls itself the "field school for environmental organizing."[6] Through Green Corps, college graduates are placed in paid positions in environmental groups for nine months of the year. As with the People's Project's other partnerships, Green Corps members are expected to serve as canvass directors, running local campaign offices during the summer months. In all of the canvass offices I visited around the country in the summer of 2003, approximately half of the canvass directors were working on the canvass through one of these three programs.

Jessica Hodge of the Sierra Club said her group worked closely with young people enrolled in this program: "[Green Corps is] really intensive. [Its organizers are] kind of poverty-stricken, [working] like sixty and seventy hours a week." Although the work is hard, the year-long program is successful in placing those who complete it in national groups. Hodge reported that "lots and lots" of the graduates of this program had gone to work for the Sierra Club.

An alumna of the program who was working for a progressive environmental group in Washington, D.C., explained to me Green Corps' attraction to recent college graduates: It "actively recruits talent and then effectively works to launch long-term careers in grassroots organizing and advocacy. It's also an effective avenue for networking between liberal environmental groups because alumni have a fairly well developed sense of loyalty to one another, and confidence that fellow alumni are talented and well trained."[7] Even this full-time employee of a progressive group in Washington admitted to having "mixed feelings" about her experience with Green Corps. But she acknowledged: I "would not be working for [this group] right now if I hadn't done Green Corps."

Others had less positive experiences with the program. In the winter 2004 edition of *Threshold* (Miller 2004: 7), the magazine of the Student Environmental Action Coalition, Nathaniel Miller, a former Green Corps organizer, cautioned students against applying to the group. He wrote that during the four months that he worked with Green Corps "they engaged in union-busting and openly opposed affirmative action, environmental justice, and other efforts to diversify the environmental movement." In addition, many of this recent college graduate's complaints about Green Corps were reminiscent of those I heard from the People's Project canvassers in 2003. He called Green Corps a "top-down organization" that required its workers to meet quantitative goals and targets, and he accused the group of having a "fundamentally undemocratic" structure. Although when hired he had been ecstatic to find a position where he would "get paid to be an activist," he was let go after reportedly trying to organize the members of his cohort and being a union agitator.

Although Miller's short tenure suggests that his personal experience with the group may be unique, I found similar accounts posted on the progressive watchdog website Nonprofit Watch.[8] This site posts personal reports and maintains a bulletin board of accounts by other young people. In contrast to claims by some on the left that this website is a front for some right-wing organization, it is not. It is run by Bernardo Issel, a self-proclaimed progressive who works for the labor-union-organizing group Corporate Campaign, Inc.[9] In his article, Miller (2004: 7) also reported that Green Corps had a very high attrition rate. In his class of thirty-one people, "only fourteen finished the year, [with] six people leaving during the first three weeks." In short, young people working for this partner group, which states its mission as training "the next generation of environmental leaders,"[10] have had problems similar to those of People's Project employees. Some who did not complete the year-long program had been so turned off by their experience with Green Corps that they were no longer interested in working for mainstream progressive politics and became anarchists instead.[11]

It is much easier to get an entry-level job at the local level than paid work in a national office. Jessica Hodge of the Sierra Club, for example, began as an unpaid volunteer in the Las Vegas chapter. She recalled slowly making her way into a leadership position at the local level and then, after four years, moving to Washington to take a paid position in the group's legislative office as a field representative.

Hodge's experience mirrors the observations of Theda Skocpol and her colleagues (Skocpol, Ganz, and Munson 2000: 541; see also Skocpol 2003) in their work on the institutional origins of civic engagement in the United States: "Local chapters [have historically] channeled indispensable resources of money and human energy to the 'higher' levels of federations." Although Hodge was able to rise through local channels into national politics, she recognized that her personal experience had become less common in recent years: "I think I'm becoming more and more an exception. . . . I wouldn't be surprised if I was one of the few [people in this office that started out as a Sierra Club volunteer in a local chapter]." In other words, her experience of entering into a national group by working her way through its local channels is unlike that of most people who have ended up working in the national offices of progressive groups in recent years.

For young people looking to start in a *paid* job in progressive politics at the local level, there are fewer options. In fact, canvassing for the People's Project provides one of the very few paid channels into left-leaning national groups from the local level. Before many national groups outsourced their canvasses, their local offices provided entry points for young people to get involved in progressive politics. John Passacantando of Greenpeace, for example, spoke to me about the ways that the in-house Greenpeace canvass had been important to his group and the role that it played in recruiting young people:

> The [Greenpeace] canvass served as a feeder track for hungry, smart people who would one day run Greenpeace campaigns [and even] run Greenpeace. . . . We lost something huge when we shut down our canvass. It's not [a] secret. So many of the heavyweights throughout the Greenpeace world, Greenpeace U.S. and Greenpeace International Amsterdam, had started in [our] canvass. . . . [It] served an amazing purpose. [And we] are now tasked with [finding other ways] to bring people in.

The executive director listed a number of high-ranking staff at Greenpeace *and* other national environmental groups who had begun working in progressive politics as members of the Greenpeace canvass. Although the group had developed some newer programs to bring in young people, he recognized that they did not replace the canvass: "The volume that we had going on that canvass . . . [which] had brought in smart, young people who were hitting the doors every night, and who were ready to do action on a moment's notice, [such as] climbing action, ship action. . . . We've not replaced that, and that remains a weakness [for us]."

With groups like Greenpeace outsourcing their canvasses, there are fewer and fewer options for young people to enter the local branches of national groups. At this point, young people who want to enter progressive politics at the local level through the canvass must succeed within the hierarchy of the People's Project to be promoted. The Project acknowledges this fact and even sees itself as a training ground for progressive activists. Jerry, from the group's national office, explained that the canvass is all about "training activists and . . . [it's] filling a void left by higher education in a lot of ways. . . . Too many schools, I think, don't teach students basic citizenship skills . . . and/or having their voices heard, and/or working with their neighbors to get the decision implemented that they want. . . . I see that as a . . . societal void that's filled by the [People's Project]." Even canvass directors in the local campaign offices of the organization saw the training of young people to be activists as one of their main jobs.

If they are successful within the Project, there are many opportunities for these young people to move up through the organization and its partners at the local, regional, and national levels. Jerry explained the role the canvass plays for his organization: "Most of our staff, period, whether they're senior, whether they're advocates, whether they're . . . in the whole [Project's] world, the vast majority of them have either canvassed or [been a] canvass director. . . . The canvass is the backbone of all these groups." Idealistic young people who are willing to work long hours for limited pay and be moved around to fill the immediate needs of the People's Project are rewarded with positions within the progressive movement. For those young people who do not fit the canvassing organization's mold, however, there are very few other options.

When speaking with canvassers from the cohort of 2003, I asked whether, in the future, they would be willing to work for one of the national groups on whose behalf they had canvassed. Most enthusiastically responded that they would *definitely* work at an outsourcing group if they were given the chance. Some, though, were concerned that they were not legally permitted to take such a job.[12]

Although the canvassers were excited about working for the outsourcing groups, very few representatives of those national groups could name staff people in their offices who had started out as canvassers for the People's Project. A representative of Save the Children reported that such opportunities were unlikely because her group had no actual contact with the canvassers. Similarly, although John Passacantando said that Greenpeace was open to hiring people who had worked for their outsourced canvass, he noted that the canvas did not provide direct channels into his group because it was "such a separate entity." Other than those who had entered the Sierra Club through the Green Corps program, Jessica Hodge also could not recall any former canvassers from the People's Project working for her group at the local, regional, or national level.

The Human Rights Campaign provided the one exception. When asked about the possibility of members of their outsourced canvass coming to work for the national group, Sally Green Heaven replied: "Yeah, it has definitely happened. There are some canvassers who just really like the organization, and the work, and the message. [They] have applied for jobs and we've hired them. One of our former field organizers actually . . . had been a canvasser . . . so she canvassed for HRC and then she came here." Unfortunately, this example was the only account of a canvasser making the transition to working for an outsourcing group. This one example highlights just how narrow the channels of entry are for young people hoping to get into national progressive politics by working at the grassroots level. As such, it is not clear that the People's Project is doing such a great job of training the future leaders of the progressive movement.

Because so few national groups now run local offices that provide paid opportunities for idealistic young people, the People's Project has become the gatekeeper for many entry-level positions within national progressive groups. But many, perhaps too many, young people are being chewed up and spit out by this standardized model of activism that treats idealistic young people as interchangeable cogs in the machine of grassroots politics in America. The fact that it quickly burns out and turns off so many of its recruits adds to its negative effect on progressive politics.

In short, the outsourcing of canvassing has significantly limited the diversity of entry points into progressive politics from the grassroots level and, as more and more national groups outsource to the People's Project and a handful of organizations like it, the problem will only worsen. One case in point is provided by the Democratic National Committee (DNC). Before the 2004 presidential election, the People's Project spun off a for-profit group called Grassroots Campaigns, whose purpose was to raise funds and organize political campaigns by running canvasses.[13] The DNC was the organization's first client. When I met with Josh Wachs, who worked at the DNC as the executive director during the 2004 election and had been working with the Democratic Party for years, he told me about the decision to hire this organization and called the outsourced canvass: a "prospecting program for donors."

This outsourcing of grassroots politics by the Democratic Party is the most recent step in the consolidation of activism that has become the norm for progressive politics in the United States. When a group's future leaders are treated like cogs, and their employers hire them out to "prospect" for donors, is it any wonder that the Left is fractured, disengaged, and losing the very fights they are raising money to win?

REFLECTION

Talking the Talk: Doing Open-Ended Semistructured Interviews So It Matters

By Dana R. Fisher

Although the practice of doing open-ended semistructured interviews can seem on the outside as if it involves just "talking to people," there is much more to this research method. In contrast to experimental research, which is about proving causality through manipulation and control, and survey research, which tends to ask mostly closed-ended questions that can be analyzed using statistical software, this method collects qualitative data in the form of narrative, which allows for more flexibility in interaction with the subject. Based on the subject's specific responses, the researcher can ask additional questions, or follow-ups, probing for more information. As a result, the interview method collects data that can answer the "why" questions that remain at the end of many types of quantitative research. Since this method is less structured than other, more quantitative research methods, it is all the more important for research that employs open-ended semistructured interviews to be conducted in a rigorous manner, involving a clear procedure that is both theoretically and empirically defensible and maintains a level of internal validity. In other words, the researcher needs to be sure that her questions are measuring what she thinks they are measuring. When done right, this type of interview data can be sorted and analyzed for trends that help us understand the how and why of social phenomena. So although this type of research is more subjective than others, by taking these steps we can make it possible for another researcher who is armed with the same access, research question, and interview protocol to be able to collect similar data that when analyzed would yield similar findings.

In the context of the work excerpted in this book, my research focused on understanding the experience of young activists who worked as canvassers for one organization, recruiting new members and renewing existing memberships for a number of progressive campaigns during the summer of 2003. This reflection piece provides some explanation about the motivation behind this research and how it was set up to ensure that the data were consistent, that the individuals who provided their stories that became my data were protected, and that the data were collected in such a way that they would help us learn about the experience of canvassing in America.

GETTING STARTED

As I relate in the introduction of *Activism, Inc.* (2006), the motivation for this project was very personal for me, because I had worked as a canvasser during the summer after my first year in college and I briefly returned to the job after graduation. During my last year in graduate school, I sat in on a class about civil society and the public sphere. As we read and discussed some of the most influential works on civic engagement in America, I found myself wondering what had happened to all of the idealistic young people whom I had trained during my time on the canvass in the early 1990s. I got excited about the idea of returning to the canvass as a researcher armed with the tools of a social scientist to study the experience of canvassing. The research project that I came up with involved data collected through multiple methods, including a closed-ended survey that was adapted from a large national survey called the *National Household Education Surveys* and participant observation within each canvass office. However, to answer my main questions regarding how young people experience this type of paid activism and what happens to the thousands of young people who spend their summers working around the country as foot soldiers for progressive campaigns, the majority of the data collected for this project came from open-ended semistructured interviews with one cohort of young people working on the summer canvass. By talking with young people who were working as canvassers and then following up with them a year later, I aimed to learn about their impressions of the work, how the experience affected them, and why they joined the canvass in the first place. Using this method would not prove causality, but it would help to understand what happens to canvassers. Moreover, it would contribute to an ongoing conversation in the literature about activism and civic participation in America.

Although securing funding for the project was less difficult than I had expected—people affiliated with the Center for Information and Research on Civic Learning and Engagement (CIRCLE), which had just been funded by the Pew Charitable Trusts, became interested in the idea in its early stages of conception—there was much more work to be done before I could even get out in the field and start talking with canvassers. In particular, preparing the study involved gaining access to the largest canvassing organization in the United States—the Fund for Public Interest Research[14]—which had never before been the subject of an academic study. After many rounds of discussions with the organization and positive support from well-known activists whom I knew from my life before I became a sociologist, the organization agreed to be the setting of my research project. However, before I could go into the field and study canvassers, I had to negotiate a memorandum of understanding with the organization that would determine who and what I could gain access to for the study. We agreed that I could select a stratified random sample of field offices based on a list of canvass offices that the organization gave to me (they provided a list of more than 60 offices that would be running across the country during summer 2003). We also agreed that I could spend a week at each of the selected field sites during that summer observing the goings-on in each office, surveying and interviewing all of the canvassers working there who were willing to participate and had completed the requisite three-day training period. Depending on the type of organization being studied, such an agreement may not be necessary or required. However, I have found in my research with political elites of all sorts that it is imperative. More than one of my research projects has been abandoned because I was unable to come to an agreement with the organization that would be the object of inquiry in the project.

At the same time that I was negotiating with the organization, I was required to gain approval from the Columbia University Institutional Review Board (IRB) for my human subjects' research protocol. This step has become a requirement for social research around the United States.[15] The process allows representatives of the university to review the methods that will be used in the research project and ensure that the research will be conducted in a way that protects the rights and welfare of the individuals participating as subjects. Although institutional review boards review all research on human subjects being conducted at universities, including medical research, the main focus of review for social research projects is that the data are collected ethically and, in cases where the data are to remain confidential, that the data are secure and adequate measures are taken to protect the identities of the research participants.

Particularly relevant to this study was making sure that whatever the canvassers said to my graduate students and me during our interviews was kept confidential. In other words, these canvassers' perspectives on the job of canvassing and the organization for whom they were working could not be traced back to the individual canvassers who shared their stories. As IRB approval was required for all social research at Columbia University during that time, the memorandum of understanding that I wrote up with the organization included reference to the fact that all data would be collected in compliance with my approved human subjects' protocol, which had been approved by the university. This step ended up being particularly important to my research.

Although social scientists frequently complain that the requirements of our universities' IRBs put unnecessary requirements on social research—particularly for projects that collect limited personal data about the research subjects—I found the IRB provided me with a welcome shield with which I could protect my research subjects from the organization. Throughout the duration of this research project, people from the organization made multiple attempts to gain access to my data. One day early on in the project, a representative from the organization who was at the field site offered to hide in the closet or surreptitiously turn on the office's intercom so that he could listen in on my interviews and hear what the canvassers were saying. In another case, the organization said that they could not support my research without seeing the data themselves. Even though we had agreed from the beginning that my data would be kept confidential and that I must follow the regulations of the IRB, the organization persisted. Thanks to the university's human subjects requirements, however, I was able to respond to these requests by pointing out that my protocol, which is required by the university and was clearly outlined in our agreement, would not permit such activities.

In addition to protecting my subjects, the IRB protected me when the organization threatened to take legal action against me. Right before *Activism, Inc.* came out, the organization heard about it and the fact that the findings from my research were less than flattering. As a result, the organization's legal team threatened to block the publication of the book (for which they had no legal grounds), stating that I had to turn over all of my data to them. Once again, the IRB and my human subjects protocol provided a welcome protection against the threats (although I still had to pay my own legal fees).

COLLECTING DATA IN THE FIELD

After gaining access, negotiating with the organization, and getting human subjects' approval, I spent the summer of 2003 traveling to each of the six selected field sites with my graduate student assistants (two students worked on this component of the data collection, and they split the field component of the research). We spent a week at each of the offices observing the daily goings-on and interviewing and surveying every canvasser working in the office who was willing to participate in the study and met the agreed-upon selection criteria. Interviews took place anytime and anywhere that the canvassers were willing and able to talk with us: in the campaign offices, as well as in nearby coffee shops, diners, parks, and bars. Since one of the ways that the organization kept the canvassers engaged in their campaigns was through what I have called "perpetual socializing" (2006: ch. 2), we had to take interviews whenever they were possible. Depending on the canvasser and what she or he had to say, interviews ranged in length from 20 minutes to 2 hours. In the end, we collected interview data from 116 individual canvassers during summer 2003.

Along with one of the graduate students who helped me collect the initial data, I also conducted follow-up interviews over the telephone in 2004. Over six months, we tried everything to track down the 108 young people who were willing to participate in this part of the study. Attrition was a big problem for us as the young people in the sample were a relatively transient population and we had met many of them while they were on summer vacation living in a place temporarily before returning to school. Another problem was that, since a number of the canvassers whom we interviewed had been working for the organization only a short time,[16] a number of them did not remember participating in an interview with a member of the research team in summer 2003. This fact is not particularly surprising when you consider that, for most people, canvassing is a short-term job that students do on their summer vacations. In the end, we successfully completed follow-up interviews with 61 people, which represented about 57 percent of those who were willing to participate in this component of the study.

COLLECTING SIMILAR INTERVIEW DATA ACROSS RESEARCHERS

Since the 177 initial and follow-up canvasser interviews were not all conducted with the same researcher, one of the biggest challenges in this project was finding ways to make sure that the two graduate students and I collected consistent data. When conducting open-ended semistructured interviews, one of the main issues is ensuring that we all followed the same line of inquiry and asked similar follow-up questions. Inherent to open-ended semistructured interviews is the fact that the research follows a line of inquiry based on the subject's responses to the questions and what the researcher thinks is important in their particular responses. However, the main challenge is that what I might think is important may not be the same point that my graduate student assistant thinks is important. Therefore, steps needed to be taken to standardize the line of inquiry among the researchers involved in the project to ensure that data collected included as much discussion of issues related to the project's main research questions as possible.

We started with an interview protocol that included eight questions. From there, we agreed upon a number of follow-ups that we would ask depending on how the canvasser had answered the original question. We also practiced conducting the interview protocol together to standardize our delivery and follow-ups. This plan worked relatively well and yielded similar data across the researchers involved in the study. However, it was a challenge collecting comparable data, and I wish we had practiced even more before going out into the field. Although this level of structure may be uncomfortable for some researchers, it is imperative when data are being collected by more than one person. Not only did this process standardize data collection across researchers, but it also helped us all get comfortable with the lines of inquiry that I believed to be most important to the project. This step was all the more useful given our long days in the field. On the day we began data collection in Portland, for example, we left New York City on an early morning flight and went directly from the airport to the field site to observe the daily announcements in that office and begin surveying and interviewing canvassers. My last interview that day did not end until 2 a.m. that night Portland time—25 hours after I had left for the airport in New York City.

By taking the numerous steps described above, this project collected consistent data across a large sample of canvassers throughout the country. Because we spoke with everyone who was working in these offices and we had a very low refusal rate, less than 1 percent of the people whom we asked to participate, the findings from this study give us some level of knowledge about canvassers across the country. Moreover, given the ways that activism in America has changed in recent years, I believe that these findings can be applied more broadly (for a full discussion, see Fisher and McInerney 2012). In short, although there are many challenges to doing rigorous research using open-ended semistructured interviews, by taking the time to set up the research so that the data collected are usable, comparable, and internally valid and that the people who provide the data are protected, research using this method will yield defensible findings that can answer the whys and hows of social research.

NOTES

1. The exact number of campaigns and groups represented by the People's Project differs in each local office.
2. When I visited these offices in 2003, Baltimore had only four canvassers on staff and Ann Arbor had about fifteen.
3. In fact, it sometimes takes a family connection even to get an unpaid internship with a national group; and, while some of these internships offer a small stipend, most are unpaid.
4. The Sierra Club's national headquarters is located in San Francisco, California.
5. Some campus organizers are able to avoid directing a canvass by running campus-based programs over the summer.

6. www.greencorps.org (accessed July 19, 2005).
7. Personal communication with the author (May 26, 2005).
8. See www.nonprofitwatch.org/greencorps (accessed September 15, 2005).
9. Personal communication with author, July 20, 2005. For more information, see www.nonprofitwatch.org/ (accessed November 22, 2005).
10. www.greencorps.org/greencorps.asp?id2=4792&id3=greencorps& (accessed September 15, 2005).
11. Personal correspondence between former members of Green Corps and the author.
12. These canvassers referred to the noncompetition agreement that they signed. Because I was unable to see a copy of the agreement, it is unclear whether it did, in fact, limit canvassers from working for these national groups after leaving the canvassing organization.
13. http://grassrootscampaigns.com/about.html (accessed May 13, 2004).
14. I chose to create a pseudonym for the organization in *Activism, Inc.* because the findings from the research were not very complimentary. Since the organization came out in an article in *The Chronicle of Higher Education* after the book was published (Glenn 2006), I name it in subsequent publications (Fisher and McInerney 2012).
15 Although IRB approval is currently required by most foundations, including the National Science Foundation, *before* grants are funded, it was only required before I started collecting data in 2003.
16. The median length of time working for the organization when we conducted the initial interviews in the field was 20 days.

REFERENCES

Fisher, Dana R. 2006. *Activism, Inc.: How the Outsourcing of Grassroots Campaigns Is Strangling Progressive Politics in America*. Stanford, CA: Stanford University Press.

Fisher, Dana R., and Paul-Brian McInerney. 2012. "The Limits of Networks in Social Movement Retention: On Canvassers and Their Careers." *Mobilization* 17 (2): 109–128.

Miller, Nathaniel. 2004. "The Problem with Green Corps." *Threshold*, Winter: 7–9.

Skocpol, Theda. 2003. *Diminished Democracy: From Membership to Management in American Civic Life*. Norman: University of Oklahoma Press.

Skocpol, Theda, Marshall Ganz, and Ziad Munson. 2000. "A Nation of Organizers: The Institutional Origins of Civic Voluntarism in the United States." *American Political Science Review* 94: 527–546.

CHAPTER 6

Research Using Available Data

Although many social scientists choose to collect their own data, a large proportion of social research involves analyzing available data. These data run the gamut—from quantitative data like the US Census to qualitative data like newspaper articles. Many sources of quantitative data are large-scale datasets that are collected by an organization that is dedicated to gathering data. The National Longitudinal Study of Adolescent Health, which is the data set that Hitlin, Brown, and Elder use in their research, for example, is collected by the UNC Carolina Population Center. Since researchers using these large-scale data sets have no say over the research design—such as sampling and the questions being asked—they are able to focus all of their attention on the analysis of the data.

ABOUT USING LARGE-SCALE DATASETS

Although researchers using this type of large-scale dataset do not have to worry about data collection, they do have to be very focused in their analysis. As with all research, studies that employ large-scale datasets aim to explain relationships between the **dependent** and **independent variables**. To achieve this goal, researchers must rule out all other reasonable explanations of the relationship observed and be sure that there is not a third factor that is causing the relationship, which is what is called a **spurious** relationship. As you may recall from the introduction, we may find an association between two variables (say, education and income), but that association (or part of the strength of the association) can be an artifact of another **extraneous variable**. So for example, it could be that education and income are related, or it could be that something else—say, parent's wealth—explains both education and income. (As it turns out, there is a strong relationship between education and income, and part, but not all, of this relationship is explained by parental wealth).

Not all large-scale datasets are the same. An important difference between large-scale datasets is whether they are **cross-sectional** or **longitudinal**. In a cross-sectional design, a representative probability sample of a population of interest is drawn and asked a series of questions. Instead of following people over time, these data ask different people the same exact questions at the same time. This kind of data can tell us what is the case, but it is not very good at telling us how things have changed. For example, let's say we do a cross-sectional study where we ask people how much money they make. And we find that 30-year-olds make, on average, $30,000 a year, 40-year-olds make $40,000 a year, and 50-year-olds make $50,000 a year. We may be tempted, on the basis of these data, to argue that people's wages increase over time. But we haven't gathered data over time. We have gathered it at a single point in time. It could be that the 50-year-olds are earning more for other reasons—perhaps they're better educated. So all we can say is that there are differences in wages by age and perhaps that those differences are associated with other variables (education); but we have to be very careful if we want to say anything meaningful about changes over time. By "careful" we mean that the research must take into account a wide range of potential extraneous variables. And if it does so, the worry remains that the data are limited to a snapshot of a single moment.

In contrast, longitudinal designs follow a single sample over several years. So if you are picked to be part of a longitudinal study and choose to participate, you become a member of their "cohort" and will be contacted every time the study is done. This kind of design is ideal for studying change. We can see what happens to a group of people as they go through what social scientists call their **life course**. However, longitudinal studies are expensive; it is difficult to follow people year after year and to convince them to continue participating in the study. In "Racial Self-Categorization in Adolescence," Steven Hitlin, Scott Brown, and Glen H. Elder Jr. analyze data from the National Longitudinal Study of Adolescent Health, which has studied the same cohort of individuals over time.

THE BIG QUESTION OF "RACIAL SELF-CATEGORIZATION IN ADOLESCENCE"

In this paper, Steven Hitlin, Scott Brown, and Glen H. Elder Jr. use data collected as part of the National Longitudinal Study of Adolescent Health to explore how multiracial adolescents self-categorize their race over time. They use psychological and social characteristics to explain who chooses to change their racial categorization from one period of data collection to another. The study comes to very interesting conclusions about how young people decide to classify their race and why such classification changes over time.

The authors also note that the race question changed on the survey between the two waves of data collection that the authors are studying. In particular, although respondents were able to classify themselves as White, Black, Native American, Asian, or Other in 1995, the "other" category was dropped from the survey in 2001. The change in the survey instrument provides an interesting opportunity to look at racial categorization.

ISSUES TO CONSIDER

As you read the following excerpt and reflection piece, there are a number of issues to consider. First, think about how the survey instrument was changed. Would you expect Hitlin, Brown, and Elder's results to be different if the "other" racial category had been kept in the 2001 survey? What are the concerns of comparing these two surveys if the surveys themselves aren't the same? Could the change in the survey (and not the change in how individuals classify themselves) explain the results that Hitlin, Brown, and Elder observe? Second, think about the survey design. This paper is based on a dataset with a longitudinal design where the same people were surveyed six years later. How might the findings change if, instead of a longitudinal design, the authors' work was based on a cross-sectional survey? What kinds of claims could the authors make with data collected at a single period in time? Finally, how might this research be different if the authors chose to conduct their own research using a different research methodology altogether—like open-ended semi-structured interviews?

Racial Self-Categorization in Adolescence: Multiracial Development and Social Pathways

By Steven Hitlin, Scott Brown, and Glen H. Elder Jr.

For a majority of American adolescents, selecting one's racial category is not problematic. But this does not apply to a growing proportion born to multiracial households. Their racial self-categorization is not straightforward. Though "race" is not a fixed, achieved entity, quantitative models of racial identification tend to assume, and thus overstate, the stability of a person's racial status. The rise in immigration and interracial relationships over the past three decades underscores the importance of longitudinal research on multiracial self-identifications.

This study investigates the prevalence and change of multiracial self-identification across the transition to young adulthood. With data from the National Longitudinal Study of Adolescent Health, we investigate the under-explored nature of developmental change and stability in racial self-identification as measured by forced-choice questions. We hypothesize that multiracial adolescents are likely to display considerable fluidity in their racial self-categorization choices as they move across this stage in the life course.

The number of multiracial individuals in the United States is increasing (Harris & Thomas, 2002). In the 2000 Census, 2.4 percent of the population (6.8 million people) reported more than one race. Interest in multiracial children has flourished in recent years owing to their increasing number as well as racial measurement changes in the Census. Most multiracials are younger adults and adolescents (Harris & Sim, 2002; Tafoya, Johnson, and Hill, 2004), the period in the life course where the development of racial self-identification typically occurs (Phinney, 1996; Stephan & Stephan, 2000). We know little about the stability in self-identification among adolescents as they age. Development of a sense of racial self-categorization is inherently social and occurs within racially structured, often discriminatory, interactions.

While adolescents work to form a coherent interpretation of what it means to be a member of a racial or ethnic group, they encounter a range of influences, from peers to families to culture, that argue for the validity of one interpretive scheme versus another. Monoracials' struggle to attach meaning to a race category is masked in forced choice tasks. Blacks, for example, will select the broad category "Black" even though at the level of the individual, one Black youth may be testing the validity of an Afrocentric meaning system for a self-interpretation of what it means to be

Steven Hitlin, Scott Brown, and Glen H. Elder Jr. 2006. "Racial Self-Categorization in Adolescence: Multiracial Development and Social Pathways." *Child Development* 77 (5): 1298–1308.

Black, while another may be drawn to an Assimilationist frame (Cross & Fhagen-Smith, 2002). Blacks with wildly divergent subjective racial identities will nevertheless select "Black or African American" as the monoracial category that best represents their overall racial self-categorization when presented with a forced-choice question, as in the Census.

In this sense, racial self-categorization masks intra-group variations in *racial identity*. For youth of biracial or multiracial heritage, the connection between subjective identity and racial identification is potentially more profound and meaningful in that the act of self-categorization may conjure a self-categorization that the larger society seems to demand. Or, it may represent a chance to celebrate or affirm that one's heritage is tied to two or more racial categories. Thus, the act of selecting a racial category may be a surface level act for youth of monoracial heritage but a developmentally significant act for youth of biracial or multiracial heritage.

In this paper, we investigate the consistency of racial self-identification across time, incorporating a developmental, longitudinal framework largely missing from the empirical literature. We address two research questions: (1) How much fluidity in racial self-identification pathways exists across adolescence, and (2) can we predict this change in forced-choice racial self-identification based on psychological and social differences? We focus on multiracial developmental pathways within a nationally representative sample of adolescents. They show the existence of fluidity in racial self-identification across time.

HYPOTHESES

We suggest that the act of forced-choice, racial self-categorization is more revealing for multiracial adolescents than their monoracial counterparts. For monoracials, racial self-categorization is an uncontested choice that is likely to be automatic. However, this self-categorization process is contested for multiracial adolescents. It is not a matter of confusion, necessarily, but rather reflects, as Ting-Toomey (2005) highlights, the necessary working out of divergent and sometimes conflicting frames of reference. When encountering a forced-choice racial category scheme, multiracial individuals are presented with a more complicated cognitive task than monoracial individuals. Though the racial options are quite bounded, they represent meaningful social categories that American citizens are often presented with, when being asked for their racial identification.

Our first analysis involves tracking individuals' racial self-categorization over time. We provide a demographic overview of the prevalence of fluidity in forced-choice racial self-categorization in American adolescents, something that does not lend itself to traditional hypothesis testing. After establishing nation-level, quantitative support for notions of racial fluidity, we provide a preliminary analysis where we attempt to predict pathways of fluidity over time. We expect that:

1. Multiracial adolescents will demonstrate more fluidity than mono-racials, as their social ecologies provide more opportunity for contested, negotiated racial identities. Over time, a larger percentage of such individuals will be significantly more likely to switch racial self-identification.

2. Social influences, mother's education and the racial makeup of the neighborhood, will be significant predictors of racial fluidity across time.

3. Multiracial adolescents' psychological orientations (self-esteem, optimism) and crystallized intelligence (PVT score) will be significantly associated with racial fluidity.

4. The contested aspect of multiracial identity will take a toll on adolescents, as expressed in lower self-esteem.

METHOD

Participants

Our data come from the National Longitudinal Study of Adolescent Health (Add Health), a nationally representative, school-based sample of adolescents (Bearman, Jones, & Udry, 1997). Students who attended one of 132 United States schools in grades 7 through 12 were given questionnaires during the 1994–95 school year. From that, a random sample of 200 or so students from each school and a linked feeder school was drawn to obtain a sample for in-home interviews. The total in-home sample size, including special over-samples based on various ethnic and genetic characteristics, is 20,745. These individuals were interviewed again between April and August 1996 and again between August 2001 and April 2002.

Descriptive characteristics of the sample are shown in Table 6.1 and Table 6.2. The sample includes slightly more females than males. Racially, the sample is predominantly white, though over-sampling of certain subgroups results in nearly one-fourth of the sample reporting black at baseline as well as almost 8% reporting Asian. About 4% of youth report more than one race in both survey waves. The average age of respondents at baseline was between 15 and 16 years.

Dependent Variable

Questions about self-identified race were asked in both the first data collection wave (1995) and in the third wave (2001). The Wave 1 in-home survey asked about the respondents' race and ethnicity with the same format as found in the 2000 U.S. Census. First, a question about the Hispanic ethnicity of the respondent was asked with a yes/no answer option (respondents could also answer "don't know" or refuse to answer).

Table 6.1. Add Health Sample Characteristics (N = 12,368)

	Wave 1	Wave 3
Female	53.3%	–
White	63.0%	62.5%
Black	24.6%	24.9%
Asian	7.8%	7.6%
Native American	0.6%	0.8%
Multiracial	4.0%	4.1%

Table 6.2. Means and Correlations

	Mean (SD)	1.	2.	3.	4.	5.	6.
1. Skin Color	4.42 (1.20)						
2. PVT Score	102.42 (14.52)	.33					
3. Self-Esteem	16.35 (2.59)	−.09	.01				
4. Optimism	12.14 (2.22)	.11	.32	.31			
5. Baseline Age	15.45 (1.88)	−.04	−.04	−.07	−.05		
6. Mother=s Ed	3.70 (1.23)	.08	.31	.06	.26	−.03	
7. Tract %White	0.81 (0.27)	.66	.31	−.07	.11	−.02	.06

*All correlations show statistical significance due to large sample size.

This was followed by a separate question that asked for the racial grouping that fits the respondent, with the opportunity to choose from more than one among: White, Black, Native American, Asian, or Other ("don't know" and refusal were also options). This question order is the same in the Wave 3 survey. However, the race question is different as the "other" option was dropped. Only White, Black, Native American, and Asian were answer options.

This difference in response categories in Wave 3 of Add Health necessitates the omission of any respondents who chose "other" as their sole race or as a part of their multiracial self-categorization. Since nearly one half of respondents who identified themselves as Hispanic/Latino defined themselves as "other," we also exclude all Hispanics from our analyses. Thus, the analytic sample is 12,368 with weighted analyses conducted on a slightly smaller subset of the sample (N = 11,671). We focus on Non-Hispanic Whites, Blacks, Asian-Americans and Native Americans.

Independent Variables

In order to better understand the developmental process of racial self-categorization, we compare the pathways on both social and psychological measures that are known to be relevant in either or both the developmental and racial identity literatures. Since developmental processes are known to vary by gender and age, we include both in these analyses.

We also examine other developmentally relevant variables. We refer to "optimism" as a measure of an emotionally charged, individual orientation toward the future. When people consider their futures, they can be optimistic for little things (e.g., finding a good restaurant) or for big things (e.g., developing a satisfying career path). We focus on the latter form of optimism. For a variety of social (e.g., structural advantages) and psychological (e.g., mental illness) reasons, individuals may differ in their sense of optimism about their futures (Peterson & Chang, 2003). A sense of having a positive future is important for mental health, and for holding a belief that agentic action is useful in the first place (i.e., Bandura, 1982). We use three measures of adolescents' expectations for their future that load adequately and have strong fit statistics within a confirmatory factor analysis (IFI = .998, CFI=.999, RMSEA=.048).

Given our focus, we utilize a notion of self-esteem as a point-in-time measure of how positively or negatively youth feel about themselves. We use four indicators of self-esteem, such as *lots to be proud of* with loadings that range from .82 to .57, that have strong fit statistics within a confirmatory factor analysis (IFI=.999, CFI=1.000, RMSEA=.026).

We also include the Add Health Picture Vocabulary Test (AHPVT), a measure of language acquisition that is an indicator of cognitive development. Specifically, the AHPVT measures hearing vocabulary for Standard American English and is an abbreviated version of the Peabody Picture Vocabulary Test (PPVT).

In addition to psychological scales, we include two more social measures as well as an evaluation of the respondent's skin color. First, mother's education, a proxy for socioeconomic status, is measured as a seven-category ordinal assessment of the highest level of educational attainment achieved by the respondent's mother. These categories are: None; Less than 8th grade; 8th to 12th grade (did not graduate and no GED); High School Graduate or GED; Some Post-High School; College Graduate; Professional/Graduate Training. The percent White of the respondent's census tract is also included to provide a measure of neighborhood racial context. Skin color is assessed by interviewers in the third wave of data collection using a five-category measure: black, dark brown, medium brown, light brown, white. Interviewers were alone, so reliability cannot be assessed.

Procedure

We conduct our examination using three sets of analyses. First, we map out the racial identification pathways present in the Add Health sample. We then proceed by examining binary logistic regressions with the measures noted above regressed on a binary racial identification measure that indicates switching. We follow this with a multinomial logistic regression analysis using those measures to examine the likelihood of being on a particular pathway versus having a stable, single race identity.

RESULTS

The adolescents were asked their race at two different time points (Wave 1 and Wave 3). Consequently, the cross-time comparison monoracial and multiracial identities exhibit six possible pathways of racial identification, all of which appear in the Add Health sample. Adolescents can (1) select the same monoracial category at both times; (2) choose the same multiple race categories at both times; (3) begin with a single race identity, and then add one or more different racial identities (Diversifiers); (4) begin with multiracial self-categorization, but end up selecting only one race (Consolidators); (5) select completely different multiracial identities at each wave (switching multiracials); (6) select different single racial identities at each wave (switching monoracials). Each pathway is shown in Table 6.3, with both the weighted and unweighted sample sizes.

For our purposes, the most interesting developmental pathways are those that switch identities; three of the four groups are large enough to meaningfully investigate. Nearly twice as many adolescents have fluid multiracial identities across time as those who report stable ones. With the exception of the "Switching Multiracials" (adolescents who report fully *different* multiracial identities at each wave), there are significant numbers of young people in each of the pathways. Indeed, the second most common pathway consists of those youth who chose a single race at baseline but added one or more races to their identification in Wave three (Diversifiers). This is a particularly important finding given the cross-sectional nature of most previous work on racial identification. In such work, this category would be considered part of the monoracial group, and their multiracial development would be ignored.

Nearly as many adolescents (306 unweighted) change from identifying with more than one race at the first wave to selecting only one race

Table 6.3. Pathways of Racial Identification

	Unweighted N	Weighted N
Non-switching	11,616	10,972
Monoracial at both waves	11,457	10,821
Multiracial at Wave I and Wave III	159	151
Switching	752	699
Monoracial at Wave I B> Multiracial at Wave III	325	305
Multiracial at Wave I B> Monoracial at Wave III	306	280
Switching Monoracial	98	93
Switching Multiracial	23	21

in young adulthood (Consolidators). There are almost twice as many of either Consolidators or Diversifiers as there are consistently multiracial individuals. Certainly, there is less stability in multiracial self-identification than we might expect, and much less stability than those who identify as monoracial. These numbers suggest that hundreds of thousands of adolescents in America fit either of these "fluid" categories.

Also of note are the nearly 100 young people who have switched from one single race in Wave 1 to a different single race in Wave 3. Here again, cross-sectional work examining race identification would place these youth within the monoracial category regardless of which survey is used and would entirely miss the "protean" nature of their racial self-categorization. Fundamentally, this table presents the complexity and temporal nature of racial identification development that is glossed over in cross-sectional analyses.

When we look more specifically at the details within each pathway, we find substantive patterns. The largest block of Consolidators (N = 130, 42.5%) are initially White/Native Americans who ultimately select White cultural assimilation paths. Only 13 (4.3%) of these individuals select Native American. There are four other types of Consolidators that are worth mentioning. Twelve percent (N = 36) initially reported White/Black multiracial self-categorization and ultimately chose Black, while less than one percent were initially White/Black and ultimately chose White. Adolescents who reported being White/Asians initially (N = 33) are twice as likely to select Asian as White (N = 22 vs. 11). All but one of the 60 Black/Native Americans selected Black, lending support to traditional notions of hypodescent underlying Black racial identification. Finally, of the 18 Consolidators that selected "three or more" races, 15 of them ultimately chose Black, again demonstrating the primacy of this identity.

We similarly examined youth in the Diversifier category. By far the largest subgroup are initial Whites who end up reporting being White/Native American (N = 181, 56% of the Diversifiers, 89% of those who start off reporting White). This group dwarfs the other cells in the Diversifying pathway. Nineteen Blacks become Black/White (5% of Diversifiers, 25% of initial Blacks) while another 42 become Black/Native American (12.9% of Diversifiers, 55.6% of initial Blacks), and still 13 (4% of Diversifiers, 17% of initial Blacks) select "three or more races." Obviously there is something enticing about including Native American as a part of one's racial identification. Asians do not follow this pattern, however. Of those initially reporting a monoracial Asian race, 93% (N = 29) ultimately chose White/Asian as their race. Table 6.4 shows the results of a binary logistic regression that examines the effects of various social and psychological characteristics on the likelihood of switching racial classifications across the two survey waves. The reference group includes all individuals who maintained the same racial classification at both time points, both monoracial and multiracial. Results are for weighted data.

Table 6.4. Binary Logistic Regression Models of Switching Racial Classification

	Odds Ratio	95% Conf. Interval
Age	0.96	0.92, 1.01
Gender	0.90	0.75, 1.08
Mother=s Education	0.81***	0.75, 0.88
Skin Color	0.94	0.85, 1.03
PVT Score	1.01*	1.00, 1.02
Self-esteem	0.92***	0.89, 0.96
Optimism	1.03	0.99, 1.08
Census Tract %White	0.57**	0.38, 0.86
	Chi-Square Tests	
Likelihood Ratio	$63.69_{(8df)}$***	
Wald	$64.46_{(8df)}$***	

Notes: N = 9,926 (587 switch); omitted category includes all respondents who have the same racial classification across both waves of data. *p<.05, **p<.01, ***p<.001

Two psychological characteristics appear to distinguish switchers from non-switchers. Youth with higher self-esteem are less likely to switch races than those who have lower self-esteem. Specifically, for each unit increase in self-esteem, the odds of switching races are lowered by a factor of .92. On the other hand, for each unit increase in PVT score, the odds of switching races are increased by a factor of 1.01. While this latter effect may appear small, it is important to note that PVT has a standard deviation of almost 15. Thus, youth who are a standard deviation higher on PVT than their peers would be about 15% more likely to switch their racial classification.

Two social factors also appear to be important in the process of race switching. Youth from higher socioeconomic backgrounds appear less likely to switch races. Specifically, for each unit increase in mother's education, the odds of changing race are lowered by a factor of .81. Living in a predominantly white neighborhood has an even more pronounced effect. For each unit increase in the census tract percent white, the odds of switching races are lowered by a factor of .57. Other social and psychological factors do not appear to affect the generalized phenomena of switching racial classifications, but this does not preclude their potential importance within any of the pathways noted above. Table 6.5 shows the odds ratio results of a multinomial logistic regression analysis comparing across the same covariates examined in Table 6.4 and explores potential heterogeneity among the various pathways. The model also uses weighted data. Non-switching monoracials are the reference group. Due to their very small sample size (weighted N = 21), we exclude the switching multiracials from these analyses.

Table 6.5. Correlates of Racial Categorization Pathways: Odds Ratios from Multinomial Logistic Regression

	Diversifiers	Consolidators	Switching Monoracial	Non-Switching Multiracial
Age	.97	.92*	1.02	1.03
Gender	.91	.83	1.17	.84
Mother's Education	.84**	.78***	.85	1.21*
Skin Color	1.08	.93	.70**	.85
PVT score	1.01	1.02***	1.00	1.01
Self-esteem	.92**	.94*	.89*	1.00
Optimism	1.01	1.02	1.17*	.95
Census Tract % White	.72	.56	.35*	.64
Subsample N	305	280	93	151

Notes: N = 9,903; –2 log likelihood = 6,122.97; df = 256; omitted category is consistent monoracial. *p<.05, **p<.01, ***p<.001

Compared to the non-switching monoracial group, Diversifiers are less likely to come from poorly educated backgrounds. They are also less likely to have high self-esteem. Consolidators are even more different from non-switching monoracials. Youth who shift from a multiple racial self-categorization to a single race category are likely to be younger. They tend to be from less-educated backgrounds and are likely to have lower self-esteem than youth who maintain a consistent single-race identity. Consolidators are also likely to have higher PVT scores than non-switching monoracials. Youth who switch single race identities across the surveys are also quite different from more consistently identifying adolescents. Switching monoracials are less likely than non-switching monoracials to be light skinned, possess high self-esteem, and live in predominantly white census tracts. However, these individuals are more likely to be optimistic than youth who maintain the same single race. Finally, consistent multiracials are more likely to come form well-educated backgrounds, but largely do not differ from consistent monoracials. Results suggest that adolescents with stable identities across time, monoracial or multiracial, exhibit more positive psychological antecedents as have more advantaged social origins. However, our data do not permit an assessment of the causal relationship in these associations.

Overall, the model shows more differences between the switching and non-switching groups than among the different developmental pathways. In other words, youth with stable racial identification, regardless of their monoracial and multiracial distinction, are more similar to each other than to youth whose racial identification is fluid across time. Similarity across the racially fluid groups is evident, particularly regarding background, socioeconomic status and self-esteem. However, some differences across social and psychological covariates suggest a more complex picture of racial self-identification development.

DISCUSSION

With the notable exception of Harris and Sim (2002), the stability of racial self-identification is generally assumed when race is used in statistical models (Martin & Yeung, 2003). This assumption is unjustified for multi-racial individuals, for whom acts of forced-choice racial self-identification are likely to be contested in terms of multiple social and ecological influences. By taking a longitudinal, developmental perspective, we highlight the fluid nature of multiracial self-categorization and recommend a variety of arenas for future inquiry.

Our results show fluidity with respect to forced-choice racial categories used by the U.S. Census. We also find particular multiracial combinations to be more likely to switch their racial self-identifications across time points.

Specifically, Native-American self-categorization is particularly likely to be involved in switching across time, suggesting that this category represents a self-identification instability in the American racial landscape. A large proportion of adolescents initially report being White and adopt a White/Native American self-identification, while the majority of White/Native Americans consolidate by reporting a White category. We might hypothesize that each type of developmental pathway represents the perceived utility of either identifying only with the majority culture, or additionally claiming membership in a minority category. Certainly this is an area for in-depth research, one that will require quite specialized samples to fully disentangle.

Patterns are less clear for African-Americans, with evidence supporting hypodescent principles rule in some combinations; Blacks are more likely to diversify than others. Future research should explore the extent to which these pathways represent individual orientations versus external judgments of respondents' color and cultural markers. Asians who diversify are likely to include White as a racial category, while White/Asians are twice as likely to consolidate to an Asian identity. These demographic findings support the attention paid to explorations of specific racial combinations, and more qualitative and quantitative inquiry is necessary.

This research offers a preliminary look at the complexity of such developmental processes. Recall that, in order to maintain measurement integrity, we dropped both Hispanics as well as those who selected "Other" as their race. Thus, we provide a conservative estimate of the fluidity of multiracial self-identification across time.

There are six logical developmental pathways of racial identification, and all are represented in this nationally representative sample of adolescents. Proportionally, some of these cells are small when compared to the overall sample, but they represent potentially tens of thousands of adolescents. Any cross-sectional study of multiracial individuals necessarily misses this vital point, multiracial identification across adolescence is quite fluid, significantly more than it is for monoracials. We briefly highlight those specific combinations that are highly represented within these developmental pathways and suggest avenues for future research.

Preliminary, multinomial analyses provide a more detailed picture regarding factors that are associated with this fluidity. Given the ecological contexts in which American multiracial adolescents live, we suggest that forced-choice self-identification is a contested act in contrast with being a relatively uncontested cognitive process for monoracial individuals. Based on previous theoretical and small-scale studies, we suggest that the process of racial self-categorization, and likely racial identity development, is less linear for such adolescents. A binomial logistic regression that compares consistent versus switching adolescents suggests that both social and psychological characteristics distinguish these two groups. Higher socioeconomic background, measured by mother's education and neighborhood racial distribution, is associated with a lower likelihood of adolescent switching across time. As we predicted, higher self-esteem is associated with a lower likelihood of switching races across time. Higher intelligence is also associated with an increased likelihood of switching racial identifications, perhaps demonstrating the capacity of certain adolescents to fluidly respond to the cognitively complex task of racial self-identification in a racially-contested society.

Fluid multiracials have less educated mothers than consistent monoracials, while consistent multiracials come from higher educated households. This proxy for socioeconomic status suggests that family background has important influences on how adolescents decide to racially identify themselves within a multiracial framework. Monoracials who switch their racial identifications stand out in our multinomial analysis. These young people are less likely than other youth to be from White neighborhoods, and they possess significantly darker skin color. Interestingly, while they have lower self-esteem than consistent monoracials, they possess a higher sense of optimism. Perhaps this reflects social comparisons with relevant groups, not including the dominant White culture, but future studies should explore this group in-depth.

Our study reinforces the need for specialized studies of specific multiracial populations. We provide a framework for such studies, situating these specialized comparisons within a broader understanding of fluidity in multiracial development. Nationally representative datasets are unlikely to provide large enough subsamples of such groups, but Add

Health points to the need for a more careful examination of multiracial samples. Our findings are conservatively estimated since we have excluded Hispanics from the sample, but they suggest that 4–5% of U.S. adolescents show racial fluidity over time, a percentage of the adolescent population which is comparable to the number of Asian Americans in the general population.

The strength of these data lies in the nationally representative nature of the sample, but our study contains limitations. We can make observations about the racial self-categorization of these adolescents, but greater detail is needed on the *process* of how one comes to feel secure and comfortable when presented with a self-categorization task. We identify different pathways but can only speculate as to the motivations and influences affecting the self-categorization of adolescent multiracials. Additionally, due to changes in the measurement of race across waves of Add Health, we dropped Hispanics and those individuals who selected "other" from our sample. Assuming Hispanics also demonstrate fluidity in racial self-categorization over time, we can plausibly assume that we underestimate the prevalence of adolescent multiracial fluidity.

Additionally, we are unable to make global claims about the cultural versus psychological influences on multiracial development. Individuals in younger age cohorts in the United States are more likely to self-categorize multiracially, lending support to the idea that period effects are a primary influence on developing self-identity. There is a historical element to this with rates of increasing racial intermarriage. Developmental processes are shaped by historical context, and the development of racial self-categorization is likely to vary in concert with social and demographic shifts around issues of race. Our study suggests such trends will lead to more changes in multiracial self-identification, but this is an empirical question.

This basic structure of American culture (see also Bonilla-Silva, 1996) underlies the individual development of racial and ethnic identities and helps explain these developmental processes. Adolescents create a sense of self that mirrors the social realities they face. Multiracial adolescents develop racial self-identities within overlapping racial contexts; we have shown that neighborhood and skin color influence this social process. Complicating the picture are potential benefits that some adolescents who are phenotypically White might acquire by claiming a minority racial category (e.g., college admission preference). Those who cannot pass, for example darker-skinned African American multiracial individuals, may have less latitude for self-definition as they encounter racially charged social structures in America. Our data do not allow us to delve into these important issues, but we show substantial fluidity in the multiracial self-identity development of adolescents, a fluidity that calls for more detailed research.

REFLECTION

Intentional Serendipity and the Research Process

By Steven Hitlin, Scott Brown, and Glen H. Elder Jr.

Research influences theory and the questions we investigate in a variety of ways. One of the most common has come to be known as the "serendipity pattern" (Merton 1968, 158ff.). Serendipity may occur in the earliest stage of research when the investigator is looking for relevant data to investigate a question but instead encounters a wholly unexpected source of data that leads in a different direction altogether. Sociologist John Laub, a specialist in criminology, encountered such data when he stumbled upon boxes of IBM cards in the basement of the Harvard Law School, data from a long-inactive but pioneering longitudinal sample of delinquent boys from the Boston area. With his collaborator, Robert Sampson, Laub wrote two books (*Crime in the Making*, 1993; *Shared Beginnings, Divergent Lives*, 2003) that show the importance of social relationships for leading juvenile offenders away from crime as they get older.

Serendipity can also refer to the experience of an investigator who observes in the data something that is not consistent with theory or with empirical facts. Additional data may be collected in order to make sense of this surprising observation, or the observation may result in a modification of theory. When theory is totally inappropriate for the observation at hand, another theory may be applied or sought. Luck is not the only factor. Ultimately what an investigator makes of an unexpected observation depends on the preparation of his or her mind to see its promise and possibilities for theory and research.

One way to increase the chances of making your own research luck is to put together the right kind of research team. People who have overlapping-but-separate interests can create fertile conditions that encourage the recognition of new observations and spur new directions for theory and research. This may involve the selection of a diverse research staff, the structuring of the work setting with common, open spaces, and incentives for collaboration. This paper is a product of such an arrangement. Out of this research environment emerged a fruitful study of multiracial development.

The Life Course Studies program at the Carolina Population Center has long been a place for training scholars with an interest in the life course, and Glen Elder (one of the paper's authors) has developed a situation that makes research luck possible. It consists of a suite of offices around a central area where a number of pre- and postdocs can work, interact, and regularly meet to discuss research. Elder's office is in the back corner, rendering him easily accessible for those times he isn't out wandering amongst the rest of us. It is a program and physical space designed to promote collaboration and the free exchange of ideas.

One author (Hitlin) was trained in social psychology. Another (Brown) had experience with longitudinal data. The research team of a social psychologist, a demographer, and a life course expert in close proximity meant that we got lucky. Brown had a burning question about a specific quirk in a longitudinal data set, the strange observation that adolescents seemed to have changed their race over time. The stage was set for serendipity to emerge.

Our research suite is called a life course setting because all projects study the lived lives of people: their life course. We have long known that the best way to study the life course of a person is to follow this individual through time in a longitudinal study (Elder and Giele 2009). In contrast to a social survey conducted at one point in time, a longitudinal study shows us whether change has occurred in a specific person's life, and it does so through a sequence of follow-up surveys. The follow-ups vary in spacing, from every year to every decade or even longer. A longitudinal study also offers researchers an opportunity to identify the explanatory processes—to ask, for instance, what factors or mechanisms account for someone's personal change? Lots of other methods, like experiments, cannot follow the same people across major events in their lives. Cross-sectional data, often the product of a single survey, allows many things but not a focus on change or development over time.

A longitudinal study enables researchers to identify the order of events and transitions, like whether someone's military service provided access to higher education or whether Reserve Officer Training in college led to active military duty. Sometimes this is done at the beginning of a survey; other times, researchers look back at a set of longitudinal data and find unexpected patterns. This is what we did.

With our primary interest in multiracial development, we decided to use longitudinal data from Add Health that are representative of the national population, especially in its race-ethnic and socioeconomic diversity. The subjects were interviewed in 1995 and again in 1996, and then five or so years later in 2001/2. The first and third interview waves are the basis of our study of multiracial development. The survey was designed to focus on the respondents' social, economic, psychological and physical well-being, using contextual information regarding family, neighborhood, community, school, friendships, peer groups, and romantic relationships. However, a strange thing happened; the original study designers changed an important question over time, which made us curious. A significant number of people in the data had different races at different times.

OUR PROJECT: COLLABORATING ACROSS DIFFERENT PERSPECTIVES

One afternoon, while playing around with the Add Health data, Brown wandered into Hitlin's office to discuss a strange quirk he had noticed in the Add Health survey design. A couple of years earlier, Harris and Sim

(2002) had written a pathbreaking article using the same data demonstrating that a significant portion of the adolescents in the study answered the "race" question differently when they were asked the question at home than when asked the same question at school. Students were more likely to consider themselves multiracial if they were taking the survey at home with a parent in the house. About 12 percent of these students were likely to give different racial answers when answering the same question more anonymously at school. Brown noticed that the question that asked about "race" had changed in the third wave of the study, as well.

The census questions about race/ethnicity were as follows:

- What is your race?
  a) White
  b) Black, African American
  c) Asian
  d) Native American
  e) Other
- Are you of Hispanic, Latino, or Spanish origin?

Because so many people answered "other" in Wave 1, Add Health researchers had removed the category for the later waves of the study so as to force respondents into more conventional categories ("White," "Black," "Native American," "Asian/Pacific Islander"). The survey followed the U.S. census convention of asking an additional question after this item on whether the respondents considered themselves "Hispanic." This meant that if you answered "Other" as your racial category in Wave 1, you no longer had this option to describe yourself later on. Brown had been exploring what some of these people had chosen and remarked on this oddity to Hitlin.

What we had was a data problem without a theory; a good many young people were forced to change their racial category because the question changed. We were curious: could we find any patterns in these changes? Hitlin, a social psychologist who studies issues of self and identity, looked at the items and realized that the categories presented by the U.S. census department did not map onto the ways that some people—often Hispanic Americans—self-identified.

The census treated "race" and "ethnicity" as different, but we suspected that people answering the question did not divide the world up in this way. The survey suggested that if you were "Hispanic," your race was likely to be "White." However, many Hispanics did not also view themselves as White; for them, being Hispanic was enough of a racial category. This incongruity could be explained by social identity theory (Tajfel and Turner 1979), which long ago demonstrated how individuals self-categorize on the basis of meaningful social distinctions. We guessed that people thought they were Hispanic, not Hispanic and White. The fact that in later waves of Add Health the "other" option was removed was going to force people to select categories they didn't feel were a true fit.

Thus a series of papers was sketched out. Brown and Hitlin, working in Elder's strategically assembled training program, collaborated on understanding these issues within a developmental framework, another strength of longitudinal data. This finding, and our social psychological theory about why these identity changes were reported, could have happened only with a lot of luck: a fortuitous quirk in the ongoing survey, the expensive capacity to follow the same individuals over time, and three academics with overlapping-but-separate interests being situated in a suite on the fourth floor of the Carolina Population Center.

WORKS CITED

Elder, Glen H., Jr., and Janet Z. Giele. 2009. *The Craft of Life Course Research*. New York: Guilford Press.

Harris, David R., and Jeremiah Joseph Sim. 2002. "Who Is Multiracial? Assessing the Complexity of Lived Race." *American Sociological Review* 67 (4): 614–27.

Laub, John H., and Robert J. Sampson. 2003. *Shared Beginnings, Divergent Lives: Delinquent Boys to Age 70*. Cambridge: Harvard University Press.

Merton, Robert. 1968. *Social Theory and Social Structure*. Glencoe, IL: Free Press.

Sampson, Robert J., and John H. Laub. 1993. *Crime in the Making: Pathways and Turning Points through Life*. Cambridge, MA: Harvard University Press.

Tajfel, Henri, and Jonathan C. Turner. 1979. "An Integrative Theory of Intergroup Conflict." In William G. Austin and Stephen Worchel (eds.), *The Social Psychology of Intergroup Relations*, 33–47. Monterey, CA: Brooks/Cole.

REFERENCES

Bandura, A. 1982. "The self and mechanisms of agency." In J. Suls (ed.), *Psychological Perspectives on the Self*, 3–40. Hillsdale, NJ: Lawrence Erlbaum.

Bearman, P. S., J. Jones, and J. R. Udry. 1997. *The National Longitudinal Study of Adolescent Health: Research Design*. www.cpc.unc.edu/projects/addhealth/design.html.

Bonilla-Silva, E. 1996. "Rethinking Racism: Toward a Structural Interpretation." *American Sociological Review* 62, 465–80.

Cross, W. E., Jr., and P. Fhagen-Smith. 2002. "Patterns of African American Identity Development: A Life Span Perspective." In C. L. Wijeyesinghe and B. W. Jackson (eds.), *New Perspectives on Racial Identity Development: A Theoretical and Practical Anthology*, 243–70. New York: New York University Press.

Harris, D. R., and J. L. Thomas. 2002. "The Educational Costs of Being Multiracial: Evidence from a National Survey of Adolescents." PSC Report no. 02–521, Population Studies Center at the Institute for Social Research, University of Michigan, Lansing.

Harris, D. R., and J. J. Sim. 2002. "Who Is Multiracial? Assessing the Complexity of Lived Race." *American Sociological Review* 67, 614–27.

Martin, J. L., and K.-T. Yeung. 2003. "The Use of the Conceptual Category of Race in American Sociology, 1937–99." *Sociological Forum* 18, 521–43.

Peterson, C., and E. C. Chang. 2003. "Optimism and Flourishing." In C. L. M. Keyes and J. Haidt (eds.), *Flourishing: Positive Psychology and the Life Well Received*, 55–79. Washington, DC: American Psychological Association.

Phinney, J. S. 1996. "When We Talk about American Ethnic Groups, What Do We Mean?" *American Psychologist* 51, 918–27.

Stephan, C. W., and W. G. Stephan. 2000. "The Measurement of Racial and Ethnic Identity." *International Journal of Intercultural Relations* 24, 541–52.

Tafoya, S. M., H. Johnson, and L. E. Hill. 2004. *Census 2000: Who Chooses to Choose Two?* Washington, DC: Russell Sage Foundation, Population Reference Bureau.

Ting-Toomey, S. 2005. "Identity Negotiation Theory: Crossing Cultural Boundaries." In W. B. Gudykunst (ed.), *Theorizing about Intercultural Communication*, 211–33. Newbury Park, CA: Sage.

CHAPTER 7

Research Using Available Data/ Historical Analysis

Historical methods use archival materials or secondary sources (the work of other scholars) to make claims about social processes. Some historical researchers argue that their methodology allows them to make causal claims—that methodology is commonly comparative; others are skeptical about the prospect of establishing causality with historical data and therefore focus more on explanations of processes without attempting to assign direct causal effects.

ABOUT HISTORICAL DATA

Students may wonder what the difference is between history and historical social science. Our answer is "not much." While there were once vigorous debates about the separation of historical sociology and history, today many social scientists do work very similar to that of historians, and vice versa. We will define **historical social science** as the use of archival material or historical accounts to make an argument that has **generalizable** implications.

Some historical social scientists look at a single case, and others look at multiple cases. Those who use multiple cases are comparativists, and they deploy what is commonly known as a "comparative historical methodology." In general, those who deploy the comparative method seek to establish causal claims.

Let's say we are interested in explaining how revolutions happened in the 1600s and 1700s. Using a comparative method, we would look at many nations where revolutions happened and see what factors they all had in common. These factors would give us potential causal explanations. However, we could not be sure that all the factors we identified were explanatory. Some could be causes, and some could simply be incidental. We would therefore take a second step to identify other contexts—nations where revolutions did *not* happen. And those factors that were present when revolutions did not happen would be unlikely causes of revolution.

So let's take an example. Let's say we look at many contexts where there are revolutions and we observe three factors that they all have in common: (A) the rise of merchants as an important part of the economy, (B) the decline and unrest of the peasantry, and (C) changes in crop yields. All three could be causes of revolution. Next, we look at places where there was *not* a revolution. And in these places we find that there were (B) decline and unrest of the peasantry and (C) changes in crop yields. This finding would lead us to eliminate these factors as causes and settle upon (A)—the rise of merchants as central to revolution.

Our example here is too simple (and not accurate regarding historical phenomena!). Often there are several causes of phenomena. Comparative historical methodologists are very sophisticated in the logic of establishing causal claims. And there are vigorous debates about their capacity to do so. But we hope this example shows how the historical method can be used to try to establish causal phenomena.

Other researchers do not care so much about causality and instead focus on how social processes work. Some of these researchers are comparativists, and others simply study single cases. One of the advantages of the historical method is that often the processes under study are complete. When we study processes that are ongoing, the outcomes cannot be known because they have yet to happen! But when we study historical events, we can often look at the beginning, middle, and end of a process.

In the end historical methods are similar to other methods. The scholar is required to gather data herself or rely upon existing sources. She must decide on the bounds of her project, define her variables, posit a relationship between them, and then interrogate that relationship with data. This interrogation means providing considerable evidence that the relationship exists, as well as trying to find and use contradictory evidence whose absence helps show that the relationship is valid.

THE BIG QUESTION OF "ISLAMIC MOBILIZATION"

In the following paper, Ziad Munson looks at the relationship between ideology and social movement mobilization, studying the emergence of the Muslim Brotherhood in Egypt. Munson takes advantage of declassified documents from the US State Department to provide a detailed account of how the organization became so widespread in the country. By integrating this unique data source with the findings from past historical studies, the author shows how getting people involved in a social movement—what social movements scholars call "mobilization"—depends on the interactions among ideology, organizations, and the social context. The case of mobilization is very similar to other cases you have read about—that of Dana Fisher's "Activism, Inc." and Michael T. Heaney and Fabio Rojas' "Partisans, Nonpartisans, and the Antiwar Movement." We have selected this case so that you can see how historical work might address a question that is related to topics discussed elsewhere in this book.

ISSUES TO CONSIDER

As you read Munson's piece and his reflection on doing historical analysis, we suggest you think about the following points. First, how would this study have been different if it had relied on a different data source? Munson discusses how he happened upon the data while looking at media coverage on microfilm; what if he had had only those data? What are the concerns of using data that come from the State Department? Are there potential **selection effects**—where the US government might have chosen to gather information not on all aspects of the Muslim Brotherhood but only on select parts that interested them? How would this concern influence Munson's findings? What can be done to address this concern?

Second, since the Muslim Brotherhood has gained significant attention lately due to the political change taking place in Egypt, how might this historical work be updated to include the more recent past? What research method and type of data source might be best for updating this study? Finally, think about the **generalizability** of Munson's findings given his data source? What can we know about mobilization beyond the context of Egypt at the time period Munson is studying? What are the strengths and weaknesses of this method for this kind of work? And how does Munson evaluate his own claims? Does he use the logic of negation, providing evidence that shows how he might be wrong?

Islamic Mobilization: Social Movement Theory and the Egyptian Muslim Brotherhood

By Ziad Munson

Since its founding in Egypt in 1928, the Muslim Brotherhood has spread to every state in the Islamic world and claimed the allegiance of millions from virtually every segment of society. At the height of its popularity, it had half a million active members in an Egyptian population of less than twenty million—proportionally more than twice as large as the AARP in the United States today. The Muslim Brotherhood also spawned many of the militant Islamic groups that exist today, including organizations such as Hamas, the Islamic Jihad, and Gamaat Islamiyah. Despite its importance, however, scholars still know very little about the remarkable rise of the Egyptian Muslim Brotherhood.

My analysis centers on two theoretically important arguments. The first focuses on the interaction between the ideational component of the Muslim Brotherhood, on the one hand, and the group's organizational activities on the other. This study suggests that our existing understanding of the role of ideas in social movements must be deepened to consider the ways in which mobilization depends on the interactions among ideas, organizations, and environments—not simply on one or the other of these three dimensions. Second, the case of the Muslim Brotherhood also suggests that our understanding of the relationship between mobilization and repression must expand its focus to include the processes within organizations that enable them to withstand repressive efforts of the state.

IDEAS AT WORK IN THE MUSLIM BROTHERHOOD

Understanding Muslim Brotherhood mobilization requires a focus on the unique political opportunities in Egypt in the period, but it requires something more as well. I suggest that the key to the mobilization of the group, above and beyond the presence of some favorable political opportunities, was the relationship between ideas and ideology, on the one hand, and the organization's structure, activities, and relationship to the regular lives of Egyptian people on the other.

ORGANIZATION RESOURCES

Past historical studies coupled with U.S. State Department dispatches provide a relatively clear picture of the structure of the Muslim Brotherhood

Ziad Munson. 2001. "Islamic Mobilization: Social Movement Theory and the Egyptian Muslim Brotherhood." *Sociological Quarterly* 42 (4): 487–510.

throughout this period. One of the basic organizational features of the Society was its federated structure of authority, in which a network of branch offices throughout the cities and villages of Egypt was unified by a central headquarters in Cairo. The branch system formed the basic structure of the Muslim Brotherhood from its very founding. Members exhibited considerable loyalty to their branch in addition to the organization as a whole, and the branch leader played a critical role as liaison between the rank-and-file membership and the central leadership. The organization also shifted coordination and communication responsibilities of the entire Society from branch office to branch office during periods of state repression.

Superimposed upon this federated system of branches was a three-tier membership structure. Established after its third general conference in 1935, the tiers divided the organization by degrees of member commitment. First-level members were called "assistants" and were required only to sign a membership card and pay dues. At the second level were "related" members, who were required to demonstrate a knowledge of the Society's principles, attend meetings regularly, and perform an oath of obedience. Third-level members were called "active" and were expected to entirely immerse their lives in the organization, including high achievement in Quranic learning, observance of all Islamic obligations, and regular physical training (Mitchell 1969).

A great deal of previous work on social movements provides the basic tools for thinking about how these organizational structures contributed to the Muslim Brotherhood's spectacular growth. John McCarthy and Mayer Zald (1977) discussed the advantages of a federated organizational structure in their original formulation of the resource mobilization perspective, focusing largely on American civil rights groups of the 1960s. More recently, Mark Lichbach (1994) included the federated organizational structure as one of several methods of overcoming free-rider problems in opposition movements. Also, Doug McAdam and his colleagues (1996) stressed the importance of different "mobilizing structures" in social movement success.

In the case of Egypt, the role of the federated structure was even more important because of the way in which this structure was linked to the ideas of the organization. The rapid sectoral transformations associated with modernization and incorporation into the world economy created vastly different conditions and interests among Egyptians in the first decades of the twentieth century. Industrial workers in the Shubra al-Khayma district of Cairo, for example, had little in common with the traditional Egyptian peasants or even the populations of the numerous mid-sized Nile delta towns. The Muslim Brotherhood's federated structure allowed it to appeal to the parochial orientations of different groups and different regions of Egypt. It used these appeals to maximum advantage, as evidenced in confidential reports by state department informants:

> The most interesting part of our conversation dealt with the manner in which the Ikhwan [Muslim Brotherhood] carries on its propaganda work in the rural areas. Either in a written document or by word of mouth the Ikhwan's line on current issues is sent to all rural centers where it is explained to four or five fairly literate leaders capable of explaining the issue to others and defending it if necessary. These leaders, in turn, each contact approximately one hundred fellow Ikhwanis and pass on the information. Subsequently it is spread in a less organized fashion among the people by both Ikhwanis and non-Ikhwanis. He claimed that this mechanism for spreading information is very effective because travelers can always be found who are going to the provinces. Therefore, the transmission of information presents no problem. (USDS 1954, #564)

The Muslim Brotherhood used what variety there was within its ideological perspective to attract people in different situations. In some ways, then, it was different things to different people—fighter for the poor in poverty-stricken rural areas, or voice for democracy within educated urban neighborhoods. This kind of ideological nimbleness was facilitated by its federated structure (along with its recruitment strategies, as I explain later). Even the various Cairo suburbs had their own separate branches so that the loyalties of the Society's members could be closely tied to their neighborhoods and the local concerns of the population. Traditional social networks were maintained and incorporated into the individual branches of the group, allowing the Muslim Brotherhood to gain access to lines of communication and commitment originally developed outside of the organization, as the state department report makes clear.

The organization also needed to negotiate a much different relationship with the state than organizations that form the typical focus of existing social movement literature. The system of branches helped the Muslim Brotherhood maintain its organizational strength during periods of state repression. The Society kept lines of communication and authority open to different branches in order to protect the larger organization from periodic government crackdowns, police raids, mass arrests, and infiltration by the state security apparatus—events that effectively eliminated many other opposition groups in the country. Another confidential state department report details one way this was accomplished through the branches:

> As a means of maintaining the nationwide coordination . . . the leader of one designated province is vested with the nationwide leadership of the entire Brotherhood organization. . . . In the event that the entire provincial organization in the leading province is uprooted [by the police], the national leadership is passed on to another province according to a planned random pattern. By this means the Brotherhood hopes to be able to maintain itself in spite of government suppression. (USDS 1959, #261)

This system allowed the organization to maintain its structure and activities even when it was formally dissolved by the state and subject to continuous police surveillance and efforts to destroy it.

While previous scholars have believed that much of the organization was destroyed by the raids and arrests of the period, my data contain considerable evidence that the Muslim Brotherhood was relatively successful in surviving repressive efforts by Egyptian authorities. The government dissolved the Society in 1948, but the U.S. State Department received reports of secret mass meetings, Society organizing in mosques, and pamphleteering throughout Egypt during this time. The group was still sufficiently organized after three years of formal dissolution to produce a demonstration of over three thousand members on less than a day's notice in early 1951 and to carry out well-organized rallies at every branch office in Egypt the day after the ban on the organization was lifted on May 1, 1951 (USDS 1954, #2439). In 1954, the Society was operating again within ten days of the major wave of arrests following al-Nasser's 1954 dissolution of it and imprisonment of its leadership and thousands of its members. By June, there were reports of a public resurgence of the Society's activities.

The Muslim Brotherhood was clearly not dismantled by government efforts. Its organizational structure was key to its ability to resist state attempts to eliminate it. This point is an important one, because by themselves political Islam and political opportunity structure explanations for the rise of the Muslim Brotherhood are based in part on the belief that the organization was considerably more ephemeral, rising and falling with the demographic or political winds of Egypt. The pressures of modernization or the changes in political opportunities produce groups such as the Muslim Brotherhood, the stories go, but grievances and organizational structure become buried when the state exerts enough repressive force. In other words, the operative determining force in each case lies outside the group itself. My evidence suggests that the organization was considerably more enduring than previously believed; its organizational structure provided a means to survive attacks by the regime.

The structure of the Muslim Brotherhood not only provided advantages to the group in the traditional ways described by a basic resource mobilization model, but it also provided an important avenue through which the ideas and ideology of the organization could contribute to the group's success. We saw this previously with the tie between the group's message and its federated structure. The Muslim Brotherhood, like any social movement organization, also faced the task of mobilizing the support and resources of individuals with a variety of different beliefs and levels of motivation for collective action. Speaking in general terms, few people in any society will share exactly the same ideological system as professed by the ideology of a particular organization, and fewer still come to a voluntary association predisposed to alter dramatically their life circumstances for the good of the group. In terms of the specific case under study, the Muslim Brotherhood was uniquely structured to tap into a diversity of social beliefs and commitment and thereby overcome this problem.

One of the most important ways that the Muslim Brotherhood negotiated the difficult terrain of ideas was through its three-tiered membership structure. This system allowed the organization rapidly to incorporate new members with a variety of different beliefs and degrees of commitment. Potential recruits were not asked immediately to plunge their entire lives into the ideology and activities of the organization. At the first level, members had to commit no more than their name and a small amount of money to the organization. This level created a membership pool that provided resources to the group and an audience predisposed to its ideas.

Each of the next two levels added further responsibilities—ideological as well as material—to membership. This graduated process bridged the space between a new member's regular life and the life of the organization. It also acted as a screening device; members who advanced to the higher levels were relatively insulated from those who lacked the same commitment to the Society and therefore were more willing to raise doubts about its ideology or its tactics. The tiers thus maintained a degree of homogeneity in beliefs among groups of members, strengthening their ties to each other and to the organization. They also allowed the organization to benefit from the support of members with a range of commitment to the group.

More theoretically, the lesson here is that the organizational structure and the ideology of a movement are intertwined in important ways. The role of ideas in social movements has recently received a great deal of attention through the concept of framing (Snow et al. 1986; Gamson 1992; Tarrow 1992; McAdam et al. 1996). In practice, the concept refers to the interpretations of events provided by social movement organizations that are intended to resonate with the beliefs of supporters (Benford 1993). While the attempt to take ideas more seriously in the study of social movements is valuable, the framing approach is limited by the conceptualization of ideology as sets of strategically chosen ideas (Benford 1997). It is an overly instrumental view that masks the interactive dimension of ideas and the range of ways in which they are embedded in the organization of the group itself. Framing arguments incorrectly suggest that the task of social movement organizations is to find the ideology or set of beliefs that best tap into a larger sympathetic population. Such an approach ignores the diversity of ideas and beliefs in society.

By contrast, the case of the Muslim Brotherhood demonstrates the importance of the relationship between ideas and the structure of the group as key to overcoming the universal problem of varying degrees of commitment and beliefs. It is not simply that the ideas of the Muslim Brotherhood were popular or that its structure allowed it to take advantage of available political opportunities, although both of these factors played a role. Even more crucial, however, is the fact that the three-tiered, federated structure of the group brought individuals into partial and incremental contact with the ideology of the organization. Thus ideas and organizational structure are intertwined: the latter provides a basis for an introduction to and education about the former in a way that is consonant with the everyday experiences and needs of Egyptian people.

It is also telling to compare the Muslim Brotherhood to the Egyptian communists in this regard. Communist groups were organized in a strictly hierarchical fashion, without independent branch or federated offices. This structure led to constant factionalism and limited the national presence of the communists. Several studies of Egyptian communism suggest that the movement was also decimated by government crackdowns on several occasions (Goldberg 1986; Botman 1988; Ismael and El-Sa'id 1990). Communist organizations were concentrated and one-dimensional. Once infiltrated, they had little defense against the security agencies of the state. Unlike the Muslim Brotherhood, the communist presence in Egypt was virtually eliminated in the 1920s and 1930s as a result of state repression (Beinin and Lockman 1987).

In contrast to the Muslim Brotherhood's three-tiered membership, communist organizations seldom made institutionalized distinctions between members and their levels of commitment. Tasht, one of the most influential communist groups in Egypt during the 1940s, had a "nomination" process for new recruits that could last as long as two years, during which time the individual was continually investigated and tested. A communist leader critical of this system equated the process to entering the priesthood (Ismael and El-Sa'id 1990, p. 45). There were thus severe ideological barriers to entry into the communist membership, and the structure made no place for members with varying levels of commitment; the movement accepted only the most dedicated and committed individuals. In contrast to the graduated way in which the Muslim Brotherhood's structure brought its ideas to members, the beliefs of potential communist recruits had to be entirely transformed before they were given any access to the movement. Thus, the communist groups made it extremely difficult for potential recruits to move from their ordinary lives to active participation in the movement.

ORGANIZATIONAL ACTIVITIES

The activities of the Muslim Brotherhood are among the best-documented aspects of the organization, as they were easily observed by those both within and outside the group. Until now, however, these activities have been acknowledged by scholars seeking to understand the Muslim Brotherhood and other Islamic groups but seldom incorporated into theoretical models. It is thus important to outline the main features of the Muslim Brotherhood's recruitment activities, how these activities related to their beliefs, and how this relationship contributed to the Society's rise to power.

Probably the most important single feature of the society's expansion was its method of establishing new branches. After its founding in Isma'liya, the Muslim Brotherhood began construction of a mosque, using funds from membership dues and grants from local businesses. A boy's school, girl's school, and social club were subsequently added to the complex as the organization grew. Each new branch of the Society followed a similar pattern of growth. The organization would establish a branch headquarters and then immediately begin a public service project—the construction of a mosque, school, or clinic, the support of a local handicraft industry, or the organization of a sports program. This private social service infrastructure grew quickly and became an important part of the Egyptian social, political, and economic landscape. State department records indicate, in fact, that the system was so large that the government was forced to fund and continue staffing the Society's extensive network of services after the organization was dissolved by al-Nasser in 1954 for fear that their collapse would lead to widespread unrest (USDS 1954, #1129).

These activities played an important role in rapidly attracting new members. Muslim Brotherhood public works brought millions of Egyptians into contact with the organization and its ideology. They helped overcome potential free-rider problems within the organization, as resources such as schools and clinics served as selective incentives for Muslim Brotherhood members and potential recruits. Perhaps most importantly, they created an institutional infrastructure in which the Society could demonstrate its ability to deliver on promises of social and economic change to the Egyptian population. They gave material legitimacy to the Society's message that Islam is the true path to development. The ideology was therefore not just a set of abstract ideas debated by intellectuals and group leaders; the Islamic message was linked to the real, practical activities of the Society. The activities of the organization and its ideology were thus two sides of the same coin. People came to see the two hand in hand, each reinforcing the legitimacy and effectiveness of the other.

This is what I mean when I talk about the importance of the interrelationship between ideas, on the one hand, and other aspects of the movement, on the other. It is not enough simply to have a message that resonates with potential recruits. As noted previously, there were many such organizations operating in Egypt during this time, but none of them achieved the prominence of the Muslim Brotherhood. Key to the organization's success is the way in which its ideas were meaningfully related to its practices. Ideas were tied directly to action in concrete, identifiable ways (e.g., "Islam is the answer, so we build mosques," or "the poor must be supported, so we provide widow pensions").

While the organization spread physically by continually expanding its social service infrastructure, it proselytized and spread its message through the use of the mosque. The mosque was the primary venue in which explicit recruitment to the organization took place. Other than sporting events, mosques were the only forum in which the government would permit large congregations of people during much of this period.

Mosques were also relatively safe from police raids or even obvious government intervention in the conduct of the services. Even the state had to play by the rules in the mosques, as a state department memo makes clear in describing government efforts to combat the organization:

> The Army has launched a comprehensive counter-propaganda campaign and is sending carefully selected Army officers into the mosques throughout Egypt. The officer, attired in civilian clothes, first sits and listens to the Sheikh and if he attacks the Regime and the new Constitution, the officer rises, questions his statements (per mosque traditions) and then gradually refutes his charges, especially by pointing up the Regime's projects for the good of the people. (USDS 1954, #2291)

Despite formal government control over both mosques and their preachers, mosques greatly protected the ability of the Muslim Brotherhood to recruit new members and publicize their views even while technically banned by government authorities.

Mosques had many other advantages as well. They gave the society's preachers an aura of respectability and morality they might not have otherwise possessed if their rallies were simply held in the street or a branch office; they tied the organization to Islam, thus legitimizing the group's oppositional message (Billings and Scott 1994). Moreover, mosques protected speakers from sharp criticism and physical attack from audience members. They also served as a self-selection mechanism for potential recruits; those in attendance were already predisposed in some way to the religious message of the Society. Mosques were thus critical to the successful rise of the Muslim Brotherhood—they created and maintained a public space for the organization not only in a material sense (they offered protection from the police and a focal point for large audiences) but also in the ideological sense (they gave the Society a borrowed religious virtuousness while also insulating discussion from alternative beliefs). While its leaders used street demonstrations and marches as displays of power, the mosque remained the primary site for new recruitment throughout 1932–1954. Only with a specifically Islamic message was the organization able to gain such effective advantages from mosques. At the same time, only through the use of mosques was the organization able to propagate an ideology that was harshly critical of the existing regime and social relations in Egypt.

Here again the interaction between the organization's activities and its ideology is important. The use of the mosque, coupled with the Islamic message, combined to produce particular advantages for the group's mobilization. This finding parallels similar conclusions about the importance of mosques in studies of the Iranian revolution (Parsa 1989; Rasler 1996). It also again suggests the need to move beyond the more simplistic formulations of ideology suggested by frame analysis. Framing approaches focus almost entirely on ideas themselves, looking for ways in which they might be aligned, extended, amplified, and so on (Snow et al. 1986). What is also needed is a focus on the relationship between ideas and organizational activities. Ideas can't be analyzed in isolation, as a separate "variable" in a laundry list of mobilization causes. It is a well-fitted interface between characteristics of an organization and characteristics of its ideology that leads to successful mobilization.

While its construction of public works and extensive use of mosques were the most visible activities of the organization, Muslim Brotherhood recruitment and leadership training also forged important links with the beliefs of its members and of Egyptian society. The group was committed to recruiting men from diverse social backgrounds. When the movement began to train its own preachers in 1938, it gave strong preference to those who had connections to the peripheral provinces of Egypt. Al-Banna consciously fostered this policy in order to build a cadre of preachers who were "sympathetic to the needs, feelings, idiosyncrasies, dialectical peculiarities, and local circumstances of the great masses of workers" (Mitchell 1969, p. 190). The organization also staged a continual series of lectures, meetings, and discussions aimed at incorporating each member's larger biography into the Society. By 1939, the organization was holding mass meetings in their headquarters in addition to the regular meetings inside the mosques. These were further supplemented by additional lectures aimed at the secondary group affiliations of the membership. Thus, the society held special meetings for workers, students, professionals, and so on.

This strategy of recruitment and propagandizing was important to the organization, because it tied individuals' secondary affiliations to the Muslim Brotherhood itself and thus served to bring members more fully into the fold of the organization. Members identified and interacted with the group not only in terms of a desire for political or moral reform but also in terms of religion, occupation, and social status. The sharp distinction between general social life and active support for the organization was thereby further blurred, easing the transition into the group and allowing the Muslim Brotherhood to take advantages of group affiliations, resources, and connections that ostensibly lay outside of the organization.

McAdam (1983; 1982) and others have already noted the importance of tactics to the ability of social movement organizations to generate resources. While the Muslim Brotherhood's strategies of recruitment led to important material resources, many of their most important effects lay not in their ability to attract direct material advantages but in the connection they created between the organization and individual beliefs. Access to secondary group affiliations, regional identities, and so forth helped the Muslim Brotherhood cement the loyalty of its members by linking itself to existing belief systems and structures of loyalty in society. The point is thus not that the Muslim Brotherhood found an effective way to frame its message in order to tap into existing public opinion. It helped formulate that opinion through strategies that eased the divide between membership and nonmembership, the requirements of the organization, and the regular lives of its members. It was therefore able to mobilize a wide variety of different segments of Egyptian society.

CONCLUSION

I have argued that the specific relationships that tied the Muslim Brotherhood's ideas to its organizational structure, group activities, and the beliefs and practices of ordinary Egyptians offer the key to understanding its tremendous popular support in Egypt in 1932–1954. The relationships ultimately allowed the group simultaneously to appeal to a broad segment of the Egyptian population and to negotiate the difficult political landscape dominated by an authoritarian state.

The U.S. State Department files have confirmed many of the observations made by others of the Muslim Brotherhood, but they also reveal important new information. First, they show clearly that the Muslim Brotherhood was never truly dismantled in the state repressions of October 1941, December 1948, and January 1954. The Society maintained its organizational structure throughout these episodes and continued its organizing activities, distributing information, and even providing social welfare to the needy. Recent research on the relationship between repression and mobilization has focused largely on the behavior of the state (Andrews 1997; Salehi 1996; Rasler 1996; Opp 1994). My findings complement this work by highlighting the importance of the organizational structure of the Society and the tactics it employed to avoid the state measures to suppress it. We need to examine not just the quantity of repression, but also its effectiveness, given the structure and message of a particular social movement.

The new data also demonstrate that the Muslim Brotherhood was not a fanatical terrorist group or radical opposition movement during this period. Translations of organizational tracts and publications reveal an ideology concerned with regular political issues of the day, such as government corruption and the need for more medical clinics. State department interviews with Muslim Brotherhood members reveal average individuals with common perspectives on Egyptian politics and demands for unremarkable social and political reforms. State department analyses of speeches and party programs found a similar lack of distinction in the ideology of the organization and their concrete proposals for change. This finding is an important corrective to the view that Society members are those either alienated or discontented with society who believe it can be transformed by some magical return to a mythical past.

The mobilization of the Muslim Brotherhood was possible because (1) its internal structure was adapted specifically for avoiding repressive efforts of the state and making it practically and ideologically easy for individuals to join; (2) its activities were intertwined with beliefs in such a way that each was strengthened and made more resilient to state repression and more attractive to potential supporters; and (3) the structure of the group's message, rooted in rich Islamic ideas and symbols, was tied to everyday Egyptian life and thus accessible to potential recruits. The analysis I have presented is rooted in existing explanations of the organization and models of social movements more generally, but it also goes beyond these explanations. First, unlike political Islam and political opportunity structure models, this analysis addresses the question of why the Muslim Brotherhood in particular became so powerful rather than one of the many other Islamic groups that existed during the same period. Second, its conceptualization of ideology and the link between organization and beliefs offers a way to think about ideas and ideology systematically without resorting to the reductionism of framing models. Ideology must be considered more systematically. Its effects and relationship to social movements are more pervasive than current models would allow. Third, the focus on the ways in which the organizational, tactical, and ideological qualities of the Society allowed it to overcome significant state repression offers insight into extending the political process model to non-liberal-democratic regimes. Future research on the Muslim Brotherhood and other social movements outside the Western fold can continue to extend and refine these insights through more comparative analysis that moves beyond the limitations imposed by a single case study.

REFLECTION

Making Sense of History

By Ziad Munson

Sociological methods are almost always taught using the framework of the scientific method: choose a topic, formulate a question about that topic, generate hypotheses or potential answers to the question, and then collect data that help evaluate the hypotheses. The reality of actual scientific research—in biology and physics as much as in sociology—rarely looks like this framework; scientific insights are seldom developed in such an orderly fashion. This point is especially true of comparative historical research. The data for this method come in many forms; it requires evaluating and making sense of an almost limitless number of historical details; and the data collection and data analysis steps of the research process are hopelessly intertwined. The comparative historical method is, in short, messy. At the same time, however, comparative historical research is also a uniquely powerful and engaging method. Studies using this approach help the past come alive while simultaneously helping to inform the present. And comparative historical research often focuses on singularly important events in a society's history.

START WHEREVER YOU ARE

As with many other research projects that use the comparative historical approach, I began collecting data without a well-formulated hypothesis. Indeed, I began my research on an entirely different topic, the Egyptian media (rather than the Muslim Brotherhood). I was collecting data on media coverage of unrest in Egypt during the 1950s and 1960s from old newspapers archived on microfilm. My plan was to analyze the different media frames of the conflict that took place between the British colonialists and Arab nationalists after World War II. The microfilm reels that I used were stored in a large drawer in Lamont Library at Harvard University. As I worked through them, I noticed the other material that happened to share the same microfilm drawer in the library: declassified documents from the US embassy in Egypt. I had never heard of these materials before and decided on a whim to take a look—and I was immediately intrigued by the richness of this document collection. One of the first that caught my eye was a Top Secret request from the embassy to send Gamal Abdel Nasser, who had recently become president of Egypt through a coup d'état, a copy of the then popular film *It's a Wonderful Life* because, as the document explained, Nasser would likely find it "touching."

I found more serious—and more important—material as I explored further. I discovered that the American embassy had excellent contacts on the ground in Egypt and that American agents made regular, detailed reports based on these contacts about commercial activity, cultural activity, and—critically—political sentiment and protest in the streets. These documents, discovered by accident in a library drawer, provided a trove of new information on a critical period in Egypt's modern history. Moreover, they repeatedly referred to the Muslim Brotherhood, an organization I knew to be a key actor during the period. The material was more interesting than the original newspaper articles with which I had started, and the historical and intellectual issues I could address with them were more important. I therefore let the data guide me to a new focus—on the Muslim Brotherhood—as well as a new question: how was this group able to mobilize so many people so often over such a long period of time, even in the face of significant repression?

My question is typical of the kind often asked in comparative historical research. The method is often used to ask questions about events that happened in the past (as the name implies). But comparative historical questions also tend to focus on unusual events; events that—with the hindsight of history—we know were particularly important or meaningful. Although many methods endeavor to find cases that are common or typical or average, comparative historical research looks for the opposite: those cases that are special or unique in some important way.

It might have been difficult to appreciate fully the importance of the Muslim Brotherhood during the period when it first rose to popularity. There had been popular mobilizations in Egypt in the past, so its rise was interesting and important at the time but not unique. It is what the organization later came to represent that made its mobilization so important: the group has played a critical role in both of the power transitions that have occurred in Egypt in the last 50 years (1952 and 2011). Perhaps more importantly, virtually all militant Islamic groups around the world today can trace their ideological origins (and many their organizational origins as well) to the Egyptian Muslim Brotherhood. It is not an exaggeration to say that the rise of the organization has proven to be of world historical importance. This follows the pattern of many comparative historical studies, which focus on events that are particularly important in history. It is a method for asking big questions about such topics as social and political revolutions, the rise of capitalism, and the emergence of human rights.

DEFINING CASES

As I changed the focus of my research to the Muslim Brotherhood, I also realized that this single organization would not be enough to sustain my entire analysis. The group is interesting, but it represents only a case study without a comparison. If I believed a particular factor was important to the rise of the group, how could I know that the many other groups that failed to mobilize during the same period didn't also have that factor working in their favor? If I believed a particular factor was irrelevant, how could I show that all of the groups possessed the same factor if I had information on only one group?

One of the key challenges in comparative historical research is finding the right "cases" to compare. A case is an instance or example of the phenomenon you are interested in studying. If, for example, you are interested in childhood obesity, each case might be a child who suffers from obesity. If you are interested in the causes of social revolutions, each case might be a nation-state that has experienced a revolution. Many quantitative, statistical methods rely on the existence of hundreds or even thousands of cases in order to insure they are making the relevant comparisons. By contrast, comparative historical research focuses on a very small number of cases, usually three or sometimes even two. Because there are so few cases in a comparative historical study, the specific cases chosen for the research take on much more importance.

Cases must be similar enough so that you are not comparing apples and oranges. If *everything* about a group of cases is different, it is impossible to determine *which* difference is the most important. In my study of the Muslim Brotherhood, I chose the Egyptian Communist Party as my comparison case because of its similarities with the Muslim Brotherhood: both were based in Egypt in a similar time period, both called for similar kinds of changes to the Egyptian political system, and both were social movement organizations vying for popular support among ordinary Egyptians. But they also differed in important ways, too, most notably in their relative success at mobilizing new members. The narrow range of differences between the two cases helped me discover how specific factors affected their ability to mobilize.

Data availability can be another important criterion in selecting cases. You obviously can only compare cases about which you can gather information in the first place. In my Muslim Brotherhood study, I originally tried to compare their success with the many other Islamic groups that had been founded in Egypt during the same period but failed to attract many members or followers. In other words, I started with groups that were even more similar to the Muslim Brotherhood than the Egyptian Communist Party. Unfortunately, however, I wasn't able to find enough information about these groups. This is a general problem in studies that use historical data; information on "failed" organizations—especially if they never gained much popularity—is hard to come by. So my decision to compare the Muslim Brotherhood with the Communist Party wasn't just theoretically driven; it was driven by the practicalities of what data I could get my hands on. The good news is that data of the kind I used in my study—historical records—are becoming easier and easier to find. Internet archives and online databases are making vast quantities of usable data available in more places, more cheaply than ever before.

CONDUCTING THE ANALYSIS

For many people, much of the mystery in comparative historical research lies in the actual analysis itself. Once you've assembled a body of data, like the US State Department documents, what are the next steps to take in actually *using* that information to answer a particular research question or compare several different cases you've chosen? This is less of a problem in quantitative studies that use statistical methods, because the "analysis" is already implied in the method itself—ordinary least squares regression, for example, represents a kind of analysis in which the researcher believes there is a predetermined, mathematical relationship between a set of different variables. Comparative historical research has no analogous procedure that presupposes a particular relationship between variables.

At the same time, however, there really is no mystery to how comparative historical analysis is actually conducted: it is no more than careful reading, observation, categorization, and a willingness to go back and forth between ideas about what you are studying and the actual data on what you are studying. The back and forth of comparative research is already evident in the few details I've laid out about my project. Instead of proceeding through a well-developed series of steps in the research process, each predicated on completing the previous step, I collected data, which led me to revise my research focus, which led me to collect new kinds of data, which in turn necessitated that I further revise my approach, which then led me to still more data, and so on. If it was serendipity that led me to my main source of data and my central research question, it was a process of constant iteration that led me to the analysis I ultimately conducted in the article.

I probably wouldn't have made much progress if I hadn't started with at least some ideas about what to look for in all of the data I was amassing. I began my research as a graduate student who had read some of the existing research on social movements and Middle East politics. Research on social movements, it seemed to me, was too instrumental (that is, it relied too heavily on the assumption that individuals always rationally pursue their self-interest), and its discussion of religion was too shallow (that is, religion was dismissed as being unimportant or important only in narrow ways). At the same time, the Middle East in general seemed to be largely ignored by sociologists. I thought at the time that these new data on Egypt might offer a way to address these concerns. It was the starting point for my analysis.

I poured over documents and historical accounts with an eye toward the issues of motivation and religion. I paid particular attention to documents that reported on the state of mind of Muslim Brotherhood members or those who attended street protests organized by the group. I noted where religion and religious issues were present—and absent—from the data. And I started documenting the ways in which the growth of the movement looked similar to and different from the more closely studied movements in the West. My answer to how the Muslim Brotherhood was so successful, which focused on how beliefs were embedded in the structure of the organization, came after only a great deal of work with my data and constantly switching between developing new ideas about my question and collecting new data relevant to my question.

A key issue in comparative historical analysis is the reliability of data sources. Historical documents can't be used without understanding how they were produced. Who wrote them? For what audience? What were the resources and constraints of the authors? Part of my analysis included finding answers to these types of questions, which helped me put the historical documents I was using in the proper context. In the case of my declassified State Department files, I learned that the United States was seen in Egypt as a distant and largely benevolent outside power during this period. With one important exception (the 1956 invasion of Egypt by Israel, Britain, and France), the United States was not centrally involved in either the foreign or domestic politics of Egypt. As a result, its agents operated (and observed) freely and were given particularly good information from their Egyptian contacts. This difference not only accounts for the richly detailed accounts I found within the documents, but it also gives me more confidence that the reports are accurate.

These documents helped me develop a much more detailed understanding of the Muslim Brotherhood than had been available to previous scholars. They contained information on communism in Egypt, too, but in the case of the Egyptian Communist Party, I relied much more on books and articles that had already been published about the subject. These kinds of secondary data are not uncommon in comparative historical research. Sociologists often build on the detailed work of historians, area specialists, and other scholars who have already published information that helps us in our comparisons. Sometimes, however, these sources will disagree about the facts of a case. In these situations, scholars must adjudicate between different sources in the same way a student would evaluate a potential source for an essay or term paper: they look at the level of detail the author provides, information on where they obtained their data, how they analyzed it, and so on. Very often, accurate information on a particular case requires "triangulating" accounts from several different sources. In other words, you need more than just one or two secondary sources that describe a particular event (or organization or time period or personality) in order to have confidence that the data are strong enough to use in your comparisons.

COMPARATIVE HISTORICAL METHODS IN PERSPECTIVE

Comparative historical methods are often criticized for lacking rigor or being too easy for the researcher to manipulate. My own feeling is that these criticisms overestimate the rigor and objectivity of other approaches, particularly statistical ones. But they also tend to confuse lack of rigor with the messy back-and-forth nature of comparative historical research. The history of human societies and institutions is complex. Comparative historical methods mirror that messiness in order to engage fully with historical complexity. They require the researcher to get to know their cases, and their data, extremely well.

As with many other methods, there is also a great deal of variability in comparative historical research. Some use historical documents for their data, as I did, while others rely exclusively on previously published histories. And while many studies focus on large, monumental events that have changed the course of the world's history, it isn't necessary to use the comparative historical approach. The method could be used, for example, to compare how two neighboring colleges have implemented diversity plans or how two businesses developed much different competing products. In other words, the approach can be very global and ambitious or very local and focused. The key to the approach is its eclecticism. Those who are interested in comparative historical methods would thus benefit from reading several different studies. A couple of good places to start are listed below.

REFERENCES

Adut, Ari. 2005. "A Theory of Scandal: Victorians, Homosexuality, and the Fall of Oscar Wilde." *American Journal of Sociology* 109: 445–95.

Andrews, Kenneth T. 1997. "The Impacts of Social Movements on the Political Process: The Civil Rights Movement and Black Electoral Politics in Mississippi." *American Sociological Review* 62: 800–19.

Beinin, Joel. 1990. *Was the Red Flag Flying There? Marxist Politics and the Arab-Israeli Conflict in Egypt and Israel, 1948–1965.* Los Angeles: University of California Press.

Beinin, Joel, and Zachary Lockman. 1987. *Workers on the Nile: Nationalism, Communism, Islam, and the Egyptian Working Class, 1882–1954.* Princeton, NJ: Princeton University Press.

Benford, Robert D. 1993. "Frame Disputes within the Nuclear Disarmament Movement." *Social Forces* 71: 677–701.

———. 1997. "An Insider's Critique of the Social Movement Framing Perspective." *Sociological Inquiry* 67: 409–30.

Billings, Dwight B., and Shaunna L. Scott. 1994. "Religion and Political Legitimation." *Annual Review of Sociology* 20: 173–201.

Botman, Selma. 1988. *The Rise of Egyptian Communism, 1939–1970.* Syracuse, NY: Syracuse University Press.

Charrad, Mounira. 2001. *States and Women's Rights.* Berkeley: University of California Press.

Dessouki, Ali E. Hillal, ed. 1982. *Islamic Resurgence in the Arab World.* New York: Praeger.

Fourcade, Marion. 2009. *Economists and Societies: Discipline and Profession in the United States, Britain, and France, 1890s to 1990s.* Princeton, NJ: Princeton University Press.

Gamson, William A. 1992. *Talking Politics.* New York: Cambridge University Press.

Goldberg, Ellis. 1986. *Tinker, Tailor, and Textile Worker: Class and Politics in Egypt, 1930–1952.* Los Angeles: University of California Press.

Huntington, Samuel. 1996. *The Clash of Civilizations and the Remaking of World Order.* New York: Simon and Schuster.

Ismael, Tareq Y., and Rifa 'at El-Sa'id. 1990. *The Communist Movement in Egypt, 1920–1988.* Syracuse, NY: Syracuse University Press.

Jansen, G. H. 1981. "Secretive Brothers." *Middle East International* 153: 8–9.

Kane, Danielle, and Jung Mee Park. 2009. "The Puzzle of Korean Christianity: Geopolitical Networks and Religious Conversion in Early Twentieth-Century East Asia." *American Journal of Sociology* 115 (2): 365–404.

Kedourie, Elie. 1992. *Democracy and Arab Political Culture.* Washington, DC: Washington Institute for Near East Policy.

Kramer, Martin. 1993. "Islam vs. Democracy." *Commentary* 95 (1): 35–42.

Lichbach, Mark I. 1994. "Rethinking Rationality and Rebellion: Theories of Collective Action and Problems of Collective Dissent." *Rationality and Society* 6: 3–39.

Marty, Martin E., and R. Scott Appleby, eds. 1993. *Fundamentalisms and the State: Remaking Polities, Economies, and Militance*. Chicago: University of Chicago Press.

McAdam, Doug. 1982. *Political Process and the Development of Black Insurgency, 1930–1970*. Chicago: University of Chicago Press.

———. 1983. "Tactical Innovation and the Pace of Insurgency." *American Sociological Review* 48: 735–54.

McAdam, Doug, John D. McCarthy, and Mayer N. Zald, eds. 1996. *Comparative Perspectives on Social Movements*. New York: Cambridge University Press.

McCarthy, John D., and Mayer N. Zald. 1977. "Resource Mobilization and Social Movements: A Partial Theory." *American Journal of Sociology* 82: 1212–41.

Mitchell, Richard P. 1969. *The Society of the Muslim Brothers*. New York: Oxford University Press.

Opp, Karl-Dieter. 1994. "Repression and Revolutionary Action: East Germany in 1989." *Rationality and Society* 6 (1): 101–38.

Parsa, Misagh. 1989. *Social Origins of the Iranian Revolution*. New Brunswick, NJ: Rutgers University Press.

Rasler, Karen. 1996. "Concessions, Repression, and Political Protest in the Iranian Revolution." *American Sociological Review* 61: 132–52.

Salehi, M. M. 1996. "Radical Islamic Insurgency in the Iranian Revolution of 1978–1979." In Christian Smith (ed.), *Disruptive Religion*, 47–63. New York: Routledge.

Smith, Christian, ed. 1996. *Disruptive Religion: The Force of Faith in Social Movement Activism*. New York: Routledge.

Snow, David A., E. Burke Rochford Jr., Steven K. Worden, and Robert D. Benford. 1986. "Frame Alignment Process, Micromobilization, and Movement Participation." *American Sociological Review* 51: 464–81.

Tarrow, Sidney. 1992. "Mentalities, Political Cultures, and Collective Action Frames: Constructing Meanings through Action." In Aldon D. Morris and Carol M. Mueller (eds.), *Frontiers in Social Movement Theory*, 174–202. New Haven, CT: Yale University Press.

Thompson, E. P. 1972. *The Making of the English Working Class*. Harmondsworth, UK: Penguin.

Tibi, Bassam. 1998. *The Challenge of Fundamentalism: Political Islam and the New World Disorder*. Los Angeles: University of California Press.

US Department of State (USDS). 1949. "Confidential Central Files, Egypt, 1945–1949." Washington, DC.

———. 1954. "Confidential Central Files, Egypt 1950–1954." Washington, DC.

———. 1959. "Confidential Central Files, Egypt, 1955–1959." Washington, DC.

Zubaida, Sami. 1993. *Islam, the People, and the State: Essays on Political Ideas and Movements in the Middle East*. New York: I. B. Tauris.

CHAPTER 8

Research Using Available Data/Content Analysis

Content analysis is the study of human communication. While it is frequently the study of the written word—books, newspapers, court transcripts, websites, laws—it can include the study of objects such as paintings, buildings, and other human endeavors that convey meaning. The purpose of this method is to reveal the meanings and associations of the content under study. Researchers who do interview work sometimes do a version of "content analysis" when studying their interview transcripts. However, the technique has become a method in its own right.

ABOUT CONTENT ANALYSIS

Humanistic scholars have engaged in versions of content analysis as far back as we have accounts of human knowledge. What does this painting mean? What is being conveyed by these words? Such questions are at the core of trying to understand the meaning behind human activity; it is what philosophers, art critics, and literary analysts do in their professions. It is very likely, in fact, that you have had to answer these kinds of questions on English essays or in art classes before. However, over the last several decades, scholars from the social sciences have begun to deploy the insights from our own methodology to answer these kinds of questions. Such work has been greatly aided by technological advances that allow us to review masses of text in new and interesting ways.

The work of content analysts begins in many of the same ways as the work of other researchers. First, you decide upon a topic of interest. Next, you ask how you might address that topic. You then figure out what the important categories or variables are, how you will observe them, and whether or not you can use your findings to make broader claims.

For example, you might be interested in how Americans understand protest events. In order to address this question, you could interview or survey people. But such projects require considerable resources: traveling around the country to talk to people or designing and implementing a survey that draws upon a representative sample. Instead, you might be able to draw upon another available source of data: newspaper reports of protest events. Some of these are even available through university libraries and online, and you can get a representative sample through online search techniques. You could then look at the content of these reports to understand how protest events are covered and understood.

Such a project requires identifying a data source—in this case newspaper articles—creating a sampling frame for these data, operationalizing important variables of interest, and then exploring the major themes associated with these variables. Scholars can use statistical tools to do this analysis. A researcher can ask how frequently certain words or ideas are associated with one another—in our example, how frequently are "protest" and "violence" or "peaceful" mentioned in the same media report, and what are the associations with other concepts (such as "youth" or racial characteristics) when protest appears frequently with "violence."

But scholars can also take a more qualitative approach with content analysis. Like ethnographic work or semistructured interviews, researchers can explore the themes that emerge within their data by spending large amounts of time with their data—visiting it and revisiting it until the researcher can make sense of its content backwards and forwards. The technique here is **inductive**. In this case, there is always the worry of **confirmation bias**—that the researcher finds what she is looking for. But this challenge to **internal validity** can be addressed by a healthy attitude of skepticism, which involves looking for cases that challenge your argument rather than support it.

As more and more of our lives are chronicled and archived online and as technologies develop that allow us to sift through and analyze this information, it is likely that content analysis will become an increasingly powerful and popular tool for social research. An important part of content analysis is its tie to the methodological tools of the social scientist, tools that consider identifying and operationalizing variables or concepts of interest, understanding their associations with other concepts, and doing so within a **sampling frame** that allows for generalizations.

BIG QUESTION OF "'CLOSE YOUR EYES AND THINK OF ENGLAND"

In the paper you are about to read, Jessica Brown and Myra Marx Ferree use an inductive research design to explore themes in the British print media around women's reproduction. Brown and Ferree are interested in how women's "reproductive responsibility" is understood in Britain. All throughout Europe white "native-born" couples are having fewer and fewer children. This fact means that in many nations, populations are declining. Such declines are important because many state programs depend on transfers of money from younger citizens to older people. Also important is that across Europe, more and more young people are the children of immigrants. This situation has resulted in what some scholars have called a "moral panic" about the future of European nations. There are fewer children, and some commentators do not see many of the children born today as truly "European." Brown and Ferree are interested, therefore, in the discourse around this transformation, and in particular, how such a discourse conceptualizes women's reproductive rights and responsibilities.

ISSUES TO CONSIDER

As you read this paper, we encourage you to think about elements of the research design. How was the population of interest defined? Here the population is, not people, but articles. And how were elements within that population sampled? How were variables defined and **operationalized**? What are the categories of analysis, and what counts as an observation? Do Brown and Ferree eliminate alternate explanations? If so, how? And given their design, what is the **external validity**? How far can we generalize from this study? But it is important also to realize that this paper is not a quantitative study of media coverage; as a qualitative study, what can we learn about people's lives by doing content analysis—in this case, exploring newspaper articles? Finally, beyond the article of Brown and Ferree, you might think of the ethical implications of using online data on human subjects. To what degree is this information in the public domain and therefore free to be used for a research project? What are the concerns of informed consent? What are our ethical responsibilities when using the content of online information?

"Close Your Eyes and Think of England": Pronatalism in the British Print Media

By Jessica Brown and Myra Marx Ferree

In nationalist discourses, the nation's strength and authenticity are tied to the biological and cultural reproduction of its people (Yuval-Davis 1997). This makes women's roles as reproducers central to nationalist projects. Since national reproduction needs women, nationalism always has feminist or antifeminist implications in how it formulates its reproductive politics. Thus, understanding the gender politics of pronatalism implies addressing the race and class context in which these struggles take place.

If analysis is limited to cases where pronatalism is part of government policies that are authoritarian, coercive, or explicitly racist, then the answer to the question of whether pronatalism can be good for women is automatically no. But pronatalist nationalist projects can also be part of democratic discourses about reproduction. Swedish nationalist discourse about the "people's home" was associated with greater support for women as both mothers and workers (Hobson 2003) and French "republicanism" defined motherhood as a contribution to the nation deserving of policy support (Cova 1991; King 1998; Misra 1998). Because the ways political cultures recognize motherhood lead to different types of policy outcomes, how population issues are framed in relation to women matters.

In this article, we examine how British newspapers frame the issue of a falling national birthrate as a social problem. Defining the nation itself as at risk from a failure to reproduce, media discourse also offers diverse diagnoses of what is wrong with women, and to a lesser extent with society at large. Our title, and guiding metaphor, is drawn from the supposed advice for women of the Victorian era to endure sex for the sake of the national good, to "close your eyes and think of England." While this saying today appears an outmoded joke, it illustrates the central role that women's reproduction has long played in British nationalist projects.

LITERATURE REVIEW

British newspapers, both the mainstream broadsheets and the flashier tabloids, have paid significant attention to the nation's falling birthrate in the past several years. The United Kingdom's birthrate is projected to fall to about 1.61 by 2005, a figure well below the 2.1 births per women needed to maintain the population at its current size (UN Population Division 2001). The effects of low fertility—overall population decline, future labor

Jessica Brown and Myra Marx Ferree. "'Close Your Eyes and Think of England': Pronatalism in the British Print Media." *Gender & Society* 19 (1): 5–24.

shortages, and budget deficits as the proportion of active workers to pensioners shrinks—are "real" macroeconomic problems that responsible news makers should present as public issues.

But most scholars of media emphasize that media attention is not distributed according to the actual severity of a social problem, either in its prevalence or impact (Hilgartner and Bosk 1988; Stone 1988). Whether recognizing violence such as sexual harassment or hate crimes (Jenness and Grattet 2001; Saguy 2003), constructing social risk from diseases like AIDS (Epstein 1996), or assessing the importance of social trends such as changes in family types (Misra, Moller, and Karides 2003), media concern reflects wider social conflicts and interests. Therefore, to say that a social problem is constructed through active media work is not to deny a material basis for concern but to focus on how those concerns are framed for a particular audience and the implications that this framing has for the political solutions seen as feasible or desirable (Cook 1998; Ferree et al. 2002).

Such media work especially comes in critical discourse moments when heightened attention to an issue provides opportunities for speakers with various interests to attempt to define its meaning (Gamson and Modigliani 1989). In such periods, the nature of what everyone knows becomes widely established and remains part of the common store of understanding even after media attention moves on to other issues. The release of the February 28, 2001 UN report on population decline and the March 21, 2000 UN report on replacement migration converted a long-standing trend into a critical discourse moment (UN Population Division 2000, 2001). The nature and tone of the media coverage strongly implied this was not a typical policy problem. In the words of the *Sunday Times* (London), what does it mean when a nation "wakes up one morning and faces the nightmare scenario of finding it cannot reproduce itself?"

Our question is why and how British media define the transition to low fertility as a matter freighted with nationalist anxiety. This analysis draws attention to their evaluation of the reproductive choices of white native-born women, relating it to the anxieties provoked by immigration and showing how race, class, and gender concerns about the future population of Britain are expressed in pronatalist stories. Pronatalism is defined here as a political, ideological, or religious project to encourage childbearing by some or all members of a civil, ethnic, or national group. Insofar as their cultural claims are successful, procreation becomes a patriotic, religious, or eugenic obligation, and motherhood is constructed as the central feature of female identity (Heitlinger 1991; Yuval-Davis 1997).

PRONATALISM AND THE PRESS IN BRITAIN

Several factors make Britain an interesting case. Political liberalism emphasizes both individual independence and reliance on the market for provision of social goods (O'Connor, Orloff, and Shaver 1999). As a liberal state, the United Kingdom has long been more reluctant than other European nations to enact pronatalist policies, including those that support mothers, families, and child-rearing labor (Gauthier 1993; Koven and Michel 1990; Siim 2000). Britain is distinctive in Western Europe for being a modern and relatively wealthy state that nonetheless offers a sparse collection of family benefits.

Moreover, the state itself cannot be said to be initiating or controlling the pronatalist project in the media. British newspapers are independent of state control, diverse in their political orientation, responsive to a wide range of organizations and interests in civil society, and have economic and cultural interests of their own. Pronatalism in the media is thus a complex and multifaceted project advanced by multiple actors, situated within multiple institutions possibly working at cross-purposes to one another, since most British newspapers are explicitly placed on the Left or Right (McDowall 1999). The long-standing confluence of these civil society actors into identifiable streams gives each newspaper its distinctive character and makes it a cultural actor that can reliably be read as having a particular type of voice and audience. We analyze the newspapers' pronatalist discourses as indicators of varying cultural ideas about normative reproductive behavior, women and their relationship to the national interest, and what immigration and the birthrate together imply for the future of Britain.

METHOD

We examined expressed concerns about low fertility in British news articles published between January 1, 2000 and May 15, 2002. The time parameter for the sample was given by the release of the UN Population Division reports on low fertility and on replacement migration as a potential solution (2/28/2000 and 3/21/ 2000). These releases created a critical discourse moment.

Comparing the release period to the 30-month period ending May 15, 1999, the dramatic increase in attention is apparent. The smallest increase in coverage was from 15 to 33 stories (*The Independent*), the largest, from 4 to 41 articles (*The Times*).

The sampling frame was 10 major British newspapers covering a range of ideological orientations and including both broadsheet newspapers and sensationalistic but widely circulated tabloids. To identify relevant articles, the LexisNexis full-text database was searched using the terms *birthrate*, *demographic*, or *population* (in full text) and *baby* or *birth* in the title. After duplicate and irrelevant articles were discarded, the sample contained 202 articles focused on declining fertility.

The definition of the sample did not presuppose that the decline in fertility would be framed as a social problem, since media could take the opportunity to attack the findings of the report rather than affirm and even magnify them. In fact, only a few articles ($n = 7$) frame the decline in positive terms, and another handful ($n = 9$) argue that there is no fertility crisis at all. It is important to note that fertility declines in less industrialized nations are almost always framed positively.

We coded articles for their overall presentation of low fertility as a social problem or crisis, and for the presence of a pronatalist message. This was defined as presenting increased childbearing as either normative for individual Britons or essential to the good of the nation. Articles that explicitly advocated solutions were coded for the types of social policies they supported. Finally, articles were also coded in terms of their attention to, and framing of, immigration as a population issue (whether it was positive, conditionally acceptable, neutral, or negative) and how population changes due to immigration were interpreted in relation to changes in natality (as part of the problem or part of the solution or both). References to immigrants, asylum seekers, and nonwhite populations in Britain were examined in these articles and in a comparison sample of articles independently selected to provide an overview of media discourse on migration and racial change in Britain. Using this independent sample ($N = 100$) of racial population discourse, newspapers were characterized as more or less favorable to immigration, and the types of pronatalism expressed in newspapers with differing stances to immigration were compared. This allowed us to place the discourse about native-born population decline into a wider framework of media concerns about racialized population change.

RESULTS

Most of the coverage of the declining birthrate in the United Kingdom and Europe presents this demographic falloff as a serious social problem (140 articles) and uses a language of acute crisis in 91 of these. These pieces weave together themes of aging with disappearance or death ($n = 43$), and many are highly emotional in tone. "Spin the clock forward 30 years and Britain will look like Hamlin after the Pied Piper—a place of sterility in which the revellers have turned into lonely old people," argues a writer in the January 3, 2002 *Daily Mail*. Three articles from the *Times* (December 10, 2000; February 10, 2002; March 22, 2002) argue that low-fertility countries are committing "cultural suicide" or "national suicide," and the *Financial Times* (2001), in a piece titled "Why We Must Go Forth and Multiply," laments that "western Europe" is "turning itself into a geriatric ward."

A subset of the 140 articles presenting fertility declines as a social problem are the 24 percent of all articles that define low fertility wholly or partly as a threat to the United Kingdom's cultural and ethnic landscape. This is not entirely surprising. According to UN fertility models, in order to insulate itself from the projected economic consequences of low fertility, the United Kingdom would have to increase immigration.

For instance, to maintain the dependency ratio at present levels (4.1 active workers for each individual drawing state support) through 2050, the United Kingdom might have to admit as many as 1 million individuals annually or increase the retirement age to 72.

These articles connect maintaining Britain's cultural identity with biological reproduction. A *Times* piece warns that populations can only adopt replacement migration as a solution to low fertility "at the risk of a loss of their original identity." Likewise, a writer for the *Daily Telegraph* asks, "If immigrants substitute for births, will British society as we know it disappear?" The *Independent*, a left-wing paper, carried a similar warning, noting that immigration levels high enough to slow population ageing would only "generate rapid population growth and eventually displace the original population from its majority position."

In all, 46% of the articles discuss both immigration and the declining birthrate, but not all of them present it so negatively. In fact, the vast majority of these 94 articles (82%) present immigration as either positive (42%), neutral (16%), or conditionally acceptable (24%). Although those we place in the "conditionally acceptable" category define immigration as necessary in light of declining fertility, they also claim that admitted immigrants will only be welcome if they assimilate to British norms, values, and customs, and/or they predict that increased immigration, while necessary, will result in spikes in the crime rate, increases in unemployment, or a souring of race relations in the United Kingdom.

It should not be surprising, then, that 81 articles (40% of the total) suggest that the preferred solution to low fertility is a decision by native-born Britons to return to the larger family sizes of the past. Although they share certain assumptions about reproduction and the nation, these pronatalist articles vary in how they diagnose the reasons for fertility decline and what policy responses they define as appropriate.

Consistent with the common assumption that reproductive work is a female duty, most pronatalist messages were aimed at women. Thirty-eight of the 81 pronatalist articles (47 percent) solely addressed a stated or implied female subject, while a further 25 articles (31 percent) addressed their message primarily to women but also contained ambiguous messages that might apply to men or to gender-neutral "Britons" or "married couples." Seventeen articles (21 percent) addressed gender-neutral subjects with no focus on women or men. Only 1 article focused solely on men.

The pronatalist rhetoric in this sample divides into four categories based on its framing of women and women's reproductive work. Articles specifically "beg," "lecture," "threaten," and/or "bribe" women to reproduce the nation. We describe these below.

Begging

This pronatalist framing is an overt, positive call for increases in childbearing. Twenty-two articles (27%) of the 81 in the pronatalist subgroup contain begging messages. An article from the *Daily Star* entitled "Give Us More Babies" and that begins "Euro chiefs yesterday urged couples to have more babies to counter an alarming rise in the proportion of old people" is a straightforward example of this frame. Begging articles state outright that couples or women should have more children. The negative framing of a population in crisis is connected to a positively framed appeal to rise to the occasion and have children for the nation.

Half of the begging articles stress the individual joys of procreation. For instance, a *Daily Mail* article notes that childless people "cannot see the wonderful way children upend material values" and continues, "Nothing in life can match the feeling of pride in your children. To the childless, the boy in the donkey costume in the primary school nativity play is just that. To you, heart in mouth, eyes brimming, he is your little boy about to make his solo singing debut. They cannot see the art in the birthday card which features a stick of pasta and a withered primrose, but to you it's worth all the Monets in the world." The article concludes, "Love, like happiness, is a gift that runs in families."

Other expressions of the joy of procreation highlight the benefits of child rearing compared to other forms of status-driven consumption. An article from the *Times* claims, "The successful conception of a child—the old fashioned way in an ongoing relationship—isn't just something to shout about, it's something that you wear as proudly as last year's pashmina or this year's Prada bowling bag. . . . The youth promoting properties of a babe in arms are—as Sharon Stone has illustrated—infinitely more effective than the most expensive jar of antiwrinkle cream or any amount of silicone injections." This message, implicitly targeted at middle-class women, encourages childbearing by arguing that having children makes one look younger and more fashionable. The assumed subject is also reminded that children are a boon to the nation, but babies are simultaneously framed as a blessing to the woman, whether as the fulfillment of maternal love or as fashion accessories.

Lecturing

Fifty-two articles (64%) contain messages in the lecturing category (45 of these 52 primarily address a female subject). This frame assumes that the childless have a duty to reproduce that they are failing to perform for some individual reason, typically diagnosed as selfishness, irresponsibility, or psychological dysfunction. In an article headlined "Sorry, baby, but our lifestyle comes first" the *Sunday Times* argues that the low birthrate occurs because "our age is preoccupied solely with the goal of individual self-fulfillment." The *Financial Times* takes up the same complaint in the article "Why We Must Go Forth and Multiply". "Many trendy types regard children as a nuisance," the author writes. "They interfere with careers, tax the bank balance and threaten a hedonistic life-style." The *Daily Mail* similarly asked, "Why ARE we too selfish to have children?" and blamed feminism for the falling birthrate. "All around is the siren voice of the feminist argument: Marriage, traditionally the Holy Grail of womanhood, is legalized prostitution. Self-fulfillment lies less in being a wife and mother than in independence and a job which delivers a fat pay packet."

Not all women who choose not to bear children are presented as selfish—one writer implies that they are mentally ill. The *Sunday Times* identified "tokophobia" as the "profound fear of childbirth" and put the number of sufferers at "one in seven women." Quoting Kristina Hofberg, Britain's "leading expert on the syndrome," tokophobics are "often career women who can't understand how they can hold down a really good job when they can't do something as simple as have a baby."

Begging and lecturing messages both assume people make decisions about reproduction based on superficial criteria and that reproducers fail to understand their own interests correctly. But whereas begging messages assume that readers could be motivated to have children by appeals to pleasure, fashion, or sentiment, lecturing messages provide the flip side of this argument. Here it is an excessive love of pleasure, career advancement, material goods, and in some cases, self-determination, that makes people, especially women, reluctant to have children. In both cases a better understanding of self-interest would align women's reproductive choices with the nation's need for more babies.

Both begging and lecturing messages imply that the desire to have children is not inherent, natural, or uncontrollable. In this regard, both define women as self-directed reproducers. Although begging frames take a positive tone by highlighting the benefits of making good choices, while lecturing frames focus on bad choices and the negative attributes of the women making them, both imply that women make unfettered choices about reproduction. By contrast, the other two types of pronatalist messages assert—with negative or positive language—that women have an essential or natural drive to have children.

Threatening

Threatening messages, present in 45 (56%) of the pronatalist articles, are typified by their use of scare tactics. Reproduction is framed as natural and essential; failing to reproduce is presented as threatening both individual well-being and social stability. Thirty-eight out of 45 threatening articles are aimed at women. Among threatening discourses that focus on individual risks from childlessness, a common subcategory (15 out of 45) features accounts of women who left childbearing too late and are now sterile. This frame assumes that all women naturally want to have children, and the failure to do so presents a personal crisis as well as a national one.

The *Daily Telegraph* quotes "Catherine," a 38-year-old women who always wanted a big family but found she'd waited "too long." After "tests and more tests," she and her husband discovered they could not conceive naturally. This necessitated a "grueling round of investigations and treatments" after which she became pregnant. "I remember making a pact with God," the grateful mother is quoted, "and saying, please let me have one child and I'll always count my blessings. I'll be content with one."

Other articles warn that women run a high risk of never finding a partner should they refuse to settle down soon (6 out of 45). The *Daily Mail* ran a piece entitled "SINGLES: Why women are leaving it too late to find a man. How most believe they will discover Mr. Perfect. They prefer loneliness to a bad relationship. Why one in four might never become a mother." An *Evening Standard* article sent a similar message, ending with a quote from conservative pundit Robert Whelan who warned, "The twin results of modern morality are sterility and loneliness. Sexual revolution has not meant that people are having lots of relationships but that millions are not having relationships at all. And those that are having relationships are not having families". The *Sunday Times* takes the threatening rhetoric a step farther in an article entitled "Women Pay for Equality with Rise in Cancer." Other articles argue that low fertility is not only personally but socially detrimental (17 out of 45). The *Daily Telegraph* warns that a society populated by increasing numbers of only children might become "a society of people who don't know much about cooperation and turn-taking". The *Telegraph* quotes sociologist Frank Furedi as finding the only-child boom particularly worrying. "I look to Japan for heightened versions of British trends," he says. "There, because of a falling birthrate, they have ended up with indulgent parents and slobbish children, in a state of perpetually delayed adolescence, who regard adults as their servants".

The *Sunday Times* focuses on macrosocial threats: "The nightmare scenario of the human race waking up one morning and realizing it cannot reproduce itself is not just scare mongering . . . if we carry on like this, it will be a reality". On May 27, 2001 the *Sunday Times* again argues that falling family sizes are a "psychological, moral, and spiritual shift whose causes may be economic and social but whose effects strike at the heart of civilisation." It also ran an alarmist article entitled "Breed or Die Out" and one warning that the low birthrate is leading humanity toward the "lightly disguised gates of hell".

These threat frames, unlike begging and lecturing ones, take women's duty to reproduce for granted. They raise an alarm about the failure to reproduce as a personal and social crisis. While the lecturing frame is often more directly disparaging of women, framing their bad values and choices as the cause of the crisis, the threatening frame positions women as unwittingly bringing disaster to themselves and society. The media presents itself as offering "facts" that an unknowing readership has neglected to face, so threatening articles draw heavily on social science experts and data to legitimate the presentation of dire personal and social consequences.

Bribing

Finally, 37 articles (46%) contain "bribing" messages. These claims rest on the assumption that the desire to have children is natural or essential to womanhood (28 of 37 bribing articles are aimed specifically at women). Assuming women want to have children, the problem this frame faces is to explain why they are not doing so. The answer is the existence of structural barriers that prevent women from following their natural inclinations. Thus, women are framed as good and government or society as deficient. The source of the problem is the lack of adequate social support for children and child rearing. Rather than the lazy, selfish, or irrational procreators presented elsewhere, women in the bribing frame are depicted positively as victims of a society that does not properly value motherhood. Both in the demand for social support and the positive view of women, this frame is most congruent with feminist analyses.

The barriers to women's childbearing that this frame identifies are difficulties combining work and family, lack of financial resources, and insufficient support from men. Thirty-two of these bribing articles argue that promother structural changes must be made in the workplace, the state welfare system, and even relationships within individual homes to accommodate women in their desires to form families. Not only in diagnosis but in policy responses, the bribing frame is actively prowoman.

It is also the only one of the four frames to engage, albeit indirectly, with the issue of class inequality. In contrast to the other pronatalist frames, which assume women withhold childbearing labor for superficial reasons, the bribing frame assumes that a growing number of Britons are making a rational choice not to have children because of real economic constraints that British employers and government need to address. Not only class, but even more explicitly, gender disadvantage is framed as the source of the fertility problem.

For instance, the *Daily Telegraph* warns that the birthrate is falling fastest in societies where women are burdened with "traditional male attitudes, weak family welfare and inflexible work arrangements," while in nations where "families are supported, where women can combine work and family, and where men (sometimes) wear the aprons, as in Scandinavia and France, birth rates are higher." Likewise, in the *Sunday Mirror*'s "Happiness Is an Early Baby and a Nice Boss", the author argues that "modern life isn't good for marriage and having children" since most employers are not willing to help women juggle the demands of career and care work.

IMMIGRATION, NATIONALISM, AND PRONATALIST POLITICS

Overall, left-leaning newspapers were less likely than the conservative ones to carry pronatalist arguments. While 50% of the right-wing news articles in this sample had some kind of pronatalist frame, only 29% of left-wing articles did. Furthermore, the negative frames of lecturing and threatening were more common in the right-leaning press: Forty-two percent of pieces in the conservative papers carried lecturing frames, threatening frames, or both, whereas 18% of pieces in the left-wing papers did so.

Surprisingly, articles that advocate changing government benefit structures, workplaces, and families to support mothers also appear more often in the conservative than in the liberal press. Nineteen percent of all articles in conservative papers contain one or more of these "pro-mother" arguments, while only 11% of those in liberal papers do so.

Conservatives' interest in bribing women to have babies seems to be related to the liberal papers' greater willingness to define immigration as an alternative solution. Although liberal papers are equally likely to express dismay about declines in the birthrate, they are more likely to name immigration and immigrants as a way of addressing this concern. Of the 34 articles in left-leaning papers that talk about immigration in addition to discussing the birthrate, 59% present increased immigration as a positive or neutral step in light of declining fertility, whereas among the 50 conservative articles that discuss both, only 20% present increased immigration as positive or neutral. When conservative papers present immigration as a necessary step, they are more likely to condition their acceptance of immigrants on their assimilation or warn of social problems (36% in these papers compared with 15%t of articles in liberal ones).

Insofar as conservative writers reject immigration as a means of addressing the population problem, they are more likely to turn to bribing women to do so. An article in the *Times* entitled "Immigration Will Not Ease Our Burden" argues, "The root cause of population ageing is a very low birthrate. An effective response must make the workplace, the tax and welfare system and gender relations as a whole more favorable to women, so they can fulfill ambitions to have more than one child. Look after women, and the population will look after itself." *The Mail on Sunday* made a similar argument in an article on immigration reform that ended with the phrase "If we look after women's interests, our population will look after itself", and the *Daily Telegraph* adopted the same message in a piece titled "Look After Mothers and the Birthrate Will Stop Dwindling".

The conservative papers sound feminist in their support for child care and ending discrimination against women. Likewise, their stated support for economic restructuring and redistribution projects seems out of character. Changes that would further women's interests, according to these pieces, are the provision of more and better day care facilities (*Daily Mail*); increased flexibility in the workplace (*Daily Telegraph*); and the extension of more government benefits to women, particularly poor and single mothers (*Daily Telegraph; Times; Sunday Times*). Aside from changes to state benefit plans and workplaces, many of these articles in the conservative press also speak to the need to, as the *Times* puts it above, "make gender relations as a whole more favorable to women" even within the home.

While one does not expect to see such messages in overtly conservative newspapers, in this particular instance, it appears racism may trump sexism and may even overcome resistance to redistributive policies. That is, the fear of large-scale ethnic and cultural changes they associate with immigration seems more threatening in the discourse of the conservative-leaning newspapers than the fear of losing power based on male and class privilege. If this is the case, then offering women incentives to combine wage work with childbearing and pushing men to participate more in child rearing and housework becomes a concession to the claims of white working- and middle-class British women. Unfortunately, this concession is traded off against these elites clinging to racial power by excluding immigrant women and men from the future British nation.

A strong nativist sentiment lies at the heart of this push for change. This framing allows for the construction of a specifically racialized nationalism, a narrow definition of who is and is not an acceptable reproducer, and sacrifices the rights of nonwhite, nonnative women and men for the interests of women in the dominant group. The racism expressed strongly and emotionally in some of these newspapers is the poisoned root from which this pro-(white) woman rhetoric springs.

Further, this rhetoric legitimates the continued ability of cultural elites to define who and what are good families. The possibility that women really would choose a lower birthrate even if they had the economic and social option to have more children is never even considered. Unlike the discourse aimed at women in less-developed countries, where lower fertility is seen as freeing women to develop other aspects of their lives, British women are culturally being defined as freer if they become more interested in motherhood.

In sum, the conservative papers' willingness to bribe women to have children, even by encouraging more gender equality in social policy and family dynamics, rests on a top-down model of defining what is in women's interests and an exclusionary definition of who is a potential member and reproducer of British culture. While offering a positive view of women, the fact that the bribing frame is most often offered in conservative papers where immigration is framed as most threatening should raise feminist concern.

CONCLUSION

British newspapers do more than report the declining birthrate; they frame the transition to low fertility as a crisis for the nation. The anxiety expressed goes beyond potential economic problems to reflect dismay at the threat to "civilization" and "culture" posed by the changing composition of the national population. How British women understand their potential to bear children and perform reproductive labor is framed as critical to national survival.

This analysis of British news media reveals the interconnectedness of raced and gendered discourses, especially in discussions of nationhood and culture. In encouraging policy makers to adopt measures that support women's employment and family work, and even encouraging British men to do more at home, this discourse supports native-born women. Yet, it also positions their childbearing as an alternative to, and bulwark against, a more open immigration policy that is presented in negative and threatening terms. Thus, the needs of immigrant women, men, and families are framed as in opposition to the needs of native-born women, and racism against the former is used to justify feminist policies for the latter.

Thus, while it is easy for feminists to criticize the negative images of women presented in the lecturing and threatening frames, the more positively toned forms of pronatalism that bribing and begging frames express should also be viewed with caution. As this case suggests, even pronatalist projects offering concrete policy benefits to majority group women are not necessarily helpful for meeting all women's interests.

REFLECTION

Looking for the Story: On inductive content analysis

By Jessica Brown

This article grew out of my master's thesis and is a good example of a largely inductive research design (wherein the researcher approaches her data without a defined hypothesis but rather allows the data itself to shape her research question.) I began the project with an indistinct idea of what I wanted to do, except that I thought I might be interested in looking at media coverage of abortion and family planning in newspapers outside North America. I chose Great Britain (rather arbitrarily, but at the time I was limited to English-speaking countries) and ran a number of sample LexisNexis searches using a few general search terms (like "abortion" and "contraception") related to my overarching theme.

I suppose I had expected to find something similar to the "pro-life"/"pro-choice" discourses that dominate coverage of this topic in the United States, where discussions about abortion generally tend to boil down to arguments about the relative rights of the embryo or fetus versus those of the pregnant woman. Instead, I found what Gamson and Modigliani (1989) call a "critical discourse moment" spurred by the release of a UN report warning that birthrates in western Europe and the British Isles had fallen below well below "replacement level" (the rate at which a population simply reproduces itself without getting larger or smaller) and these countries would soon face worker shortages and tax shortfalls as a consequence—unless, that is, they were willing to pursue a strategy of "replacement migration" (opening borders to greater numbers of immigrants to keep population sizes stable). Strictly speaking, this was not news, but rather the result of a long-term trend. Nevertheless, the UN report gave the issue salience (that is to say, made it noticeable and newsworthy) and provided a space for anxious discussion of what more immigration coupled with fewer native-born ("native born" was often code for "English-speaking" and "white") children meant for Great Britain. Within this debate, abortion and contraception were discussed but only insofar as they allowed people to stay childless or choose small families. Likewise, some journalists and commentators made emotional appeals to women to choose motherhood, but this was not for the sake of their potential unborn children but rather out of a sense of duty to their nation.

Having discovered that my data had a different "story" to tell me than the one I may have initially been looking for, I was able to change and narrow my search terms (I substituted terms like "population" and "birthrate" for the earlier ones) and time frame down to focus on specific coverage of national fertility rates and the UN Population Report (there simply wasn't much discussion of the declining birthrate beforehand, although I did run searches of the same terms in earlier time periods to check this). This rewarded me with another big stack of articles to read and an only slightly less vague idea of what I was looking for. Now I had a better sense of what my topic was, but I still didn't know what I was going to say about it.

Moreover, I wasn't entirely certain how I should go about the process of coding and analyzing the articles in my sample. In the end, I printed out each article and purchased as many different colors of highlighter pens as I could find. I read through each piece and assigned a separate highlighter color to all of my very broad initial codes ("gender," "immigration," "family planning," etc.). As my own sense of what I would be arguing took shape, my codes became more specific and focused, and I moved on to a hybrid system of colors, symbols, and written notes to help me keep track of what I was seeing. (As an aside, I'm sure I looked like a crazy person muttering to myself while drawing strange hieroglyphics all over a giant stack of newspaper printouts with a bucket of colored markers.) Once I knew exactly what I was looking for, I returned to each article to reread and recode it: a process that I repeated dozens of times as I built and developed my argument. Although I didn't realize at the time that this particular research method had a name, I was essentially pursuing a "grounded theory" coding strategy (Glaser and Strauss, 1967)

I now use qualitative research software to help me manage data, but this kind of media analysis is still a very time-consuming method requiring the researcher to patiently reread and recode each item in her sample multiple times. This process can feel frustratingly slow, but it also provides the kind of close reading that enables the researcher to get to know her data and to spend time reflecting on it. Repeated close readings are also good because they facilitate the researcher's ability to think about the data in new and innovative ways. Ultimately, the ability to think creatively is the most important part of sociological research. Usually the researcher does not have someone standing over her shoulder telling her exactly what to do and what to look for; rather she approaches each data set or research site open to whatever new and interesting stories it has to tell.

One thing time spent mulling over my data allowed me to do was to formulate a typology of pronatalist appeals ("pronatalism" refers to an ideology or argument encouraging women and men to produce children) based on the assumptions these appeals made about people, mostly women, and how they make reproductive decisions. For example, some writers seemed to assume women could be motivated to have children so long as they could be convinced that motherhood was "trendy" or "fashionable," while others framed childless couples as "selfish" or even mentally ill. What I called "threatening frames" warned women that they needed to stop looking for "Mr. Perfect" and "settle," lest they end up "old," "sterile," and "lonely," an argument that readers often find in American media as well, only without the additional warnings that women who refuse to do so are failing their country as a whole.

Another common theme in my sample dealt with the fact that Britain, like other low fertility nations, will probably need to start recruiting more immigrants to offset labor shortages. This caused many writers to remark on the possibility that the UK of the future could be significantly racially and culturally different than that of the past and present. This was also clearly a source of anxiety, both for many writers and for their readerships at large and was a major theme in the discourse. Since newspapers in the UK are more openly allied with various political ideologies or parties than are US newspapers (which generally attempt to position themselves as "objective" or "impartial"), I broadened my sample out, not just to look at the two or three London-based papers with the largest total circulation, but to sample from papers across the political spectrum. This gave me the opportunity to find out if left-wing/liberal papers and right-wing/conservative papers differed in the way they framed these issues and in the solutions they posited. Not surprisingly they did. To me, one of the most interesting findings to come out of this work was the discovery that conservative newspapers seemed more comfortable advocating changes that would allow women to more easily combine careers with having children. These writers argued for the creation of more government-funded welfare programs for poor, working, and even single mothers and suggested that employers create more flexible working environments for women with children. These writers also urged men to "help out more" at home, reasoning that if domestic work and childcare were more evenly shared, overtaxed women might be willing to have more babies. All of these proposals seemed out of character for political and social conservatives (who are generally opposed to the expansion of government programs and who are often more traditional with respect to the roles of men and women), but given the choice between changing gender relations or increasing immigration, writers for conservative papers seemed more comfortable with the former. Writers for left-wing newspapers proved to be more supportive of increasing immigration, on the other hand, so fewer of these writers focused on ways to increase birthrates among native-born or white citizens.

Part of the challenge of doing sociological research is learning to see what isn't there as well as what is. This requires transcending one's own culture and learning how to imagine alternate social worlds. An example of this is the fact that, while the decision to have a child is one that is usually made as a couple, *men's* reproductive behaviors and choices were almost completely absent from these discussions. Instead, reproduction was treated as a "woman's issue," and thus low fertility was framed solely as a consequence of women's decisions. That men might also be deciding to delay parenthood to pursue educations, careers, or the freedoms of early adulthood or, alternately, could be choosing smaller families due to the same economic and work-life balance constraints that women face was never considered. To say that men make decisions about when and whether to become parents seems pretty obvious, but because American culture also tends to erase men from discussions about reproduction, it took me several read-throughs of my data before I noticed that very few of these pronatalist appeals were aimed at men. Those few that did target men essentially reaffirmed fathers' auxiliary status by presenting them as occasional "helpers" in the home and not as full-time parents. These frames still assumed that having babies was a woman's decision (and raising them still more or less her responsibility) but urged men to be more supportive precisely so that women would go back to choosing larger families.

While some of the things I've talked about in this research reflection will be of use only to those intending to do media analysis or qualitative research, there are two bits of advice that I think are applicable to everyone. The first concerns the inherently collective nature of research itself. Although I did the research for my master's thesis, I was able to look to my advisor, Myra Marx Ferree, for the guidance and support that I needed to construct a workable method and develop my arguments. Later, when I was ready to move on to the publishing stage, she worked with me as a coauthor to refocus and redraft it and to help me navigate the intimidating process of peer review. Learning to do good sociological work requires an apprenticeship of sorts, wherein new researchers must be open to learning from many others simply because there is so very much to learn. Even an established researcher, however, will find that she often needs to turn to others for feedback, help, and inspiration. Second, when I began this work I assumed that if I chose a topic that interested me and spent enough time with the data, I would inevitably find something there worth writing about. This particular article of faith has served me well since then, because within any societal phenomena or social world, even those that seem very small or insignificant, there are always stories waiting to be told.

REFERENCES

Cook, Timothy.1998. *Governing with the News: The News Media as a Political Institution*. Chicago: University of Chicago Press.

Cova, Anne. 1991. "French Feminism and Maternity: Theories and Policies, 1890–1918." In Fiona Montgomery and Christine Collete (eds.), *The European Women's History Reader*. London: Routledge.

Daily Mail. 2001. "How Summertime Is Start a Family Time." July 2.

———. 2001. "SINGLES: Why Women Are Leaving It Too Late to Find a Man. How Most Believe They Will Discover Mr. Perfect. They Prefer Loneliness to a Bad Relationship. Why One in Four Might Never Become a Mother." January 15.

———. 2002. "Why ARE We Too Selfish To Have Children?" January 3.

Daily Star. 2002. "Give Us More Babies." April 9.

Daily Telegraph. 2000. "Does Every Couple Need a Child?" March 15.

———. 2001. "'Little Emperors' Taking over the World: Research Shows an Increase in the Number of Families Having Only One Child." April 19.

———. 2001. "Look After Mothers and the Birth Rate Will Stop Dwindling." August 7.

———. 2001. "The One and Only." June 30.

Epstein, Steven. 1996. *Impure Science: AIDS, Activism, and the Politics of Knowledge*. Berkeley: University of California Press.

Ferree, Myra Marx, William A. Gamson, Jürgen Gerhards, and Dieter Rucht. 2002. *Abortion Discourse: Democracy and the Public Sphere in Germany and the United States*. Cambridge, MA: Cambridge University Press.

Financial Times. 2001. "Why We Must Go Forth and Multiply." January 13.

Gamson, William A., and Andre Modigliani. 1989. "Media Discourse and Public Opinion on Nuclear Power: A Constructive Approach." *American Journal of Sociology* 95 (1): 1–37.

Glaser and Strauss (1967) *The Discovery of Grounded Theory*. Piscataway, NJ: Aldine Transaction.

Gauthier, Anne. 1993. "Towards Renewed Fears of Population and Family Decline." *European Journal of Population* 9: 143–67.

Heitlinger, Alena. 1991. "Pronatalism and Women's Equality Policies." *European Journal of Population* 7: 343–75.

Hilgartner, Stephen, and Charles Bosk. 1988. "The Rise and Fall of Social Problems: A Public Arenas Model." *American Journal of Sociology* 94 (1): 53–78.

Hobson, Barbara. 2003. "Some Reflections and Agendas for the Future." *Social Politics* 10 (2): 196–204.

Independent. 2001. "Science: When Millions Walk the Planet: Mass Migration Presents the World with a Human Crisis on an Unprecedented Human Scale." October 26.

Jenness, Valerie, and Ryken Grattet. 2001. *Making Hate a Crime: From Social Movement Concept to Law Enforcement Practice*. New York: Russell Sage Foundation.

King, Leslie. 1998. "France Needs Children: Pronatalism, Nationalism, and Women's Equity." *Sociological Quarterly* 39 (1): 33–52.

Koven, Seth, and Sonya Michel. 1990. "Womanly Duties: Materialist Politics and the Origins of Welfare States in France, Germany, Great Britain and the United States, 1880–1920." In Fiona Montgomery and Christine Collete (eds.), *The European Women's History Reader*. London: Routledge.

Mail on Sunday. 2001. "Sorry, Ms. Roche, We Are Not a Nation of Immigrants." February 25.

McDowall, David. 1999. *Britain in close-up*. Boston: Longman.

Misra, Joya. 1998. "Mothers or Workers? The Value of Women's Labor: Women and the Emergence of Family Allowance Policy." *Gender & Society* 12 (4): 376–99.

Misra, Joya, Stephanie Moller, and Marina Karides. 2003. "Envisioning Dependency: Changing Media Descriptions of Welfare in the 20th Century." *Social Problems* 50 (4): 482–504.

O'Connor. Julia, Ann Orloff, and Sheila Shaver. 1999. *States, Markets, Families: Gender, Liberalism and Social Policy in Australia, Canada, Great Britain and the United States*. Cambridge, MA: Cambridge University Press.

Saguy, Abigail. 2003. *What Is Sexual Harassment: From Capital Hill to the Sorbonne*. Berkeley: University of California Press.

Siim, Birte. 2000. *Gender and Citizenship: Politics and Agency in France, Britain, and Denmark*. Cambridge, UK: Cambridge University Press.

Stone, Deborah. 1988. *Policy Paradox: The Art of Political Decision Making*. New York: Norton.

Sunday Mirror. 2002. "Happiness Is an Early Baby and a Nice Boss." February 17.

Sunday Times (London). 2000a. "British Babies Die of Neglect." June 25.

——. 2000b. "Call Me a Eurosceptic, but Give Me Boston not Berlin." December 10.

——. 2000c. "'Timebomb' Alert As Births Tumble." January 16.

——. 2000d. "Women Pay for Equality with Rise in Cancer." July 9.

——. 2001. "Sorry, Baby, But Our Lifestyle Comes First." May 27.

——. 2002. "A Fear Is Born." January 27.

Times (of London). 2000. "Immigration Will Not Ease Our Burden." June 22.

——. 2000. "Stars, Status and the Infant Phenomenon." July 26.

——. 2001. "Breed or Die Out." November 15.

——. 2002. "A Civilisation with No Belief in Its Own Values Will Collapse." February 2.

——. 2002. "Shrinking Nations Offer Families Cash for Babies." March 22.

UN Population Division, Department of Economic and Social Affairs. 2000. *Replacement Migration: Is It a Solution to Declining and Ageing Populations?* Report, March 21. New York: UN Population Division.

——. 2001.*World Population Prospects: The 2000 Revision*. Report, February 28. New York: UN Population Division.

Yuval-Davis, Nira. 1997. *Gender and Nation*. London: Sage.

CHAPTER 9

Multiple Methods/Mixed Methods

Mixed methods, or what are sometimes called "multiple methods," are becoming increasingly common in social science research. Mixed methods are often deployed in research situations where there are research teams. In this case, researchers agree on a problem and deploy multiple methods to address different aspects of it. That said, it is not necessarily the case that mixed methods require multiple people. Sometimes a single researcher undertakes a research project that uses multiple methodologies to address different components of the research question.

ABOUT MIXED METHODS

The basic idea behind mixed methods is that there is no ideal methodology. And therefore, when undertaking a study, it is wise to compensate for the weaknesses of one approach with the strengths of another. If a survey is good at telling you about an association between variables but cannot tell you about whether that association is causal, it might be augmented by an experiment (this example is actually what we saw in the first chapter, with the experiment on gender). Or if you want to know about how the themes that emerge within a content analysis influence people's day-to-day lives, you might do an ethnography exploring them in practice.

It might seem, then, that there is an ideal methodology: mixed methods! But there are some limits to mixed methods. The most important are time and resources. While researchers wish it were otherwise, we neither have limitless time nor limitless resources to do research. And so sometimes we must balance our desire to know every aspect of a situation with our capacity to know something about it thoroughly, even if what we learn is limited. A second, less pressing concern is that sometimes situations change. And if this happens over the course of a research project, then the advantage of mixed methods can be lost. Let's say you were interested in studying residential ownership in the United States and designed a project where you first did a survey of mortgage lenders and then did an ethnography of people going through the process of applying for a mortgage. And let's say between your survey and your ethnography the United States went through a major financial incident where banks collapsed. Suddenly you would be studying two different situations: one with a survey before a financial crisis, and another with an ethnography after the crisis.

While such a situation seems far-fetched, it happens all the time; the world around us is constantly transforming. If you were a researcher in this situation, it might prove very interesting, and you could use the changing conditions of the field to say something about how the world is changing. But your research design of informing your ethnography by the responses to a survey might no longer work.

That said, mixed methods can create a wonderful research dialogue. This kind of dialogue often happens between projects—say, when an interview researcher builds upon the insights of an experimentalist. So researchers need not "do it all"—the scholarly enterprise is built upon the idea that we all rely upon and build off one another's work. Mixed methods research is a part of this enterprise, and rather than create dialogue between projects using different methodologies, it can create dialogue in the very same project.

As Mario Small, the primary author of our selected excerpt has noted in other work (Small 2011), "mixed methods" can mean many different things. It can mean gathering together different kinds of data—newspapers, surveys, interviews, census data—in a single project. Or it can mean designing a study where you actually use multiple data-gathering techniques (combining a survey with an ethnography). Or it can mean using different kinds of data analysis (regardless of your data source), such as using statistical techniques to analyze your interview transcripts (Small 2011, 59–60). Regardless of how you do mixed methods, the aim is to get the most out of each piece of data or each method in order to address weaknesses in your analysis with other types of analysis.

THE BIG QUESTION OF "WHY ORGANIZATIONAL TIES MATTER"

The excerpt you are about to read uses a mixed methods approach to explore how organizations in poor neighborhoods provide parents with resources that help them. The work uses qualitative interviews with parents to explore how parents rely upon and use organizations to help them navigate their lives. Then it tests the findings of these interviews with a survey of childcare centers. Through their findings, the authors argue that when looking at poverty, we often focus on poor people or the neighborhoods in which they live. Yet we often ignore the organizations in those neighborhoods: churches, childcare centers, and the like. These organizations are important resources to recognize if we are to imagine ways to help transform the lives of these people and their neighborhoods.

ISSUES TO CONSIDER

The first and perhaps most important question to ask yourself is what you learned in this paper from using more than one methodology. That is, did you learn something from the survey results that you did not learn from the interview results? If you did not, is that a problem? If a finding is confirmed using multiple methods, does this help us overcome some of our skepticism of that finding?

This project involves a research team. Three researchers visited 23 different childcare centers across four different neighborhoods in a city. What are the advantages and disadvantages of having multiple researchers engage in a project? Why do you think the researchers chose four different neighborhoods? Finally, how reliable and valid are the results of this study? How does using multiple methods influence the **reliability** and **validity** of the qualitative findings, if at all?

Why Organizational Ties Matter for Neighborhood Effects: A Study of Resource Access through Childcare Centers

By Mario Luis Small, Erin M. Jacobs, and Rebekah P. Massengill

One of the most important factors affecting well-being among the poor is the ability to access resources the middle class takes for granted, such as health care, legal representation and information about jobs. How does neighborhood poverty affect this ability? The "neighborhood effects" literature has provided two answers (Sampson, Morenoff and Gannon-Rowley 2002; Small and Newman 2001). One, social isolation theory, argues that neighborhood poverty disconnects people from middle-class social networks containing resources such as information about jobs and education (Fernandez and Harris 1992; Wilson 1987, 1996). The other, de-institutionalization theory, argues that concentrated poverty leaves neighborhoods without the middle-class capital or leadership to support strong local organizations (Wilson 1987; but see Small and McDermott 2006). Thus, residents have a harder time locating resources such as childcare and medical services (Ellen and Turner 2003; Ludwig, Duncan and Ladd 2003). Through different mechanisms, both theories expect neighborhood poverty to reduce the available resources important to well-being.

This study examines one factor neglected by the neighborhood effects literature: the networks of local organizations. While such networks concerned sociologists in the 1970s and 1980s (Laumann, Galskiewicz and Marsden 1978), they have all but disappeared from the most recent research on neighborhood poverty (Sampson, Morenoff and Gannon-Rowley 2002; Small and Newman 2001).

This neglect is problematic for two reasons. First, while local organizations matter because of the resources they sell or offer directly, they also matter because of those they give access to through their organizational ties (Chaskin et al. 2001). Second, it is unclear how neighborhood poverty affects organizational ties. The de-institutionalization perspective would expect neighborhood poverty to weaken them, given the absence of the middle class. However, a neighborhood's organizational ties are influenced not merely by the demographic traits of its residents but also by external institutional factors, such as pressures by the state and the non-profit sector, both of which may develop and sustain ties in otherwise disorganized areas (Logan and Molotch 1987; Smith and Lipsky 1993). This is especially likely if the interaction among organizations in for-profit, non-profit and government sectors has increased, since additional parties are

Mario Small, Erin M. Jacobs, and Rebekah P. Massengill. 2008. "Why Organizational Ties Matter for Neighborhood Effects: A Study of Resource Access through Childcare Centers." *Social Forces* 87: 387–414.

potential actors (Austin 2000; Marwell and McInerney 2005; Smith and Lipsky 1993). Do such institutional factors have a measurable effect? If so, do they reinforce, cancel out or counteract the effect of local demographic conditions? Tests of the general neighborhood effects hypothesis have yielded mixed results (Goering and Feins 2003), and the failure of most tests to account for organizational ties may be part of the reason.

This study examines how neighborhood poverty affects access to resources important to well-being from a perspective missing from the neighborhood effects literature. In social isolation theory, the individual is the unit of analysis, and the question is whether individuals have access to fewer resources in poor neighborhoods; in de-institutionalization theory, the neighborhood is the unit, and the question is whether poor neighborhoods are more resource-deprived. In the present study, the organization is the unit, and the question is whether local organizations are less connected if they are in poor neighborhoods. The particular connections of interest are those providing the organization's patrons access to resources important to well-being.

The study examines one of the most important local organizations—the childcare center. We present results of a qualitative study of 23 New York City childcare centers that examines whether and how centers provide their adult patrons access to resources through organizational ties. We formalize these findings into hypotheses and then test them on a unique quantitative dataset of the organizational ties of nearly 300 randomly-selected childcare centers in the city. Findings uncover that centers provide access to important resources through their ties, and that, due to the influence of institutional factors, neighborhood poverty is associated with more, not fewer organizational ties. We suggest that the neglect of organizational ties may help account for inconsistent findings in the neighborhood effects literature.

THEORETICAL PERSPECTIVE

As bureaucratization and specialization have increased, neighborhoods become connected to society less through a "sense of community" than through the ties between local organizations and larger organizations throughout society. Thus, organizations as different as grocery stores, churches, schools and local union offices represent versions of a common entity, local units that, through their vertical ties, link the neighborhood to wider society—to the national supermarket chain, the denominational board, the education department and the national union, respectively. The resources available to a resident in a given neighborhood are shaped substantially by external systems, rather than just local demographics. The foods sold in groceries, the curricula taught in schools, the services offered in community centers, and the health plans accepted in local clinics would all be shaped by external systems.

We view the childcare center as an organization with vertical ties that may carry resources "for distribution within the community" and subject to both economic and institutional pressures. Our expectations about organizational ties in poor neighborhoods differ from those of de-institutionalization theory. The latter expects the demographic conditions of the local neighborhood to be the primary causal factors, such that the higher the poverty rate, the less viable local organizations such as childcare centers. We expect the institutional conditions of both local and external organizations to play equally important roles, such that the higher the poverty rate the less or more connected local organizations, depending on the norms of local and external actors and the presence of coercive pressures. Our specific empirical questions are the following: Do childcare centers provide access to resources important to well-being through their inter-organizational ties? If so, how is this process affected by neighborhood poverty?

CHILDCARE CENTERS AND ORGANIZATIONAL TIES

The childcare center presents an auspicious opportunity to examine these questions. First, childcare centers are local organizations, since, given client preferences, they typically serve residents within the neighborhood. 77.8 percent of the centers we surveyed reported that "all or almost all" of their clients live in the neighborhood. Second, the childcare center is an increasingly important organization for the poor in light of dramatic policy shifts over the past decade. The Personal Responsibility and Work Opportunity Act of 1996 toughened eligibility rules for welfare recipients and instituted a work requirement, forcing more low-income mothers to work, and heightening the importance of childcare. Third, unlike other local organizations, childcare centers may be for- or non-profit, publicly or privately funded, and religious or secular, yielding a rich variety of forms, sectors and interests.

QUALITATIVE DATA AND FINDINGS

We interviewed, in person, directors or other personnel of 23 childcare centers in four New York City neighborhoods: one low-income black, one low-income white, one low-income Latino and one upper middle class. Centers were observed as many as eight times. In each center, we collected field notes on physical conditions of the center, social interactions and available resources. The staff interviews provided data on motivations for establishing inter-organizational ties, the nature of those ties and the resources available to parents. We complemented these data with in-depth interviews of 64 parents, and selected key-informant interviews with leaders in the government or non-profit sectors in New York City. See Table 9.1 for basic neighborhood and center characteristics in the qualitative study.

Table 9.1. Characteristics of Neighborhoods* and Centers in Qualitative Study

	Low-income white	Low-income black	Low-income Latino	Upper-middle class
Neighborhood characteristics				
Median household income	$21,000	$14,000	$23,000	$56,000
% in poverty	40	46	34	13
% black	0	66	7	5
% Latino	8	27	84	17
% white	88	2	5	69
% in same unit in 1995	74	68	65	56
Total population	25,000	7,000	17,000	23,000
Center characteristics				
Number of centers	6	6	6	5
Served low income parents	6	6	4	1
ACS/Head Start	3	2	3	1
Free services/sliding scale	5	4	4	1
Average slots per center	100	108	68	64

*Source: 2000 U.S. Census. Neighborhood figures rounded.

Before disentangling what we observed, we briefly describe the Family Focus Head Start, which highlights several of the issues at play. On our first visit to the center, Rachel, the parent coordinator, described a center well connected to external agencies and providers. She arranged workshops and events for parents of the center's 200 children, and coordinated social services with other organizations in this poor, predominantly white neighborhood. The workshops were run by other organizations. For example, the owner of a haircutting business had recently led a well-received haircutting workshop. Parents appreciated learning a marketable skill and a way to cut costs at home, especially in large families. When mothers enrolled in the center, Rachel noted if they were pregnant, and when the newborn arrived, she referred them to a neighborhood nonprofit that sends free household and childcare help to mothers postpartum. She also referred parents experiencing emergency food or clothing needs to nearby nonprofit and government agencies. Through the center, therefore, parents accessed several resources conducive to well-being—including cost-saving skills, household post-partum help, food and clothing—from other organizations.

Diverse Resources

Our fieldwork uncovered that childcare centers' organizational ties provided access to a remarkably heterogeneous set of resources conducive to well-being. The resources included information, services and material goods, and they centered on the following domains: housing, physical and mental health, health care, child development, schools, adult education, legal issues, government programs, immigration, employment and the arts and entertainment.

Not surprisingly, much of the information pertained to child-related issues, such as asthma, lead poisoning and school enrollment. Other information addressed adult issues such as domestic abuse, health care and work-life balance. This information was provided by businesses, health organizations, government agencies, schools, and others. The centers provided access to many services, most for free or at low cost, either on center premises or elsewhere. Many were services for which patrons would normally have to pay. Several involved child-related issues, such as free health and dental exams, speech therapy and cognitive development screening; others were relevant to parents, such as free or low-cost health and vision exams, assistance in dealing with landlords, temporary relocation apartments for women leaving abusive spouses, HIV/AIDS testing and treatment, adult literacy and work training. Finally, centers provided access to material goods. Several centers collaborated with the city-wide "Cool Culture" program, which gave patrons free passes to approximately 50 museums and cultural outlets in the city. One center was tied to a soup kitchen that served parents regularly; another offered toys (sponsored by a department store) during Christmas.

Referral Ties and Collaborative Ties

How did centers provide access to these resources? The fieldwork uncovered many types of relationships between the center and the external organization but we can identify two general types of relations: referral ties and collaborative ties.

Formal referrals—through which centers forwarded the name of a parent to or formally informed the parent of an organization providing a resource—were ubiquitous. Some referrals stemmed from parental requests. For example, Francis, a white mother at Little Friends, a center in a middle-class neighborhood, needed a referral for her child, who, in their bilingual Russian/English household, was not speaking by age 2. An evaluator had recommended therapy; Francis then spoke to the center's director:

> [The director] had the name of a speech therapist who was located in [the neighborhood] so it would be very convenient for [the therapist] to see him at the school. So . . . the speech therapist [my son] has is actually the one that we got the recommendation from [the director] for.

Other times, referrals occurred at the request of a teacher or staff member after noticing something during the provision of care. We asked Denise, a black mother whose three children were in a center in a low-income black neighborhood, whether she had ever received a referral from the center:

Well, actually they referred me to check my kid's eyes. They got the Health Department to come. . . . That's something we gotta work on over the summer, 'cause my son has . . . a hand-eye coordination problem.

Often centers did more than refer parents; they collaborated with the organization by providing a room or arranging a meeting for the organization to provide or sell its resource. Collaborative ties were less common, though by no means rare. Often centers held workshops in which outside speakers led training sessions on mental health, nutrition, child discipline or other issues. Other times, experts—such as speech therapists or dentists—conducted their practice at the center. One center prepared "a whole transition piece" for parents with children entering elementary school: it included school visits, presentations from school teachers, tours of school grounds, and enrollment assistance.

Role of the State and Large Non-profits

Not all childcare centers provided equal access to resources. The fieldwork was consistent with the theory that the state and the non-profit sector play a role. Two findings emerged. First, the state contributed to tie formation through coercive pressures. Second, large non-profits contributed to the process in response to government retrenchment and state contraction.

Many government-funded centers had mandates to establish ties. From their inception, Head Start programs were envisioned as collaborative enterprises. Accordingly, the federal government requires Head Start centers to provide resources for families, which effectively mandate that directors develop organizational ties. For example, the centers are required to determine whether "each child has . . . continuous, accessible health care." (Department of Health and Human Services 2005: Section 1304) If not, the center must help the parent find care. In addition, the center, working with the parent, is required to screen children to assess "developmental, sensory (visual and auditory), behavioral, motor, language, social, cognitive, perceptual, and emotional skills." (DHHS 2005: Section 1304) The government does not provide extensive funds for these assessments (Zigler and Muenchow 1992); instead, it expects centers to "take affirmative steps to establish . . . collaborative relationships with community organizations," such as "health care providers . . . , mental health providers, nutritional service providers . . . and any other organizations or businesses that may provide support and resources to families." (DHHS 2005: Section 1304)

Large non-profits in the city also encouraged centers to form such ties. One of our informants, Robert, spent decades as the director of a major children's non-profit in the city. He explained the current predicament:

[Today] there is no money in day care centers for health or mental health. . . . Head Start eliminated years ago from the federal level any substantial amount of money for [these services], and greatly cut back on three categories of staff—social worker, family assistant, and family worker—that were once part of the Head Start machinery.

His and other non-profit organizations "have compensated for those limitations" by collaborating with businesses and other organizations that provide or sell resources.

Role of Professional Norms

Our fieldwork suggested that professional norms among practitioners in all sectors and at all levels of the hierarchy contributed to tie formation. Two norms were key: (1). a "holistic" approach to childcare, expressed in the idea that one cannot care for a child without caring for the family; (2). a belief in expertise and specialization, expressed in the idea that staff should not perform a role for which they are not qualified.

The dual mantra of holistic provision and specialization was ubiquitous. Kaitlin, an officer at the city homeless agency, explained a pilot project by which a small non-profit would "bring multiple agencies together at the local level in the event there are at least three government agencies involved in a household's life." She elaborated:

> [S]o, if there's a . . . brother getting out of jail, a child who's at risk of dropping out of school . . . and the mom is just getting referred to child welfare . . . the brother's about to come back, that's gonna screw up the household. The kid's already acting out and the mother is having all this stress and then suddenly she has to defend herself to child welfare. The goal is that . . . the public agencies [will] come together to see the family holistically and then develop plans that are gonna support the family in the best way. So the probation officer, the child welfare specialist, the education guidance counselor, all [are] working together about how to bring resources that solve the problem . . .

She explained that a major funder "buys into this argument [and] gives us money to fund a program, as [have] a number of other foundations." We witnessed versions of this belief—in a holistic approach and in specialization—in both for- and nonprofit centers.

Role of Neighborhood

Our fieldwork uncovered that the actions of large external organizations were affected by the perceived poverty of the neighborhood. Businesses, non-profits and the state all used perceived need in the neighborhood as a proxy when seeking populations to which to distribute or sell resources. Kyle was an officer in the city's education bureaucracy who addressed community affairs. As he explained:

And, again, we know where the areas . . . are [in which this is] happening. If you had to ask me what are the five areas where this is happening, where there's the greatest need: Harlem, Washington Heights . . . South Bronx, central Brooklyn, southeast Queens. . . . those are the five areas where . . . we have the most problematic schools, most challenging schools, where our kids are generally under-performing and also. . . . Seventy to 75 percent, I believe, of the prison rate of the State of New York [comes from] those five zip codes.

When he came across businesses or large non-profits seeking to distribute resources, his office directed them to schools in the poorest neighborhoods. Notably, these were place-based strategies: it was the neighborhood, not the organization that served as a proxy. Kyle, for example, did not assess the percent of children in the school on free lunch to determine where to send businesses with resources; instead, he assessed whether the school was located in The South Bronx, Washington Heights or other known high poverty neighborhoods. Below, we test the significance of this distinction.

Hypotheses

Returning to our two empirical questions, our qualitative research suggests that organizational ties provided access to resources important to well-being and that this process was not affected by neighborhood poverty as expected by the de-institutionalization perspective. Our fieldwork suggests examining not merely local demographics but also institutional factors, such as state pressures and professional norms. We formalize these qualitative findings into hypotheses below.

Our first hypothesis reflects our initial qualitative findings:

H1. *Because of their organizational ties, childcare centers will provide access to multiple resources important to well-being.*

The fieldwork also suggested that coercive pressures by the state and large non-profits would contribute to tie formation. The effect of these pressures should be greatest where state influence is strongest and market-derived demands like the need for profits are weakest. Therefore, we expect the following:

H2. *For-profit centers will exhibit the fewest, and government-funded centers the greatest number of active resource-rich organizational ties.*

Nevertheless, it was also clear that professional norms played a role. Consistent with the idea of centers as loosely coupled entities, staff pursued these ties even when, as in the case of "victim's services," it was not required, if staff believed there was a need. This leads us to hypothesize the following:

H3. *Despite H2, sector differences will not fully account for the variance in number of ties—even after controlling for the center's sector, centers serving poor patrons will exhibit a greater number of ties than centers not serving the poor.*

Finally, our fieldwork made clear the importance of location. We would expect centers with a high proportion of poor parents to maintain more ties than other centers. However, we expect that demand at the center level will not fully account for the connectedness of the center. If many resource providers are using the neighborhood, not the center, to assess need, then, after accounting for demand, centers in high poverty neighborhoods should still exhibit more ties. In this respect, our expectations would differ from both a demand model (which would expect more resources in high-demand centers, regardless of location) and the de-institutionalization model (which would expect more resources in low-poverty neighborhoods):

H4. *After controlling for the poverty level of the patrons served, centers in high-poverty neighborhoods will still exhibit more ties than those in other neighborhoods.*

DATA AND METHODS

We test these hypotheses using data from a unique random-sample survey of centers in New York City. The survey was conducted by an independent firm (SRBI); the sample, drawn from a list of all licensed centers provided by the city's Bureau of Day Care. At the time of the survey (summer-fall 2004) there were an estimated 1,683 centers. The number of centers interviewed was 293, and the response rate was 60 percent. The telephone survey, conducted with the director, lasted approximately 25 minutes. We obtained data on basic organizational structure, services provided other than childcare, referrals to other organizations, ties to other organizations, and address. We geo-coded addresses and matched centers to census tracts and used tract-level demographic data.

We used the qualitative interviews to develop questions about formal referral ties and collaborative ties. We asked in the survey about six specific referral-tie-resources and five collaborative-tie resources with an additional question for collaborative resources not asked about. We asked respondents, "The next questions are about services (other than childcare) that the center may offer to parents and families, either as referrals or directly by the center. I'm going to start with referrals. In the last 12 months, has the center directly referred parents to a specific agency or organization for any of the following reasons?" We then listed each of the six issues of interest to parents. For each referral, we asked specific questions about the organization, including organization's sector (government, for-profit, or private non-profit), its name (verbatim), and its location. This helped prevent over-reporting of ties, since respondents who reported a false referral would have to lie multiple times to support the false statement. We then asked, "Now I'd like to ask about services the center may provide directly or by bringing in staff from outside orga-nizations. This question does not include referrals. During the last 12 months, did the center provide . . . " each of five different services. As a validity check, we allowed the respondents to tell us about one addi-tional service we did not suggest. For each, we asked whether the service was provided by the center or by an outside organization, and if the lat-ter, we asked for the organization's sector and name. Figures will refer only to services provided by external organizations, not those provided by the center.

FINDINGS

Organizational ties

Centers surveyed maintained both referral and collaborative ties, and multiple resources were transferred through them. The first row of Table 9.2 shows that only 51 centers had made no formal referrals in the previous year; 83 percent of centers (242 of 293) referred parents for at least one issue, while 37 percent (109/293) referred parents for at least two. Collaborative ties were less common, with 150 centers having provided no service in partnership with outside entities in the previous 12 months. Forty-nine percent of our sample had at least one collabora-tive tie and 20 percent had at least two.

Table 9.3 presents the percentage of centers with active ties by type of resource transferred. On average, centers formally referred parents for 1.6 separate issues, which varied widely. Child-related referrals were common; nearly 80 percent of centers reported referring parents for child learning disability services at least once during the previous year. Although centers were less likely to make referrals for issues not specifically related to children, many did so. Nearly 8 percent provided

Table 9.2. Number of Active Ties of Centers in Quantitative Study, by Type of Tie

	Number of Centers	
	Formal Referral Ties	Collaborative Ties
No ties	51	150
One tie	133	83
Two ties	50	34
Three ties	24	21
Four ties	16	0
Five ties	11	4
Six ties	8	1
Total Centers	293	293

Table 9.3. Percentage of Centers with Active Tie by Type

Formal Referral Ties	%	Collaborative Ties	%
Children's learning disabilities services	79.0	Dental services for children	29.8
Drug abuse/addiction services for parents	7.8	Physical health exams for children	5.2
Mental health services for parents	26.8	Children's learning disability services	24.6
Immigration services	15.6	Counseling for spousal abuse	8.1
Legal advice	16.2	Services for child neglect/abuse	6.8
Spousal abuse	17.9	Other services	10.9
Average number of referral ties	1.6	Average number of service ties	.8
N = 293			

referrals to parents for drug problems while more than a quarter referred parents for mental health services. Further, referrals for immigration services, legal advice and spousal abuse were provided in 15 to 18 percent of centers.

Centers also maintained collaborative ties to organizations that provided services to parents, averaging .8 of these ties. As with referrals, services directly related to children were most common: children in nearly 30 percent of centers received dental services provided by another organization during the previous year, while in approximately 5 percent of centers, children received physical health services. Further, nearly 25 percent of centers provided learning disability services by outside organizations. Parents also received services not directly related to children: in nearly 18 percent of centers, they received spousal abuse services from an outside organization. Finally, 11 percent of centers provided at least one additional service through a collaborative tie. The variety and number of referral and collaborative ties shown in Table 9.3 support our first hypothesis.

Sector

We hypothesized that for-profit centers would exhibit the fewest number of active ties. The results presented in the top two rows of Table 9.4—which show the coefficients for government-funded and privately-funded non-profit (with private for-profit as the baseline category)—support this hypothesis. Government-funded centers made 49 percent and private non-profit centers made 50 percent more formal referrals than for-profit centers. Turning to collaborative ties, while there was no difference in the number of services transferred by for-profit and private non-profit centers, government-funded centers provided the most by a large margin, with 220 percent more service ties than for-profit centers.

Our expectations are confirmed in a different form in Table 9.5, which presents the distribution of ties by the sector of both the childcare

Table 9.4. Poisson Regression Estimates of Number of Active Ties of Center, after Controls

Variable	Referral Ties	Collaborative Ties
Center is a:		
Government nonprofit	.402** (.157)	1.163** (.242)
Private nonprofit	.404** (.163)	.437 (.277)
Center has high proportion of poor children	.422** (.109)	.218 (.154)
Center located in a high poverty neighborhood	.243** (.123)	.368** (.164)
N	293	293

*p, .05; **p, .01

Privately funded for-profit is the base category for center sector. Our measure of high poverty neighborhood is an indicator variable coded 1 if the center is located in a neighborhood with a poverty rate of 40 percent or higher. Our proxy for need in the center is an indicator variable coded 1 if at least 30 percent of the children in the center were on government vouchers or some type of government subsidy (regardless of the center's location). Thirty-nine percent of centers were in this category. The models control for neighborhood characteristics, the variables *percent black, percent white* and *percent Latino* control for the racial composition of the neighborhood. We control for the percentage of residents who lived in a different home five years before the 2000 U.S. Census. We control for *population density*. Finally, we control for the *borough* in which the center is located (Manhattan is the omitted category), as some resource providers are located in and focus on specific boroughs.

Table 9.5. Distribution of Active Ties by Sector or External Organization

		Percentage of ties to		
Number of ties to any organization		For-profit organization	Non-profit organization	Government organization
For profit centers (n = 59)				
Referral ties	44	17.8	8.9	73.3
Collaborative ties	21	33.3	14.3	52.4
Private non-profit centers (n = 99)				
Referral ties	146	12.3	47.3	40.4
Collaborative ties	46	23.9	54.3	21.7
Government non-profit centers (n = 135)				
Referral ties	247	8.9	51.0	40.1
Collaborative ties	166	22.3	41.0	36.7
All centers (n = 293)				
Referral ties	437	11.0	45.5	43.5
Collaborative ties	233	23.6	41.2	35.2

center and the outside organization. This table includes all three sector types because it does not present regression results. As shown in the bottom two rows, referral ties among all centers were more likely to be made to private non-profits (45.5 percent of all ties) or government organizations (43.5 percent) than to for-profits; collaborative ties exhibit a seminal pattern. It is notable, however, that the business sector was highly involved in the provision or sale of resources, particularly as collaborators with the center. Among all collaborative ties, 23.6 percent were to businesses.

Center Poverty

We hypothesized that the number of ties would also depend on the proportion of poor families served by the center. The third row of Table 9.4 shows that centers with a high proportion of poor patrons have 53 percent more referral ties than other centers. We do not find an effect on collaborative ties.

Neighborhood Poverty

We hypothesized that centers in high poverty neighborhoods would have more ties, even after accounting for sector and demand, because institutional actors higher up the vertical chain use neighborhood poverty as a proxy for need. The fourth row of Table 9.4 shows that centers in high-poverty neighborhoods had 28 percent more referral ties and provided 44 percent more collaborative ties than centers in non-poor neighborhoods.

CONCLUSION

How does neighborhood poverty affect access to resources important to well-being? Most of the neighborhood effects literature has answered this question by focusing on either neighborhoods or individuals. This study, focused on organizations, has argued that an important part of the answer is the role of organizational ties. Childcare centers provided access to multiple resources through both referral and collaborative ties to other organizations. And, net of the poverty level of patrons in the center, those located in high poverty neighborhoods exhibited greater, not fewer, active ties.

Our findings would suggest that standard tests should not always show a negative neighborhood effect, which is consistent with what has been reported. If other organizations were to exhibit the patterns childcare centers do, then ignoring the role of organizational ties in resource access would lead scholars to underestimate the negative consequences of neighborhood poverty—that is, the consequences associated with other neighborhood mechanisms—since organizational ties would be an attenuating factor. Part of the inconsistency in the neighborhood effects results may result from differences in both individuals' connections to local organizations and the connections of those organizations themselves. Neighborhood effects research, then, should rely not only on multiple methods but also multiple units of analysis, with the organization as a conspicuously understudied unit.

Our study also emphasizes the importance of considering not merely local but also extra-local factors, and the interaction between the two. We should reconsider the state and the non-profit sector, especially under the current political economy. The state and professional norms often encourage organizational collaboration, and social ties among professionals across the state and non-profit sectors likely enhance this collaboration.

Finally, the study suggests exploring possible unanticipated consequences of de-concentration policies with respect to the ability of the poor to access resources important to well-being. Such policies are likely to have positive effects on feelings of safety and access to higher quality schools. However, they may also undermine some organizational channels through which non-profits and federal or local governments have distributed resources to the poor, since actors use concentrated neighborhood poverty as a proxy to reach poor individuals.

REFLECTION

The Map and the Compass

By Mario Luis Small

Sociology has always lain, at times comfortably and other times uneasily, in a space between the sciences and humanities. The discipline's mix of highly diverse approaches and methods both inspires creativity and generates tension. One easy way to incite that tension is to insist, in a crowded room of sociologists, that all good research requires good design. To sociologists who spend their days fine-tuning survey questions and controlled experiments, the statement is a truism, barely worth defending; to those who spend their days hanging out on neighborhood corners or buried deep in dusty archives, the statement is preposterous at best and scientism run amok at worst.

Sociologists of the latter kind will insist that many of the best ethnographies and historical case studies were produced by authors who jumped into their projects blindly, coming across small discoveries and unexpected dead ends that worked their way into a question and, eventually, a finished product. This largely humanist perspective on research is so pervasive that as early as 40 years ago it became the first principle of the grounded theory model: begin your project without even a question in mind. The scientists insist, by contrast, that testing theories convincingly is impossible without specifying, ahead of time, which research design will provide the right answer. In fact, this plan-dependent procedure is the foundation of hypothesis testing through statistical analysis; anything else, its proponents believe, is data mining. Furthermore, proponents would argue that haphazard approaches, where researchers can change their minds after the study has begun, will likely induce biases and undermine the credibility of the finished product. Even worse: a researcher stumbling along without thinking clearly about design may spend years producing something that, only after the fact, is discovered to contain a fatal flaw.

The mixed method researcher inevitably faces some version of this tension. A mixed study is a composite of two or more smaller ones, with their own data collection and their own position on whether preplanned design is necessary for good research. The smaller studies might proceed independently, even adopting different positions on the humanities-versus-sciences approach to design. But the mixed method study as a whole must be clear on where it stands. The researcher must have an overall perspective, lest the project—already burdened by the task of reconciling different methods—comes across as incoherent.

A MAP

The article you have read is an excerpt from my book *Unanticipated Gains*, a study of how childcare centers affect the networks of mothers of young children; the book is a mixed method study whose design has appealed to many readers. It is a multimethod, multilevel study, one that seems to exemplify the advantages of clarifying one's design—the design of the entire enterprise—before beginning a study. To understand what I mean, consider Table 9.6, below. The book, concerned with the conditions of both mothers and centers—that is, individuals and organizations—collected both qualitative data and quantitative data at each level of analysis. It included two surveys, in-depth case studies of centers, and in-depth interviews of mothers (and some fathers).

One way to think of tables such as this one is to see them as a roadmap for the project to be executed. The researcher—having attained some clarity on the core questions, the budget, the scope of the project, the length of the time in the field, and the desired outcomes—traces the map that will guide her or him on the vast wilderness to be traversed. The simplicity and comprehensiveness of Table 9.6 comes across as a reliable map, the kind guaranteed to keep me from veering too far from the right path.

But tracing a map is not how I arrived at that table. In fact, if the project was a journey, it was one I embarked on with no map whatsoever. While I had some sense of the core question, I was unclear about the

Table 9.6. The data used in *Unanticipated Gains*

	Quantitative	Qualitative
Individual	Representative survey of mothers	Case studies of mothers
Organization	Representative survey of centers	Case studies of centers

budget, scope, field time, or expected outcome. I was not even sure, over the project's long gestation, that I would eventually write a book. I was not convinced I would discover anything worth reporting. My path was circuitous, fraught with missed turns and occasional dead ends, unpredictable, at times surprising, and often difficult.

Yet it was not an aimless trip. While I did not require a map, I did need a sense of direction, and it is the latter, more than the former, which sustained my progress in the wilderness, which made my scientific work cumulative, consistent, and informative rather than unproductive. To explain what I mean, I must retrace my steps.

THE FIRST STEPS

I stumbled onto the project in my penultimate year in graduate school, after I was hired as research assistant on a study of the conditions of low-income Boston neighborhoods. My job as a neighborhood ethnographer was to visit three such neighborhoods repeatedly, talk to residents, take field notes, and report on what I saw. An important part of my job was to contact "neighborhood institutions" to learn how they contributed to the community. Trained as an urbanist, I shared the concern of many in my field that neighborhood institutions were poorly understood. My strategy was to walk every major street, to enter every establishment I saw, and to approach anyone who would speak to me about the establishment, its clients, its core business or service, the neighborhood, and anything else they cared to share. It was a classic fishing expedition, but I learned a lot about the neighborhoods rather quickly.

One day, in one of the neighborhoods, I walked into a childcare center. I asked the staff person with whom I met my standard battery of questions, adjusted to the particular locale; I asked about the center's clientele, programs, enrolled children, curriculum, after-school program, and other routine miscellany. At the end of the interview, I asked, as I always did, if there was anything else I should have asked about. She responded immediately that, yes, I had neglected to ask about the parents. She explained that the childcare center did much more than provide childcare, that it was as much an institution for the parents as it was for the children. For example, it helped people find jobs. Many of the clients (who until shortly before my visit were not required to provide proof of citizenship) were undocumented immigrants and had learned that the center, through its various connections to establishments in the neighborhood and city, had helped people find low-skilled jobs in the service industry. The center also helped people find social services, connecting them to health and other providers in private and public agencies throughout the city. The center, finally, seemed to be a space for social connections among parents, the kind of foundational entity that made the figurative grapevine operate effectively as a grapevine; it was a place where parents met, gossiped, exchanged information, and seemed to support one another. Having no prior exposure as an adult to either centers or preschools, I was surprised. More importantly, I was curious.

My curiosity lingered as I moved from Boston to New York, where I lived as I began my stint as an assistant professor. I wondered whether the childcare center I had come across was unique or, instead, was exemplary of the contemporary neighborhood institution at the dusk of the twentieth century, an entity whose core purpose was, in part, establishing and maintaining social and organizational connections. I knew no other way to satisfy that curiosity than to visit other centers.

I ran a pilot study, a short-term but open-ended exploration to see whether I was on to something. With a research assistant, I visited about 20 centers in one poor and one nonpoor neighborhood in New York City. We simply knocked on all doors and talked to any staff members who would talk to us about what the centers did, on an everyday basis, related to the lives of parents rather than children. We asked whether they helped people find jobs, connect people to social services, or facilitate community among parents. Surprisingly, many of them did. Certainly, some centers provided nothing more than day care, but others were buzzing with activity, consistently charged social networks.

New questions arose: How common was this practice? Why did centers differ so dramatically in how much they tied parents to services? Why did parents in some centers seem to have built community while those in others hardly knew other parents? Were these networks actually useful? And was adopting a network perspective the best way to think about "the neighborhood institution," this entity that had consumed so many of us in urban sociology? At a minimum, the childcare center seemed to be a strategic site to examine one thing: how neighborhood organizations affected parents' social and organizational ties. That core question became my focal point.

Having been trained the way most sociologists are trained, I proceeded to design a study, to create a map of the intellectual trajectory to be traversed as I pursued these questions. (The fact that, for all practical purposes, I had actually begun the study many months earlier did not deter me.) I decided to study four neighborhoods of different racial and class composition: three high poverty neighborhoods, each predominantly either white, black, or Latino; and one upper-middle-class neighborhood of mixed but mostly white racial composition. I figured that this racial and class diversity would help me answer not only the questions that had arisen in the field but also my theoretical concerns about whether neighborhood cultural differences might affect differences between centers. Perhaps the collective differences between the cultural practices of, say, predominantly Latino and predominantly black centers could help account for the differences in networking among parents. The plan called for locating all 23 centers across the four neighborhoods, interviewing directors and staff about their activities, talking to carefully selected parents, and attending whatever events we could. With a small research fund from my university, I hired two terrific research assistants, and we embarked on the study, our (small and admittedly crude) map in hand.

We started learning quickly and consistently over our many months of fieldwork. We learned the varied ways that centers connected parents to other organizations—sometimes by simple referrals, other times through ad hoc collaborations, still others through stable partnerships. We unraveled the many factors that motivated centers to engage in these activities. We found out how parents met other parents, why some did more than others, and why some centers seemed to sparkle with community while others seemed lifeless. We uncovered why some centers failed to generate strong community in spite of the intentions of their directors. We began to develop an inkling about which kinds of centers would likely be effective brokers of social networks and which would not. We also learned that, contrary to the expectations that informed the original design, cultural differences between neighborhoods did not seem to matter. Centers in the predominantly Latino neighborhood differed more from one to the next than they did collectively from those in the black neighborhood. In fact, our slow realizations made two things clear.

A FLAWED MAP

One, much of what we were learning did not derive from our perfectly conceived roadmap. The core, preplanned design decision—to compare centers by type of neighborhood—played little role in what seemed to be our most important and interesting discoveries about what motivated directors, staff, and parents. In fact, I began ignoring the map soon after entering the field. For example, we learned that many directors were motivated to connect parents to resources because they wanted to please external organizations that were not childcare centers and were not even located in our four neighborhoods. So we went to the headquarters of those organizations and agencies, regardless of where they were, and interviewed managers there about their own motivations. Even our plans with respect to parents were upended. Since I had wanted to learn how parents became either well connected or isolated, the original map called for us to interview a set number of parents at each extreme. But if we came across a parent who did not follow our pattern, we interviewed the parent anyway, and many did not follow our pattern.

My map quickly became obsolete. It was a perfectly drawn representation of a landscape different from the one before me. But all was not lost. Throughout the process I kept returning to that persistent curiosity: figuring out how the centers affected parents' social and organizational ties. So while I abandoned the map, I was not wandering aimlessly; I was guided by a strongly calibrated compass—my curiosity about that core question—that helped me determine which leads to pursue, which paths to let go, and which predetermined rules to ignore.

The second thing that became clear is that I needed more data. I was especially frustrated that I did not know whether what we saw was unique to our centers—which, after all, overrepresented high-poverty centers by design. As I result, I found some funds and commissioned a survey of just under 300 randomly sampled childcare centers in the city. The questions for the survey were deeply informed by our ongoing fieldwork, which made clear what specific issues to ask about, how to ask questions, and even how to frame the project as a whole. Because of our ongoing fieldwork, we even knew to instruct the firm that would conduct the telephone survey to call the centers between noon and two in the afternoon. The reason? The directors we observed seemed to spend most of their time running from classroom to classroom, putting out small fires related to the teaching and managing of children. But early afternoon was nap time, the only chance directors had 20 or 30 minutes to do us the favor of taking our survey.

Other questions beckoned me. To understand how centers affected the lives of parents, we needed to know more from parents. Our in-depth interviews were revealing a great deal about how centers were shaping parents' lives and why, if at all, these changes might make a difference. But the time and investment required to conduct effective in-depth interviews precluded our executing hundreds of them. I was dissatisfied at being uncertain whether, in a representative sample of parents, centers would in fact make any difference.

At some time during the course of figuring out where I was headed, I came across a golden opportunity, which, guided by my compass, I took without hesitation. A colleague was preparing to launch the third wave of her national study of mothers of newborns. By the time the third wave was launched, the former newborns would now be about five, and many of those newborns would be enrolled in childcare centers. An exceptionally generous person interested in spreading the use of her survey, my colleague allowed me to add a few questions to the survey about the networks of mothers, their connections to services, their experiences in centers, and their general well-being. I now had an opportunity to see not only whether the experiences of our mothers were representative but also whether, on average, such experiences improved the mothers' lives.

As these various bits of data slowly trickled in, I was faced with the daunting task of making sense of them, a task complicated by the fact that no prior map I had envisioned represented the full body of data I was now forced to understand. In fact, that small, partial, prior map that informed the four-neighborhood design was not only inaccurate; it was worthless, calling attention to the wrong set of issues. The actual data collection and the small questions that seemed crucial to understand the core larger one were far beyond the scope of anything represented in that earlier map. And yet I had a compass. If I knew nothing else, at least I knew which question needed answering.

And that compass proved useful not only when determining which data to collect next but also, more importantly, when figuring out how to think about my question: any approach, theoretical perspective, or model that seemed to veer me off path by not answering that question was replaced. It was the compass that made clear to me that thinking of childcare centers as "neighborhood organizations" was an obstacle to finding my path. As I wrote much later:

> First, it soon became clear that the neighborhood mattered less than the organizational characteristics of the center. In the phrase "neighborhood organization," the adjective had turned into an assumption what should have been an empirical question. Yes, centers were local organizations, but their local nature was not what mattered most about them, except for the fact that what is local is also convenient and therefore likely to be used. What mattered more about them, for the formation of ties and the benefits mothers could gain from these ties, was whether organizational and institutional processes were in place that allowed parents to meet other parents, to contact outside organizations, and to coordinate tasks with center staff. Following current trends in urban sociology . . . I had always instinctively focused on neighborhoods, believing, like many urban ethnographers and not without reason, that neighborhoods in urban areas played important roles in the formation of ties. The danger was that too much attention on the neighborhood had directed my thinking away from one of the most important aspects of contemporary life: that we are, in Charles Perrow's words, "a society of organizations." As [a] result, I began to think of childcare centers as the one thing I knew they were—organizations—and assessed the role of neighborhoods only to the extent they shaped patrons' social or organizational ties. (Small 2009, 203–4)

I faced many more obstacles along this theoretical path—difficult new questions, alien literatures, apparent contradictions—obstacles made more daunting as I resolved to make sense of all of it in a book. Still, my general direction was more or less clear. I was a ship in the dark guided steadily by my North Star. Without it, I would likely still be wandering.

Somewhere along the way, my collaborators and I extracted a small question and a thin slice of data—the case studies in the poor neighborhoods and the survey of childcare centers—and produced the paper that is part of this collection. Sometime later, I drafted the book. Somewhere in between, I realized I had a multimethod, multilevel set of data and produced what you see here as Table 9.6.

UNCHARTED PATH, BUT NOT AIMLESS WANDERING

The precise field that any researcher encounters will not have been traversed in exactly the same way—informed by the same questions, curiosities, or anxieties—by anyone. By necessity, to begin a field-based project, whether mixed-method or not, is to take a step onto unknown territory, because the territory itself is ever changing and the questions that motivate us depend in part on the idiosyncrasies of that moving landscape. Even the most accomplished map will be humbled by reality. This much the grounded theorists had right.

But an adventurer who cannot tell north from south will inevitably get lost in a difficult and frustrating trek. Without a sense of direction, a traveler with enough persistence will continue to clear brushes and cross rivers for months and years on end in the hopes of arriving somewhere. The expedition is as likely to fail, even if for different reasons.

In unpredictable terrain, therefore, a few tools will always prove useful—an open mind, a sense of curiosity, and a well-calibrated compass.

REFERENCES

Small, Mario Louis. 2011. "How to Conduct a Mixed Methods Study: Recent Trends in a Rapidly Growing Literature." *Annual Review of Sociology*. 37: 57–86.

Glossary of Terms

Abstract hypothesis—A form of hypothesis that specifies the population to be studied, under conditions that are of interest, and a possible relationship that might be between the variables of interest.

Association—A condition where a change in one variable is related to a change in another, but the direction of this relationship is unknown. It is unclear whether one causes the other or whether both changes are caused by a change in a third variable; also know as a correlation.

Categorical data—See NOMINAL DATA.

Causal relationship—A condition where a change in the dependent variable is determined to be the effect of a change in the independent variable

Confirmation bias—The possibility that an observed phenomenon reflects the results desired by the researcher prior to beginning an analysis; or the tendency to grant greater authority to confirming rather than disconfirming evidence.

Correlation—A condition where a change in one variable is related to a change in another, but the direction of this relationship is unknown. It is unclear whether one causes the other or whether both changes are caused by a change in a third variable; also known as an association.

Covariation—A necessary condition to observe a relationship between variables, covariation occurs when the independent and dependent variables each have more than one value.

Cross-sectional—A form of research design in which a representative probability sample of a population of interest is drawn and asked a series of questions. Instead of following people over time, these data ask different people the same exact questions at the same time. This kind of data can tell us what is the case, but unlike longitudinal data, they are not very good at telling us how things have changed.

Deductive—A research technique in which researchers begin with a general idea of how the world works and use their observations to "test" this idea—not just whether it is right or wrong but also what its limits are and how it might be amended.

Dependent variable—The variable the researcher expects to change in response to a change in the independent variable. For this reason, the dependent variable is sometimes referred to as the outcome variable.

External validity—A condition wherein research findings about the study population can be said to apply to the entire population of interest.

Extraneous variable—A variable that is not considered in the research design but has an effect on the observed association between the independent and dependent variables.

Field notes—Detailed notes of what the researcher observes while collecting data. These notes include a strict account of what happened as well as the researcher's impressions of the situation.

Generalizability—See EXTERNAL VALIDITY.

Historical social science—The use of archival material or historical accounts to make an argument that has generalizable implications.

Hypothesis—A statement about how variables relate to one another. Hypotheses are generated during research design and tested through the analysis of data.

Independent variable—The variable whose change the researcher expects will cause a change in the dependent variable. For this reason, the independent variable is sometimes referred to as the predictor variable.

Inductive—A research technique whereby, instead of starting with a theory about how the world works and testing it, researchers try to keep as open a mind as possible and use their observations to generate a theory or an account that is generalizable beyond the particular observations made.

Informed consent—A principle of data collection that all human subjects must be informed about the research project before they agree to participate. As part of this process, subjects must be made aware of any risks to their person and rewards to general knowledge.

Institutional review board (IRB)—A regulatory body of faculty and administrators at every research institution that impartially evaluate the ethical implications of every research project involving human subjects before that project can begin.

Internal validity—An assessment that an observed association in a research study actually occurs and is not the result of an extraneous variable.

Interval data—Numerical data that are expressed as an ordinal scale in which the intervals between values are the same size but the highest and lowest values are arbitrary. Temperature scales are examples.

Life course—The successive range of social institutions and roles that are experienced throughout a person's lifetime.

Longitudinal—A form of research design in which a single sample is followed over several years. As opposed to cross-sectional designs, this kind of design is ideal for studying change.

Measurement assumptions—A rendering of an abstract idea, such as education, to something more concrete about which we can gather data, such as years of schooling. In this example, the researcher assumes that "years of schooling" measures the concept of "education."

Nominal data—Data that deal with categories of things that do not have a meaningful numerical value, such as eye color or gender. Nominal data are classified by categories.

Nonprobability sample—A sampling frame in which participants from among the population of interest have either an unknown or zero probability of selection.

Nonresponse bias—A condition where particular types of people in a sample are participating at lower rates than others for a systematic reason or where the likelihood of response to a research instrument is systematically correlated with a variable of interest

Nonspuriousness—See SPURIOUS RELATIONSHIP.

Operational hypothesis—A statement about the predicted relationship between variables of interest for a certain population that specifies the conditions of interest and measurement assumptions that produced the data.

Operationalization—How the researcher converts an abstract idea into something concrete that can be measured and observed. See MEASUREMENT ASSUMPTIONS.

Ordinal data—Nominal data that are assigned to a numerical scale that expresses the order of variables but not the distance between one value and another. An example of an ordinal scale might be the final position of swimmers in a race.

Population of interest (also known as a "population")—The group of people that the researcher wishes to draw conclusions about.

Probability sample—See RANDOM SAMPLE.

Quantitative—A method of research that collects and analyzes numerical data (quantities). Quantitative data are well suited for explaining the *what* of a research question.

Qualitative—A method of research that collects and analyzes data that speak to thematic qualities related to a research question. Qualitative data are well suited for answering the *how* of a research question.

Random sample—A sampling frame in which each element of a population has a known, nonzero probability of being selected. In a simple random sample, every unit selected has an equal probability of selection. In other forms of random samples, units may have a greater or lesser probability of selection, but all probabilities of selection are known and nonzero.

Ratio data—Numerical data expressed on an ordered scale with fixed intervals between values and a meaningful zero point, such as annual income in dollars.

Reliability—An assessment that all measurements were taken in the same way throughout the data collection process.

Research question—The question that the researcher wishes to answer about a topic of interest.

Sampling—The way in which social scientists select a representation of their population of interest.

Sampling frame—The technique determining how the study population will be identified and contacted to be a part of the sample. For example, a researcher could use a telephone book, randomly select home phone numbers, and call these numbers for a telephone survey. In this instance the telephone book would be the sampling frame.

Secondary data—Data that are analyzed by a researcher that an unrelated researcher or entity gathered.

Selection bias (also known as "selection effects")—When the sample drawn for a study is not representative of the population of interest.

Social network analysis—A form of analysis that focuses on the connections, or "social ties," among social actors, such as individuals or organizations.

Spurious relationship—A relationship where a researcher observes an association between two variables (Variable A and Variable B), but some other variable (Variable C) has an association with both variables (A and B). Variable C thereby explains part or all of the association between Variables A and B.

Stratified random sample—A random sampling frame in which some units have a greater probability of selection than others. A researcher may choose this approach when an element of the population is comparatively small but desired to be an assured part of the sample.

Study population—The subset of the population of interest that the researcher has the possibility of accessing.

Unit of analysis—The social entity that the researcher wishes to observe and analyze. A unit of analysis may be an individual, a group of people, a company, a nation, or another kind of organization.

Unit of observation—See VARIABLE.

Validity—An assessment about whether an association observed in a research study actually occurs for the sample and can be said to apply to the population of interest. See also INTERNAL VALIDITY and EXTERNAL VALIDITY.

Variable—The dimension or aspect of your unit of analysis that has various values, which can be either quantities or qualities.

Printed in the USA/Agawam, MA
December 27, 2022

803515.026